Our Science
Trinidad and Tobago

Tony Seddon

Shameem Narine
La Romaine High School

Jerome Ramdahin
Waterloo High School

2

CAMBRIDGE UNIVERSITY PRESS
Cambridge, New York, Melbourne, Madrid, Cape Town,
Singapore, São Paulo, Delhi, Mexico City

Cambridge University Press
The Water Club, Beach Road, Granger Bay, Cape Town 8005, South Africa

www.cambridge.org
Information on this title: www.cambridge.org/9780521607155

© Cambridge University Press 2007

This publication is in copyright. Subject to statutory exception
and to the provisions of relevant collective licensing agreements,
no reproduction of any part may take place without the written
permission of Cambridge University Press.

First published 2007
Reprinted 2013

Printed in India by Replika Press Pvt. Ltd

A catalogue record for this publication is available from the British Library

ISBN 978-0-521-60715-5 Paperback

Cover artwork: Karen Ahlschläger
Typesetter: Meridian Colour Repro Ltd
Illustrators: Oxford Designers & Illustrators

Cambridge University Press has no responsibility for the persistence or
accuracy of URLs for external or third-party internet websites referred to in
this publication, and does not guarantee that any content on such websites is,
or will remain, accurate or appropriate.

Every effort has been made to trace copyright holders. Should any infringements have
occurred, please inform the publishers who will correct these in the event of a reprint.

Contents

TOPIC 1: The amazing human body 6
1. The amazing human 'machine' 6
2. Different sense organs for different jobs 8
3. Sight and 'super' sight 10
4. 3-D vision and a world of colour 12
5. Things to do with eyes 15
6. It's a smelly old world 18
7. A matter of taste 21
8. Waves of sound 24
9. Hearing things 26
10. Balancing act 29
11. Super brain 32
12. More about how the brain works 34
13. Skin – living inside an elastic bag 37
14. Keeping warm and cool 40
15. Chest changes and breathing 42
16. The bags you breathe with 44
17. Energy release and oxygen debt 47
18. The perfect pump 49
19. Pulse rates and fitness 51
20. Pressure and lifestyle 54
21. The body's transport system 56
22. Blood – the body's taxi service 58
23. A balanced diet 60
24. Different diets for different people 62
25. Tests for food 64
26. Biting and grinding 66
27. Chewing and swallowing 68
28. Journey to destruction 71

29	Food is the stuff of life	73
30	What happens to digested food?	76
31	Getting rid of metabolic waste	79
32	More about kidneys	81
33	Creating new life	83
34	Fertilisation and beyond	85
35	Reproduction technology	87
36	Skin and bones hold you together	90
37	Bones, big and small	93
38	Moving parts – joints	95
39	Muscle power	98
40	The science of moving	101
41	Diseases	104
42	Living the right lifestyle	107
43	The cost of being unhealthy	110

TOPIC 2: Solutions and solubility ... 113

44	Temperature, surface area and solubility	113
45	Water – the wonder solvent	116
46	Dissolved gases and life in water	118
47	Solutes cause problems for life in water	121
48	Carbonic acid and caves	123
49	How solutes affect our tap water	125
50	Acid rain is the result of soluble gases	128
51	Ground water – an important solvent	130
52	Solutes and solvents in everyday life	133
53	Getting things clean	136
54	Separating solvents from solutes	138
55	Separating a mixture of solutes	141
56	Separation techniques in industry	144
57	Changing melting points and boiling points	147
58	Water – an important solvent in industry	150
59	What is in crude oil?	153
60	Turning crude oil into useful products	155

TOPIC 3: Electricity ... 157

61 Static electricity – electricity at rest ... 157
62 Static electricity at work ... 160
63 Static electricity – a nuisance and a danger ... 162
64 Electrical circuits ... 165
65 More about cells and circuits ... 167
66 Series circuits ... 170
67 Parallel circuits ... 173
68 Different kinds of switches ... 176
69 What is in a cell? ... 178
70 Good and bad conductors of electricity ... 181

TOPIC 4: Magnetism ... 184

71 Magnets and magnetism ... 184
72 More about magnetic force ... 187
73 Magnetic fields ... 189
74 Making an electromagnet ... 191
75 Things which affect magnets and magnetism ... 193
76 Magnetism in the workplace ... 195
77 Magnets in the home ... 198
78 Magnetic Earth ... 201

Science dictionary for Book 2 ... 204
Index ... 214
Acknowledgements ... 216

1 The amazing human body

The amazing human 'machine'

The human body is amazing

The human body is an amazing 'machine'. By the time you are an adult, you will have nearly 100 000 km of blood vessels running through you. You will have about 5 litres of blood in your circulatory system and, if you live to be 75 years old, your heart will have pumped your blood round your body about 2.5 billion times. When you are fully grown, you will be supported by 206 bones and moved by 639 different muscles.

You can detect light, sound, smell, taste, pain, heat, cold and pressure. In your lifetime, you will consume about 75 tonnes of fuel and take in 10 million litres of oxygen to release nearly 400 million units of energy. Even though your brain is more complicated than the most powerful computer, it operates on the same amount of electric power needed to light a 10 watt bulb. Your communication system is made up of 12 billion nerve cells which carry messages at nearly 300 km per hour. You can repair yourself when you become damaged and, when you are grown up and have a partner, you will be able to produce offspring.

Each of us is a finely tuned 'machine' with more parts than there are people in the Caribbean. And, after all this, you are still mainly water! You are a truly amazing living organism.

All living things are made up of tiny structures called cells

In Year 1, you learned that cells are the microscopic building blocks of all living things, including humans. They make up the skin, bones, muscles, nerves, heart, brain, kidneys, liver and every other part of your body. All your activities involve about 50 trillion cells of different shapes and sizes, all working together.

In Year 1, you also learned that, although all cells have the same basic structure, they vary in size and shape. Some cells are thinner than others, some are fatter than others, some are longer than others and some are flatter than others. The reason cells vary in shape is because they have different jobs to do. Cells are **specialised** to carry out specific functions.

In the body, there are different levels of cell organisation. Cells of the same type which specialise in the same activity are usually found grouped together. A group of cells like this is called a **tissue**. The cells that line the inside of your stomach are specialised. They make special chemicals called enzymes which help you digest the food you eat. These cells make up one kind of tissue. But your stomach also contains other tissues. For example, there is a layer of muscle in the wall of your stomach which is made up of cells that can move. These cells form another type of tissue called muscle tissue. This tissue makes the wall of the stomach move in and out. This movement speeds up digestion by mixing the food with the stomach's enzymes.

All the tissues in the stomach work together, even though they each have their own special job to do. A group of different tissues like this makes up an **organ**. So the stomach is an organ. Other organs in the body include the heart, lungs, liver and kidneys.

The stomach is only one of the organs which help in the digestion of food. Some of the other organs involved include the tongue, the liver, the small intestine, the pancreas and large intestine. All these organs together make up a **system** called the digestive system. There are other systems in the body. The heart is part of the circulatory system, each kidney is part of the excretory system, the skull is part of the skeletal system, each lung is part of the respiratory system and the brain, eyes and ears are part of the nervous system.

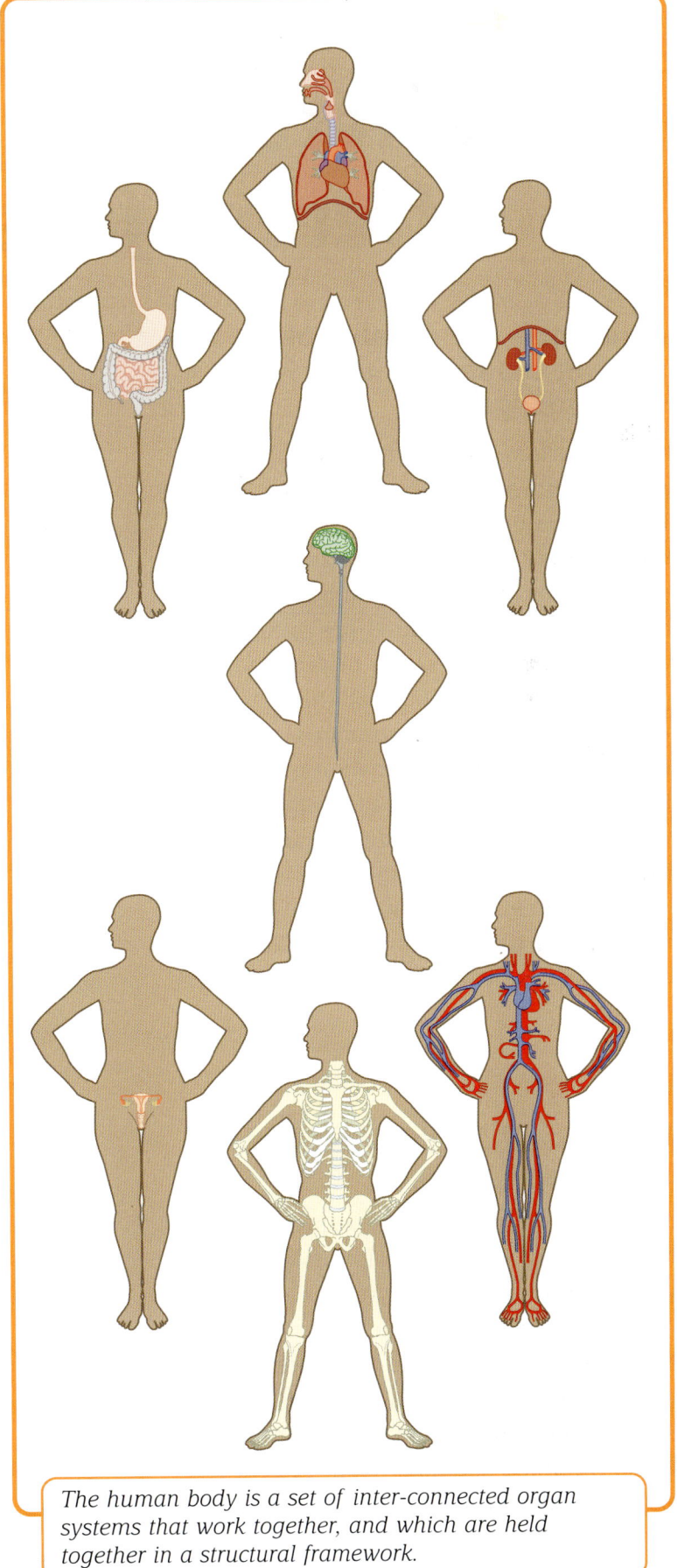

The human body is a set of inter-connected organ systems that work together, and which are held together in a structural framework.

The amazing human 'machine'

2 Different sense organs for different jobs

All animals are capable of sensing changes in their surroundings

It is important for animals to be able to pick up information about changes in their environment. A change in the environment is called a **stimulus**. A stimulus can be a change in light, sound, smell, touch, temperature, pressure or pain. Animals have **sense organs** to gather information about all these changes. Sense organs contain sensitive cells or **receptors**. Information received by these receptors is passed to the brain by means of nerves. Some animals, like humans, use a wide range of sense organs. Others rely mainly on only one or two sense organs to tell them about changes in the world about them.

Humans rely on five main sense organs to tell them about the world around them.

Whales and dolphins are highly sensitive to sound

Some animals rely mainly on hearing. Whales, porpoises and dolphins get most of the information from their surroundings by using their sense of hearing. They have their own special sonar system. They send out high-pitched sounds and listen to the echoes bouncing back. Dolphins use their sonar system to navigate and hunt for food.

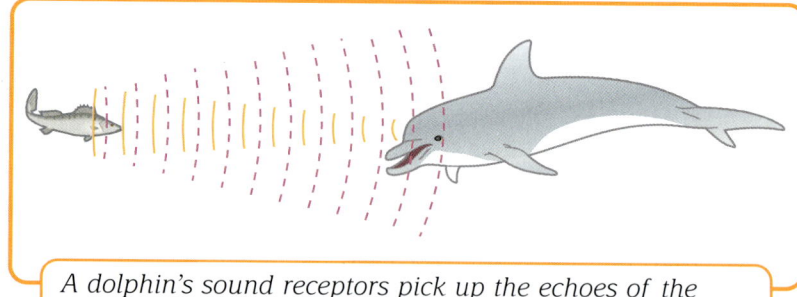

A dolphin's sound receptors pick up the echoes of the sounds it makes when they bounce back off a group of fish in front of it. These echoes tell the dolphin the exact position of the fish and how far in front of it they are.

Some animals depend more on their nose

A dog's sense of smell is very much better than our sense of smell. Some dogs have such a well-developed sense of smell that they can detect one particle of a substance when it is mixed up in a million particles of air!

Policeman with his cadaver dog in search of possible bodies following Hurricane Katrina on Rhode Island.

Other animals depend mainly on sight

Predatory animals often use their eyes more than their other sense organs. The white hawk lives in forests in northern Trinidad. It has very keen eyesight which it uses to catch small animals including lizards and snakes. Its eyesight is so sharp that it can spot the smallest lizard on the forest floor, even when it is perched high up in a tree 30 m above the ground.

Some snakes can 'see' heat

The bushmaster snake lives in forests in Trinidad. It has small, heat-sensitive pits below its normal eyes which it uses to build up a heat picture of its surroundings. The bushmaster can 'see' the heat given off by small birds and mammals, even in complete darkness. At night-time, it can 'see' the heat image of a rat as easily as we can see it in bright daylight.

The bushmaster snake from Trinidad is a night hunter which can detect the heat being given off by other animals.

Oilbirds listen to their own echoes

During the day, the oilbird, or diablotin, rests in dark caves in some parts of Trinidad. But at night it flies out to feed in nearby forests. Even in the daytime, it is too dark in the caves for it to use its normal eyes. Instead, it finds its way around by means of its own sonar navigation system. It sends out clicking sounds and listens for their return echoes. Once it flies out to feed at night, it uses its big 'night-seeing' eyes to find its way about.

The oilbird, or diablotin, from Trinidad never sees daylight.

Different sense organs for different jobs

3 Sight and 'super' sight

Eyes are our most important sense organs

Eyes are sensitive to light. They work like a camera. Each eye has an **iris** which controls the amount of light entering the eye. It has a **lens** inside to focus the light from an object onto a sensitive area at the back of the eye called the **retina**. The retina picks up the light stimuli and passes them as electrical impulses to the brain along a nerve called the **optic nerve**. The brain interprets the electrical impulses and allows you to see an image of what you are looking at.

If you have 3:6 vision, it means you have to be as close as 3 m to see an object which a person with normal eyesight can see clearly at 6 m. If you have 3:6 vision, you probably have to wear glasses. But some people are lucky – their eyesight is better than normal. In other words, their eyesight is better than perfect! If your eyesight is 6:5, you can see objects at 6 m which a person with normal vision can only see clearly at 5 m.

FACTFILE

Eyes

A human eye is about the size of a table tennis ball.

The retina at the back of the eye covers an area the size of a small postage stamp.

Each eye contains about 130 million light receptors.

Each eye can receive 1.5 million stimuli per second.

In good light, the human eye can distinguish 10 million different shades of colour.

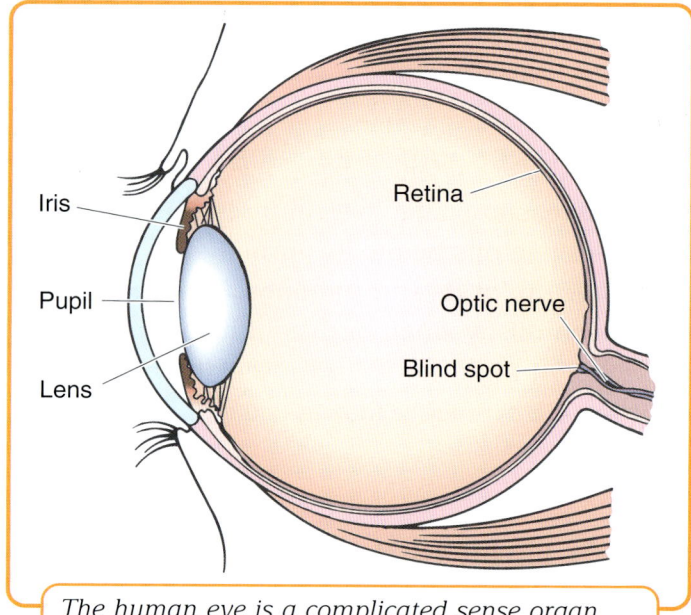

The human eye is a complicated sense organ designed to pick up information about light.

Some Australian Aborigines have amazing eyesight

Aborigines were the original inhabitants of Australia before the arrival of Europeans more than 200 years ago. Some Aborigines have the sharpest vision of any humans on our planet. A doctor called Professor Fred Hollows found Aborigines in Western Australia whose eyesight is 6:1.5. This means that they can see at 6 m what a person with normal vision can see at only 1.5 m! Their eyesight is four times better than normal eyesight!

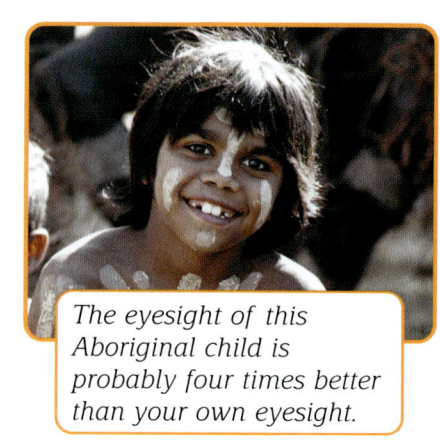

The eyesight of this Aboriginal child is probably four times better than your own eyesight.

INVESTIGATION Test your eyesight

Work with a partner.

- Ask your partner to hold your book open at the eye chart so you can see it.
- Put a mark on the floor 6 m from where your partner is holding the eye chart.
- Now stand on the mark, read the eye chart and record your results.
- When you have completed your eye test, hold the chart and let your partner test his or her own eyesight.

1. How many letters could you read from 6 m?
2. Do you have 6:6 vision?
3. Did your partner have 6:6 vision?

30

15

6

On this eye chart the letter marked 6 should be readable at 6m. If you can do this you have 6:6 vision – you have perfect eyesight. If at 6m you can hardly read the letter marked 15, you have 6:15 vision. If you can read only the large letter, your vision is 6:30.

Professor Hollows corrected an elderly 50-year-old Aboriginal man's vision back to 6:6 with glasses. In other words the glasses gave the patient perfect vision. But when the patient looked through his new glasses he said: 'Thank you for trying doctor, but this is hopeless. I used to be able to see much better.'

When the Professor told his patient a European would think that 6:6 was excellent eyesight, his Aboriginal patient said he felt sorry for the poor European people who had such hopeless eyesight, and who would never know anything better!

Technology used by astronomers now makes 'super' human sight possible

Some scientists are developing technology that will give humans 'super' eyesight. They are adapting technology originally developed by astronomers to obtain better images of the stars and planets. One scientist has even improved the eyesight of people who have perfect 6:6 vision!

Activity

- Read the information in the 'Did you know?' box.
- By using the two numbers doctors use to measure a person's eyesight, try to write down what Veronica Seider's eyesight must have been like in 1972. If you find this difficult, ask your teacher for help.

Did you know?

In October 1972, a university student in Germany called Veronica Seider had an eye test. The result was amazing. It showed her eyesight was 20 times better than normal vision. She could identify a person's face at a distance of 1.6 km!

4 3-D vision and a world of colour

Have you ever wondered why you have two eyes facing forward? A simple experiment will explain why this is.

These students are investigating why we have two eyes.

INVESTIGATION

Find out why we need two eyes

Work with a partner.

- Put a plastic cup on a table and stand about 3 m away.
- Cover your right eye with your hand.
- Ask your partner to hold a small coin at arm's length above the cup but slightly in front of it.
- Keep looking at the cup and the coin.
- Ask your partner to move their arm until you think the coin is directly over the cup.
- When you think the coin is over the cup, ask your partner to let it drop.
- Record the result.
- Repeat four more times and record the results.
- Now repeat five times with your left eye covered and record the results.
- Now reverse roles and let your partner try.
- Record your partner's results.

1. How many of your ten attempts were successful?
2. How many of your partner's ten attempts were successful?
3. Combine your scores and work out what percentage of your combined scores were successful.

- Repeat the investigation with both eyes open and record your results.
- Ask your partner to do the same and record their results.

4. Combine your scores and work out the percentage of successful drops with both eyes open.
5. Did your success rate improve when you used two eyes?

Two eyes give us 3-D vision

Because our eyes are set apart from each other, they each see things from slightly different angles. This means that the brain gets two slightly different images, one from each eye. The brain combines the two images into one and this produces a 3-D (three-dimensional) image which is what you see. This 3-D picture helps you judge distance because it allows you to see depth. Scientists call this stereoscopic vision. When you cover one eye, you no longer have **stereoscopic** vision so you can't judge distance so easily.

Did you know that you see the world upside down? Well, you don't but your eyes do. So when you see Brian Lara bat, you see him upside down. The lens in each of your eyes turns light upside down as it passes through. This means that the image of Brian Lara which forms on your retina is also upside down. But your brain changes Brian Lara back again so you do see him the right way up after all.

Can you explain why a batsman would find it difficult to play cricket with only one eye open?

Would a slip fielder take a catch more easily using one eye or two eyes?

Humans have a good sense of colour vision

If you have ever seen a rainbow, you know the range of colours humans can see. Different wavelengths of light produce different colours. The band of colours we can see is called the **visible spectrum**. Humans have good colour vision but they can't see beyond the ends of the visible spectrum – they can't see ultraviolet light and they can't see infrared light. But many birds and insects can see ultraviolet light and some snakes – you already know about the bushmaster snake – can even see infrared light.

Some people cannot tell the difference between red and green.

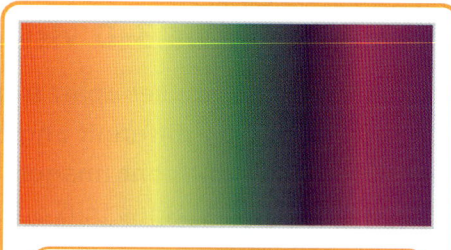

This is a spectrum showing the visible light we see and the ultraviolet and infrared light which some birds, insects and snakes see.

Do you think being red–green colour blind affects a car driver waiting at the traffic lights?
Can you think of any jobs which people do that might be affected by colour blindness?

Did you know?

The human eye is so perfect that, in total darkness, it can see a burning match from a distance of 10 km.

Some people live in a black and white world

Have you ever wondered what it would be like not to be able to see colour? The world would look like a black and white photograph. About one in every 30 000 people cannot see colour. They see only in black and white. But there is a small island in the Pacific Ocean called Pingelap where nearly 10% of the population cannot see colour.

When you look at a rainbow, you see the seven different wavelengths of light which make up the visible spectrum. You see red, orange, yellow, green, blue, indigo and violet.

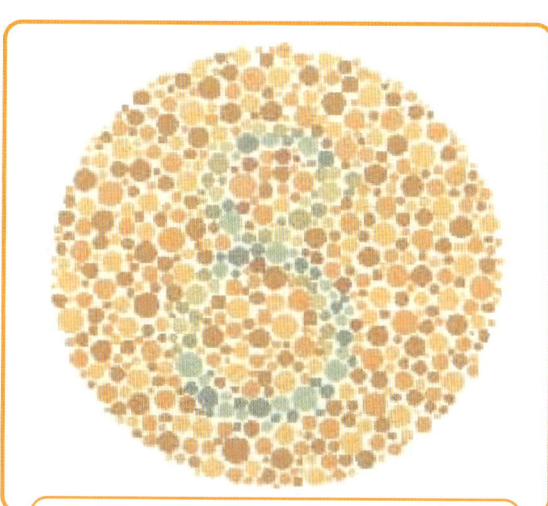

Can you see a figure 8 in the circle above? If so, you have normal colour vision. If not, you are red–green colour blind.

Things to do with eyes

INVESTIGATION Watch your iris at work

You will need a torch and a mirror.

- Stay in a dark room for 2 minutes.
- After 2 minutes, hold a mirror in front of your eyes.
- Shine a torch on your eyes.
- Record what happens to your pupils, but be quick!

You should see your pupils get smaller when you shine the torch on your eyes but you will have to look quickly. Each iris acts very quickly to close the pupil down. When you were in the dark, your irises opened your pupils wider to allow more light into your eyes. As soon as you shine a torch on your eyes, your irises close your pupils down to reduce the amount of light entering your eyes.

Write a sentence to describe what would happen in your eyes if you went from bright sunlight into a dark room.

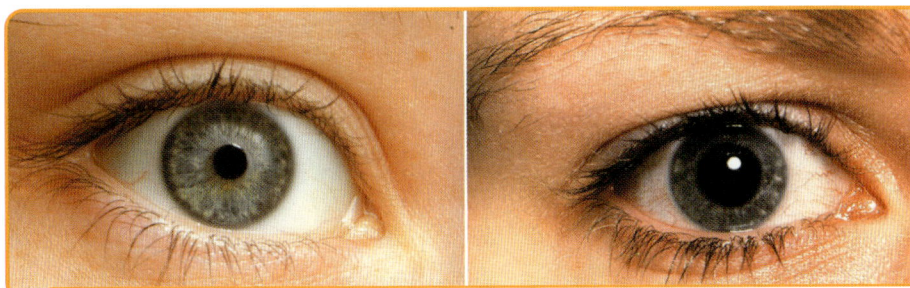

In bright light, the iris closes the pupil so less light enters the eye. In dim light, the iris opens the pupil wider so more light enters the eye.

Everybody is a little blind

There is one small part of your retina which doesn't contain any light receptors. It is the small area where the optic nerve leaves the eye to go to the brain. Because this area cannot pick up light stimuli, it is called the **blind spot**.

INVESTIGATION Find your blind spot

- Close your left eye.
- Look at the batsman with your right eye.
- Move the page backwards and forwards until the cricket ball disappears.

When the cricket ball disappears, its image is falling on the blind spot of your right eye. This is why you cannot see it.

Everybody is one-eyed

Although we have two eyes, we use one of them more than the other. Everybody has a **dominant eye**. Which eye is dominant depends on whether your brain is right-sided or left-sided.

INVESTIGATION Find your dominant eye

- Hold out your right arm.
- Keep both eyes open and point at a distant object with the index finger of your right hand.
- Keep your index finger pointing directly at the object.
- Now close your left eye.

Is your index finger still pointing at the object?
If so, your right eye is your dominant eye. You are right-eyed.

- To check your result, repeat the investigation but close your right eye this time.

If your index finger moves away from the object when you close your right eye, your left eye is your dominant eye. You are left-eyed.

- Ask your teacher to collect the results of all your classmates.

1. Are you right-eyed or left-eyed?
2. How many of your classmates are right-eyed?
3. How many of your classmates are left-eyed?
4. What percentage of your classmates is right-eyed?
5. What percentage of your classmates is left-eyed?

Activity

- Design an investigation to find out if there is a connection between eye dominance and right or left handedness.
- Show your plan to your teacher.
- When your teacher has approved your plan, carry out the investigation.
- Record your results.

16 Things to do with eyes

Did your results show a connection between eye dominance and whether someone is right or left handed?

INVESTIGATION Make a 'hole' in your hand

- Role a sheet of A4 paper lengthwise into a tube.
- Hold the tube to your right eye.
- Hold your left hand in front of your face with your palm facing you. You will need to hold your palm about 10 cm away from your face.
- Slowly move your palm backwards and forwards until you see a big 'hole' appear in your hand.

You see a 'hole' in your hand because your two eyes are working together to produce a confusing image for your brain to work out. Your brain does the best it can. It combines the tubular hole made by the rolled-up paper and the flat surface of your left palm. You end up seeing a 'hole' in your hand.

INVESTIGATION Make a floating 'sausage'

- Hold your index fingers in front of your eyes about 2 cm apart.
- Now look above them and focus on a distant object.

Can you see a 'sausage' floating between your two fingertips?

Each eye is seeing a slightly different view of your two fingertips so your brain gets two slightly different images to interpret. It does its best to sort out the confusion. It interprets your two fingertips as overlapping images. This is why you see a floating 'sausage'.

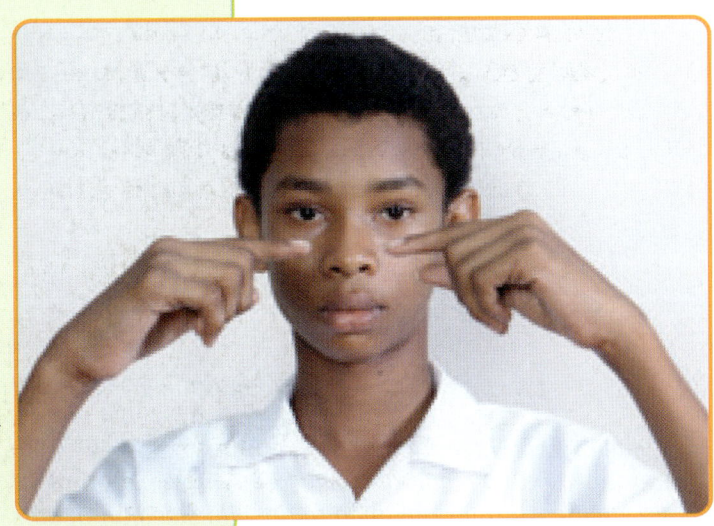

Things to do with eyes **17**

6 It's a smelly old world

Noses are for smelling

The world is full of strong smells, weak smells, nice smells, nasty smells and all kinds of smells in between. The part of your body that picks up information about smells is your nose. Your nose is your body's smell detector. Scientists have a special word for different smells. They call them **scents**.

> What is your favourite smell?
> Which smell do you most dislike?

Your smell receptors are found in the roof of your nose cavity. Each smell receptor is a tiny hair, and there are millions of them. Chemicals in the air dissolve in the mucus lining the nose cavity and are absorbed by the sensory hairs. The sensory hairs send messages to the brain along nerves and the brain interprets these as smells, or scents, of different kinds.

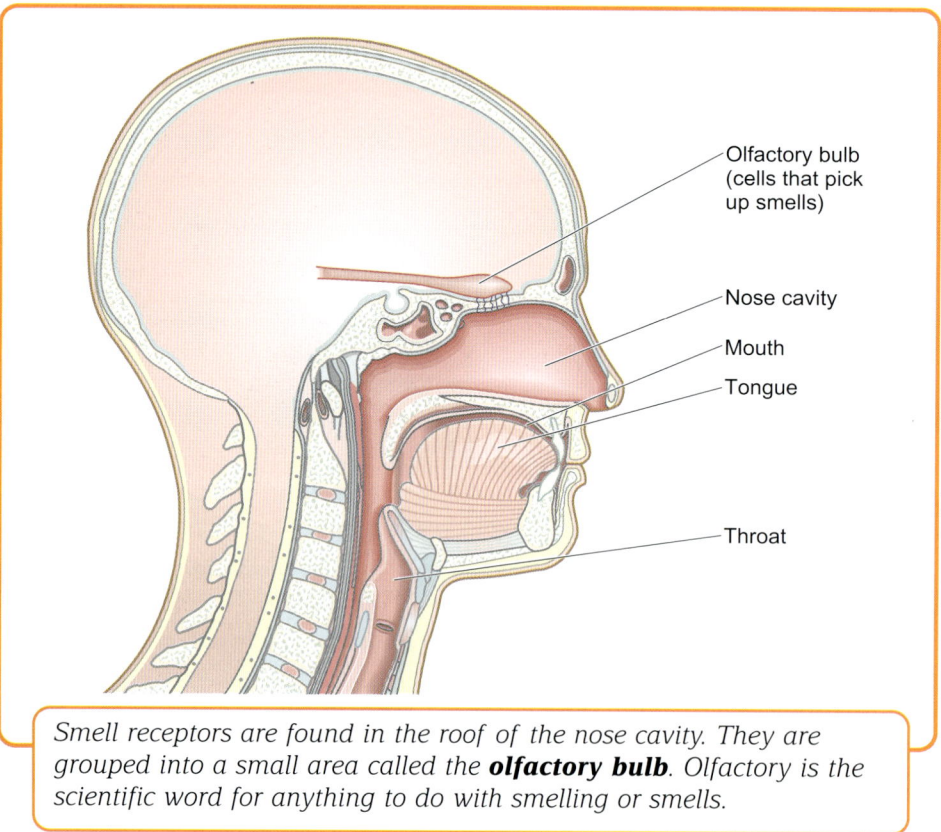

Smell receptors are found in the roof of the nose cavity. They are grouped into a small area called the **olfactory bulb**. Olfactory is the scientific word for anything to do with smelling or smells.

A smell is caused by particles of a substance mixed with air

If you think back to the work you did on particles, you will remember that air is a mixture of particles. Most of these are particles of the gases nitrogen, oxygen and carbon dioxide. Pure air doesn't have a smell – it is odourless. But air contains other particles and these are the things you smell. These are the scents your nose picks up.

Sniffing helps you to smell

When you breathe in normally, only a small amount of air floats into your nose cavity so you only pick up small amounts of scent. But when you sniff hard, you draw a lot more air onto your smell receptors. This is why things smell stronger when you sniff them. When you smell a beautiful flower, you don't smell it gently. You take in a deep breath – a big sniff – in order to draw lots of the flower's scent into your nose and onto your smell receptors.

You may have noticed that when a dog wants to smell something, it sniffs very hard. When it does this it is bombarding its smell receptors with different scents.

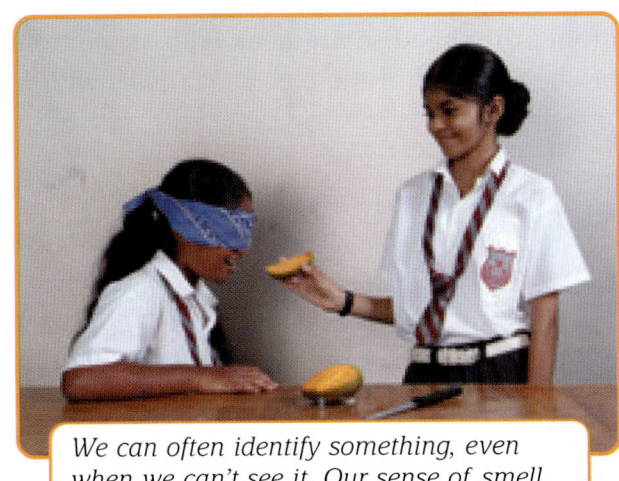

We can often identify something, even when we can't see it. Our sense of smell helps us to do this.

INVESTIGATION — Try to identify different things by their smell

Work with a partner.
Your teacher will give you 10 different items hidden in a bag.

- Let your partner put a blindfold over your eyes.
- Ask your partner to take five items out of the bag, one at a time.
- Sniff each item and try to identify it by its smell.
- Ask your partner to list the items 1–5 and record your identification against each item on the list.
- Now blindfold your partner and let them try to identify the other five items.
- Record their identification in another list numbered 6–10.

1. Did you identify all the items 1–5 correctly?
2. Did your partner identify all the items 6–10 correctly?
3. Has your partner got a better sense of smell than you have?

Did you know?

Your nose can identify at least 4000 different kinds of smell.

Our sense of smell is linked to our memory

Have you ever noticed that some smells remind you of past experiences? The smell of a certain perfume might remind you of an older sister. The smell of rotis being cooked might remind you of Carnival time. The smell of cut grass might remind you of the time your father took you to the Queen's Park Oval to watch the West Indies play cricket against England. Our sense of smell seems to be strongly linked to our memory. This probably happens because the messages going to the brain from the nose are dealt with at the front of the brain. This part of the brain also deals with memory.

FACTFILE

History

In October 1954, a dog called Henry set an amazing record. A young boy was reported missing by his parents after going for a walk. The police looked for him for 13 days but couldn't find him. Then a man called Mr Wilson lent the police his dog, Henry, who was a champion at following scent trails. The police gave Henry a piece of the missing boy's clothing so he could smell the boy's scent. Then Henry set off from the boy's home to follow his scent trail. Henry found the boy's dead body a few hours later. Henry was able to follow the missing boy's body scent left on the ground when he went for his walk, even though it was 13 days and 10 hours old!

Could you have performed as well as Henry?

Only people with the best sense of smell are employed to test different perfumes. There are probably less than 100 people in the world whose sense of smell is good enough to work as a 'sniffer' in the perfume industry.

A matter of taste

Taste is one of the first senses you experience

The main reason you have a sense of taste, apart from making life much more enjoyable, is to tell you if food is safe to eat. Your tongue is one of the first parts of your body to meet things as they come in from the outside. It works both as a tester and a taster. Food that has gone bad, or food that might harm you, tastes so awful that the first thing you want to do if it gets into your mouth is to spit it out. Babies try to taste everything. They often put things in their mouth and then spit them out quickly because they don't like the taste.

> **Did you know?**
> Your tongue is your main organ for tasting.

Your tongue is a big piece of flat muscle

Normally, your tongue fits neatly into your mouth. But sometimes, when you get over excited, it seems too big and then you bite it. But usually it behaves itself and stays snug and safe between your teeth.

The surface of your tongue is covered with little bumps. Many of these are full of **taste buds**. There are about 9000 taste buds on your tongue. Taste buds contain tiny receptors sensitive to taste. Substances entering your mouth start to dissolve in your spit, or saliva. These dissolved chemicals stimulate your taste receptors and they send messages to your brain. Your brain interprets the messages as different tastes.

> What is your favourite taste?
> Which taste do you most dislike?

Spicy foods, like curries, feel hot on your tongue

A curry with lots of hot pepper in it can make your tongue feel as if it is on fire. This is because spicy foods create 'heat' in your mouth by reacting with the taste buds. Sometimes a very hot curry takes away your sense of taste for a short time until the 'heat' has died down. It's a good idea to drink lots of water with a curry. This helps cool your mouth down and prevents your taste buds from being 'put to sleep' temporarily.

 **INVESTIGATION** — Map the taste areas of your tongue

Work with a partner. Wash your hands before you start.

Your teacher will give you four different solutions, labelled salty water (salt taste), black coffee (bitter taste), sugary water (sweet taste) and lemon juice (sour taste).

- Draw an outline shape of your tongue (a tongue map) in your book.
- Let your partner put a blindfold over your eyes.
- Ask your partner to put some drops of salty water on the tip of your tongue using a cotton bud or wooden spatula.
- Record whether you can identify the salt taste by putting a tick (for yes) or a cross (for no) on your tongue map.
- Ask your partner to put the salty water on the sides of your tongue and record the result on your tongue map.
- Ask your partner to put the salty water on the back of your tongue and record the result on your tongue map.
- Wash your mouth out with clean water.
- Ask your partner to repeat the above steps, using each of the other three solutions in turn, and record the results.
- Remember to wash your mouth out before trying each new solution.
- Now blindfold your partner and let him or her do the taste test.

1. Did you find that you could taste all four solutions equally all over your tongue?
2. Where on your tongue did you identify a sweet taste?
3. Where on your tongue did you identify a salt taste?
4. Where on your tongue did you identify a sour taste?
5. Where on your tongue did you identify a bitter taste?
6. Did your partner's results agree with yours?

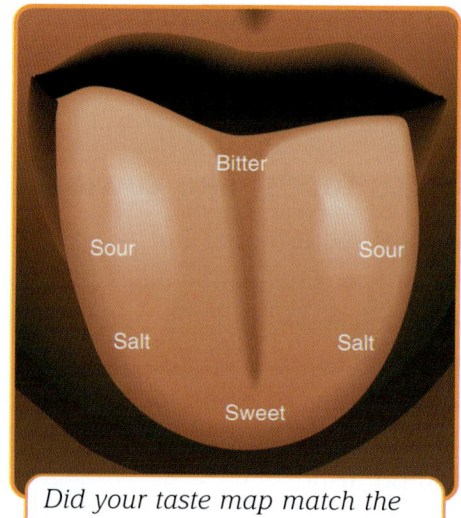

Did your taste map match the one shown in this photograph?

Activity

Can you tell the difference between the taste of Pepsi-Cola and Coca-Cola?

- If you think you can, carry out a taste test like the one above, but this time use Pepsi-Cola and Coca-Cola, and see how good your taste buds are.

INVESTIGATION Taste with and without the help of your nose

- Put a clothes peg on your nose so you can't use it to smell with.
- Now drink some orange juice.
- Remove the clothes peg from your nose and have another drink of orange juice.
- Try eating different foods with and without a peg on your nose.

1 Can you taste the orange juice when your nose is out of action?
2 Is it easier to taste the orange juice when your nose is not pegged?
3 Can you taste food easily when your nose is blocked off?

Taste and smell work together

The senses of smell and taste are closely related. When you eat, molecules from the food in your mouth travel up into your nose cavity where their smell is picked up in the usual way. If you have a cold, you often lose your senses of taste and smell. This is because the lining of your nose develops a thicker layer of mucus. This extra thickness stops molecules reaching your smell receptors. You can still taste the basic tastes of salt, sweet, sour and bitter, but you can't identify all the delicate flavours in between.

8 Waves of sound

Activity
- Find the island of Krakatau in an atlas, or on a map of the world.
- Try to work out which countries would have heard the sound made when the volcano on Krakatau erupted.

FACTFILE History
On 28 August 1883 at 10 o'clock in the morning, a volcano on the island of Krakatau, an island between Java and Sumatra, in Indonesia, erupted. It produced the loudest sound in recorded history. The sound of the explosion was heard 5000 km away to the west and 3000 km away to the east.

Sound is a form of energy

In Year 1, you learned that sound is a form of energy. All sounds occur because of vibrations. When a drum is hit, its skin moves up and down – we say it **vibrates**. As the drum's skin moves up, air molecules immediately above it are squashed together and air molecules immediately underneath it are thinned out. When the skin moves down, air molecules are squashed together underneath and thinned out above. Meanwhile, the first group of 'close-together' air molecules is now expanding and squashing together the next group of air molecules above it. And so the squashing and expanding goes on. The vibrating drum skin is pushing air into a pattern of molecules that are at first close together and then further apart. These bands of 'squashing' and 'thinning out' of air molecules form **sound waves**. So sound waves are caused by vibrations.

Activity
- Write a short account of what happens to the surrounding air molecules when a person hits a steel pan in order to play a tune.

Scientists use a special piece of equipment to 'see' sounds

A machine called an **oscilloscope** enables scientists to 'see' sound patterns. An oscilloscope turns sound vibrations into electrical patterns. These electrical patterns appear on the screen of the oscilloscope as wave patterns.

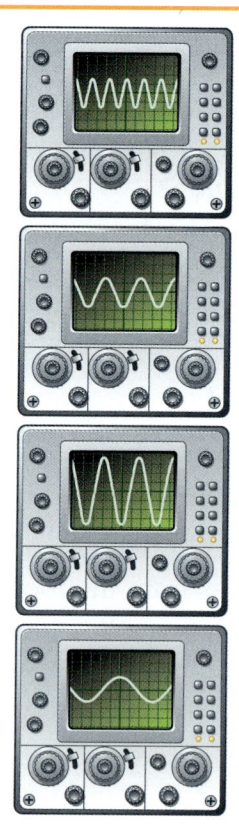

Short waves mean soft sounds while tall waves mean loud sounds. The closer the waves are, the higher the sound is. The further apart the waves are, the lower the sound is.

Scientists use special units to measure sound frequency

Some sounds are very low (deep) while other sounds are very high. The thing that makes a sound high or low is the **frequency** of the waves. Frequency is a measure of the number of waves produced every second. A low frequency sound has a small number of waves per second. A high frequency sound has a large number of waves per second. Sound frequency is measured in units called **hertz** (Hz). A sound with a frequency of 10 000 Hz is higher than a sound with a frequency of 5000 Hz.

Too much exposure to loud disco music may damage your ears. Often the sounds are well above 110 decibels and sometimes they may be close to the danger point of 130 decibels.

Humans can hear only within a specific frequency range

We cannot hear all sounds. The range of frequencies humans can hear is between about 20 Hz and 20 000 Hz. But some animals can hear sounds which are well beyond our frequency range. For example, a dog can hear sounds above 100 000 Hz and bats and whales can hear even higher sounds than this. Some bats can hear sounds as high as 200 000 Hz. In other words, they can hear sound 20 times higher than we can.

Scientists use special units to measure loudness

Some sounds are very loud, other sounds are not very loud, and there are all ranges of loudness in between. The thing that decides the loudness of a sound is the **height** or **amplitude** of the sound waves. The taller the waves, the louder the sound. The unit used to measure the loudness of a sound is the **decibel** (dB). The higher the number of decibels, the louder the sound. A sound above 130 decibels is so loud it can damage your ears.

Loudness (dB)	Object or activity
10	rustling of paper
20	cat purring
30	whispering
40	noise in the classroom
50	dog barking
60	shouting
70	car engine running
80	motorcycle engine
90	large truck or lorry engine
100	thunderclap
110	disco music
120	jumbo jet taking off
130	danger – sound beyond this point damages your ears

Activity

- Look at the table. It shows the loudness of sounds produced by different objects or activities. Where would you place the sound produced by Krakatau's volcano on the loudness table?

9 Hearing things

Ears are the body's organs of hearing. Sound waves enter your ears and stimulate the receptors specially designed to receive them. The stimuli are sent to your brain from your ears and your brain interprets them as the sounds you hear.

The things we call ears are really sound collectors

Your **earflaps** (the bits we call our ears) collect sound waves and direct them into the ear canals. Many animals have extra large earflaps for collecting as much sound information as possible. Animals are also able to move their earflaps to help work out which direction sound is coming from.

Can you move your earflaps?

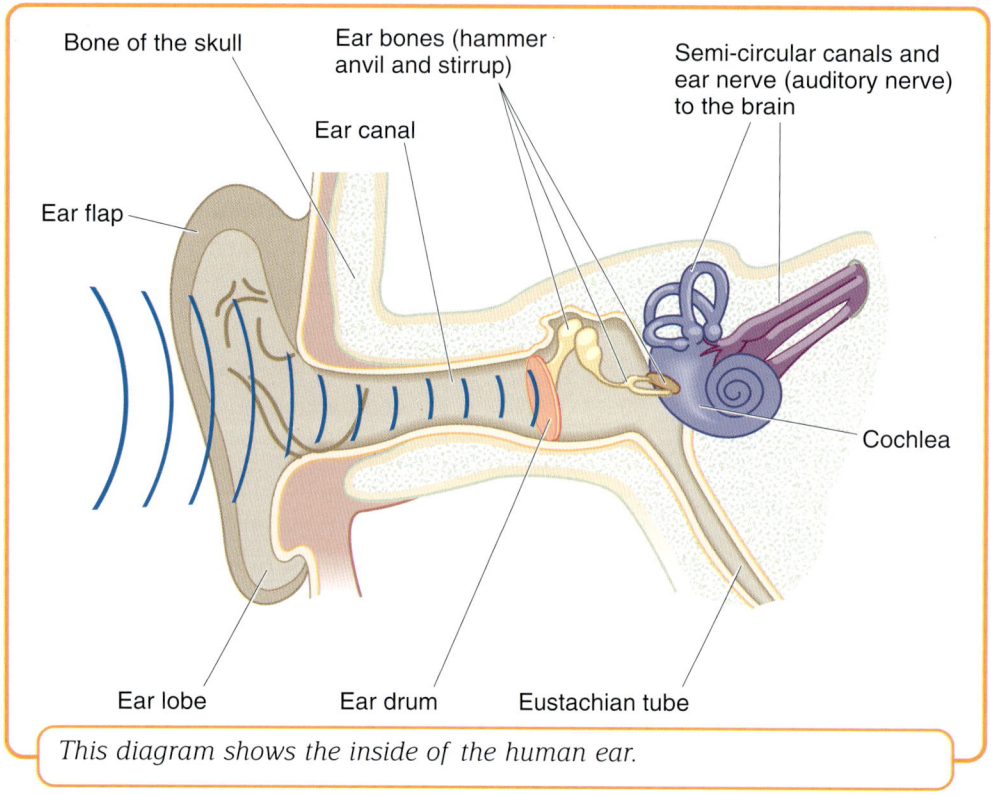

This diagram shows the inside of the human ear.

26 Hearing things

INVESTIGATION: Improve your sound collecting

Work with a partner.
- Go outside and ask your partner to stand about 20 m away from you.
- Now ask you partner to talk to you softly. They need to speak so softly that you have difficulty in hearing them.
- While your partner is talking, put your hands behind your ears and cup them like the girl is doing in the photograph.

1. When you cup your ears, does your hearing improve?
2. Can you hear more clearly what your friend is saying?
3. Why does cupping your ears improve your hearing?

When you cup your ears, you increase the size of your earflaps – the 'sound collecting' parts of your ears. Now they can pick up more sound information and your hearing improves.

The hidden parts of the ear deal with sound stimuli

When sound waves enter each ear, they travel down the **ear canal** and hit the **eardrum**. This makes the eardrum vibrate. The vibrations are then passed onto the three tiny bones in the ear called the **ear bones**. Each bone vibrates in turn and the last one vibrates against a tube called the **cochlea**. The cochlea is coiled like a snail's shell and is filled with liquid. Tiny hairs hanging in the liquid in the cochlea pick up the vibrations and also start to vibrate. Each hair is attached to a small nerve. The nerves send messages to the brain. Your brain picks up information about the strength, rhythm and speed of the vibrations and interprets all this information as the different sounds you hear.

INVESTIGATION: Find out if two ears are better than one

Work with a partner.
- Carefully put a piece of cotton wool in one ear.
- Close your eyes.
- Now ask your partner to put a ticking clock somewhere in the room.
- Try to find the clock by listening to the tick. Your partner will need to prevent you from bumping into things.
- Now try the same experiment with both ears 'open'.
- Let your partner try the experiment.

Was it easier to find the clock when you used two ears?

Hearing things

You have an interesting way of protecting your eardrums

Eardrums are very delicate structures. They can easily become damaged. If this happens, doctors say the person has a 'perforated' eardrum. The space behind each eardrum is connected to your nose and throat by a tiny tube called the **Eustachian tube**. These tubes are important in protecting your eardrums.

INVESTIGATION: Feel your Eustachian tubes at work

- Hold your nose and swallow.
- Now let go of your nose and yawn.
1. What did you feel when you swallowed?
2. What did you feel when yawned?

Your Eustachian tubes help keep the air pressure the same on both sides of your eardrums. You sometimes have to use them when you go up or down in an elevator or lift because of pressure changes. If you have flown in an aeroplane you will probably have used your Eustachian tubes, especially when coming into land.

Did you know?

Sound travels about four times faster in water than in air. Humpback whales make use of this. They keep in touch by 'singing' to each other. Each whale has its own special songs which are different from those of other whales. Because sound travels more easily in water than in air, whale songs travel for hundreds of kilometres under the sea. A whale can probably 'talk' to another whale on the other side of the world!

Balancing act

Every object has a centre of balance

You can balance a ruler by positioning your finger halfway along the ruler's length. The ruler balances because its weight is equally distributed on both sides of your finger. Your finger is positioned at the ruler's centre of balance. If you move your finger away from the centre of balance, the ruler becomes unbalanced and falls to the ground.

Every part of your body has weight

When you are standing still, your weight is balanced and you stay upright. Keeping upright is all about moving your weight about in order to maintain your centre of balance. When you are moving, you constantly transfer your weight from one part of your body to another. When you walk, you transfer your weight from one foot to the other. If you don't do this, you lose your balance and fall over.

> Predict where your body's centre of balance is when you are standing still.
> Why do you sometimes trip over when you tread on an untied shoelace?

You always know where your body is and what's happening to it

Your balance sensors are inside your ears. They tell your brain if you are moving forwards or backwards, upwards or downwards or spinning round. They tell your brain if you are moving fast or slow, whether you are leaning forwards or backwards, tilting sideways, the right way up or upside down. Your balance sensors also tell your brain when you are accelerating, slowing down or when you have stopped. They even tell your brain when you are standing still.

INVESTIGATION — Find out how long you can stand still

- Stand upright with your feet together and your arms at your sides.
- Time how long you can stand completely still without moving, apart from breathing and blinking your eyes.
- Record the result.
1. How long did you manage to stand completely still?
2. Did it surprise you that you can't stand completely still for very long?

You have two main types of balance sensor

One kind of balance sensor tells your brain about up-and-down movements and about change-of-speed movements. The other type tells your brain about change-in-direction movements. Each of these sensors works in the same way. They contain tiny hairs hanging down in a fluid. Each hair is connected to a tiny nerve which goes to the brain. When you move, the fluid moves. The tiny hairs detect the fluid moving and stimulate the tiny nerves. These send messages to the brain and the brain works out what your body is doing.

INVESTIGATION — Try the one-leg no-eyes test

- Close both eyes and time how long you can stand on one leg.
- Record the result.
- Now try again with both eyes open.
- Record the result.
1. How long can you stand upright with both eyes closed?
2. How long can you stand upright with both eyes open?
3. Do your eyes help you to balance?

Your body has a series of balance reflexes

Normally you don't think about balancing. If you trip over something, you automatically move one foot forwards to try and correct your balance. When you start to run, you automatically lean forward to counterbalance the force of the air pushing backwards against your body. If you suddenly stop after running quickly, you automatically raise your arms upward to try and throw your weight backwards so you can stop more quickly. These automatic muscle actions are called **balance reflexes**.

When an athlete does the pole vault he receives information from all his balance sensors.

Activity
- Look at the drawings of the pole-vaulter.
- Make a list of all the 'balance' sensations he will experience from the time he stands on the run-up waiting to start his vault to the time he lands on the other side of the bar.

There is only so much your body can do about balance

While you are awake, your body is constantly making thousands of adjustments to help you keep your balance. But, even so, there is a limit to what you can do about balance. Try these simple tests to see what some of these limits are.

INVESTIGATION Sit down, stand up

- Sit upright in a straight-backed chair with your hands in your lap and your feet flat on the floor.
- Now try standing up without leaning forwards.
1. Can you stand up?
2. What do you have to do to be able to stand up?

INVESTIGATION Touch your toes

- Stand upright with your back and heels touching the wall.
- Now try to touch your toes without moving your back and your heels away from the wall.
1. Can you touch your toes?
2. What do you have to do to touch your toes?

Super brain

The brain is one of the biggest organs in the body

If you could remove the top of someone's skull and examine their brain it would look like a big ball of folded up sausages or a large, wrinkled walnut. The brain is a very complicated structure made up of millions of nerve cells called **neurones**. It continually receives information about changes in your external and internal environments and decides what to do about them.

FACTFILE

The brain

It is much more complicated than the biggest and best computer.
It has a volume of about 1500 cm^3.
It weighs about 1.4 kg.
If you could unfold your brain and spread it out flat, it would cover an area the size of a sheet of newspaper.
It contains about 100 billion neurones.
It is about 2% of your total body weight.
It is made up of more than 75% water.
It operates on the same amount of electric power needed to light a 10 watt light bulb.
It uses about 25% of all the oxygen you breathe in.

Different parts of the brain have different functions

The largest part of the brain is called the **cerebrum**. It consists of two halves called **cerebral hemispheres**. Mammals have much bigger cerebral hemispheres than other animals, and humans have the biggest cerebral hemispheres, compared to the overall size of their brain. Different parts of the cerebral hemispheres have

Different parts of the brain deal with different kinds of information and control different actions. Your brain co-ordinates all the actions of your body.

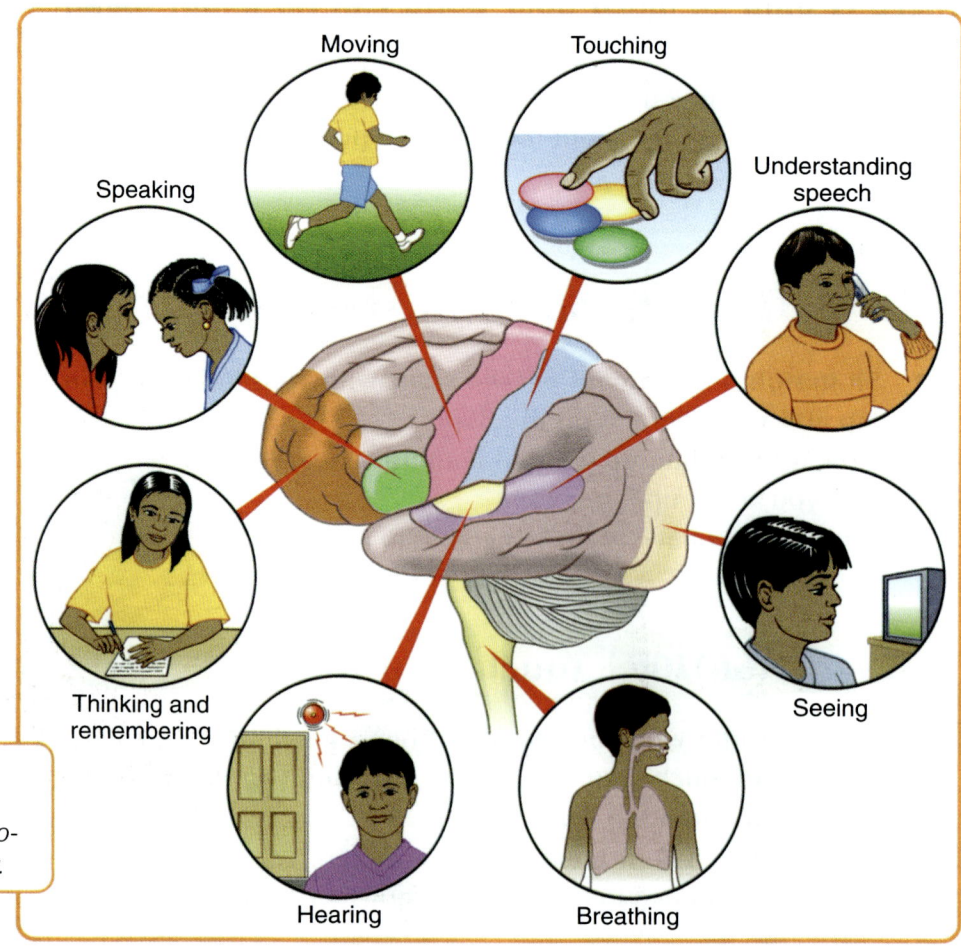

different functions. One part deals with conscious thought and memory. Other parts deal with things such as sight and speech. The part of the cerebrum near the front even determines certain aspects of your personality.

Another part of the brain called the **cerebellum**, found at the base of the brain, deals with balance, co-ordination of body movements and posture. The part which joins the spinal cord is called the **medulla oblongata**. This part is concerned with activities such as the control of heartbeat and breathing.

Did you know?

After the age of 18, you lose about 1000 nerve cells (neurones) from your brain every day.

Your brain receives signals from all parts of your body

Your brain receives millions of bits of information every second. The nerve messages travel in tiny electric currents called **impulses** along neurones that connect your sense organs to your brain. These impulses come from all parts of your body. Your brain analyses these impulses, and then sends messages back telling different parts of your body what to do. For example, an arriving impulse may say 'itch' or 'smell'. The brain then sends a return message telling you to 'scratch' or 'sniff'.

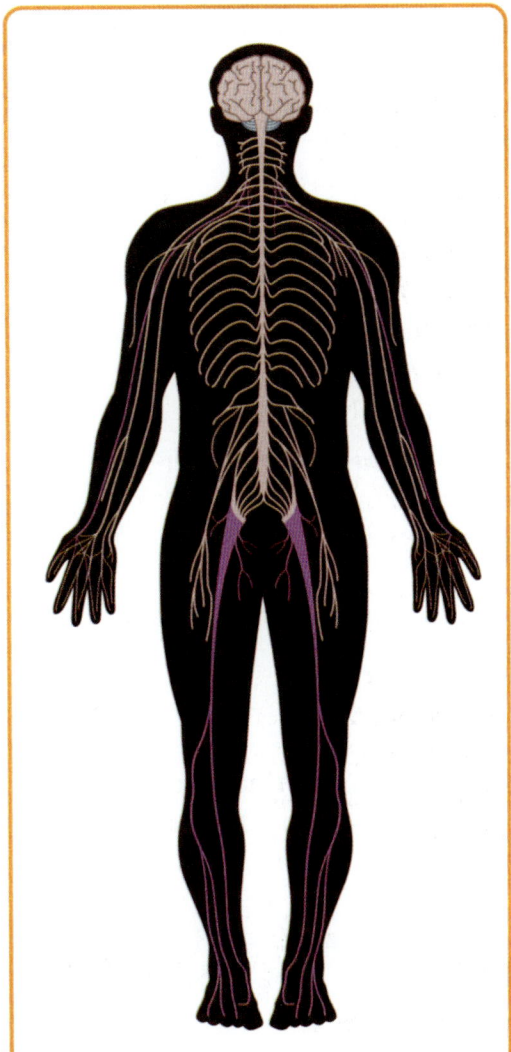

You have thousands of kilometres of nerves inside your body. They stretch from your brain to your fingertips, the tips of your toes and to every other part of your body. Your brain is your body's central processing unit for all information.

Super brain 33

12 More about how the brain works

Your brain is your body's piece of 'thinking equipment' which allows you to carry out important activities such as problem solving and making conscious decisions. But many of the activities and reactions you carry out or make every second of the day, and even when you are asleep, are automatic reactions. They happen without you having to think about them or make decisions about them.

> **INVESTIGATION** — **Watch automatic reactions**
>
> Work with a partner. Be very careful.
>
> - Stand about 1 m in front of your partner.
> - Quickly flick a handkerchief in front of their eyes, but be very careful not to touch their face.
> - Now let your partner try the same thing with you.
>
> Did you find that you and your partner both blinked your eyes when you each flicked the handkerchief?

The blinking of your eyes is a **reflex action**. You don't have to think about a reflex action. It takes place automatically without your brain having to make a decision.

> Can you think of any more reflex actions you make?
> Why do you think we have reflex actions?

Reflex actions allow you to respond quickly

Reflex actions allow you to make a very quick response to a sudden change in your surroundings. If your hand touches a hot plate, a message is picked up by a sensory receptor in your finger. The message travels from the receptor along a nerve to your spinal cord – it may also travel to your brain. Here it is passed on to other nerves and finally to a nerve which runs from your spinal cord, or your brain, to the muscles in your arm. When your arm muscles receive the incoming message, they contract and make you pull your hand away from the hot plate. The whole process happens very quickly and you don't even have to think about it. Your brain is made aware of it, but only after your arm muscles have pulled your hand away from the heat.

Reflex actions are very useful because the message gets from the receptor to the part of the body which reacts as quickly as possible. You don't waste time thinking about what to do. In the case of touching a hot plate, a reflex action prevents you from getting burned.

INVESTIGATION: Experience automatic arm raising

- Stand in the middle of a doorway.
- Press your arms as hard as you can against the doorframe for 30 seconds.
- Now take one step forwards so your arms are free to move.

What happens to your arms?

The reason your arms started to move upwards after you stopped pressing is because they remained programmed to keep pressing, even though your brain stopped sending signals to them to keep pressing.

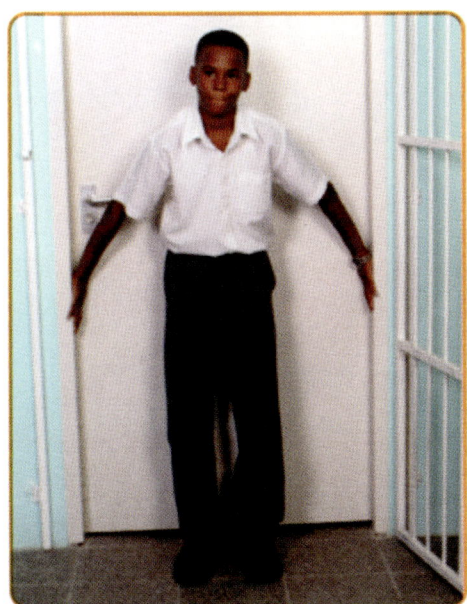
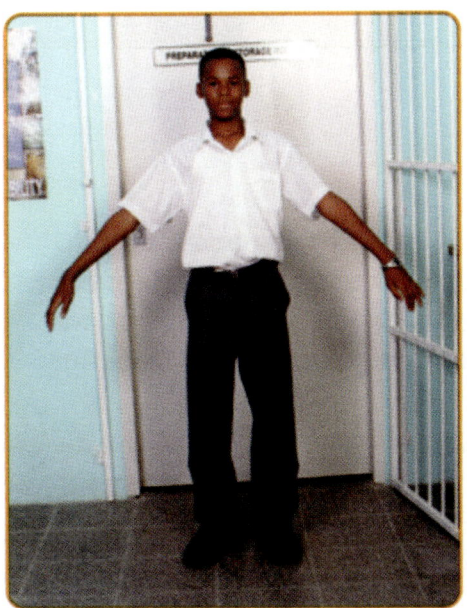

More about how the brain works

Which side are you on?

In Unit 5 you discovered that you have a dominant eye. This is because of the way your brain develops. By the time you are finishing primary school, one side of your brain has become dominant. It works the opposite to what you would expect. If the left-hand side of your brain is dominant you will be right-sided. If the right-hand side of your brain is dominant you will be left-sided.

INVESTIGATION Try some dominance tests

Record which hand (or leg) you use for each test.
- Write your name on a piece of paper.
- Clasp your hands and place your thumbs one on top of the other.
- Sit down and cross one leg over the other.
- Pretend you are throwing a stone.
- Pretend you are kicking a ball.
- Open a door.
- Pick something up off your desk.

1. Which hand do you write with?
2. Which thumb or leg was on top?
3. Which arm, foot or hand do you use most?
4. Are you right-sided or left-sided?
5. What percentage of your class is right-sided?
6. What percentage of your class is left-sided?
7. In most populations, 90% of the people are right-sided and 10% are left-sided. Are these the kinds of percentage figures you found for your class?

Activity

Some nerve impulses travel at nearly 300 km per hour.
- Imagine your younger brother or sister is 1 m tall. Assume their nerve impulses travel at 300 km per hour. Work out how long it would take for an impulse to travel from their foot to their brain.

36 More about how the brain works

Skin – living inside an elastic bag

Skin separates your inside from the outside world

Your body is covered by a thin, stretchy bag called **skin**. On the outside, skin consists of dead cells, but underneath it is alive and well. Every time you rub your skin, you brush off millions of dead skin cells. But don't worry because your body produces a new bag of skin every few weeks.

Although skin looks smooth, it has plenty of wrinkles and ridges. You only have to look at your fingertips to see the ridges that form your fingerprints. You may remember fingerprint patterns from Year 1.

Skin is important for lots of reasons

- It is waterproof so it protects your body from drying out.
- It stops bacteria, dirt and the Sun's harmful rays from entering your body.
- It controls your body temperature so it doesn't get too hot or too cold.
- It has lots of tiny sensors to keep you up-to-date about the world around you.
- It helps you get rid of waste substances.

Our skin becomes more wrinkled as we grow older. The old man in the picture is Emiliano Mercado Del Toro who was born on 21 August 1891. This photograph was taken in August 2006 at the time of his 115th birthday, when he was reputed to be the oldest living man in the world.

The hairs on skin are very important

The hairs on your skin act as protection. They grow at the entrance to your nose and ears and also around your eyes to keep out dust and other bits of debris.

The hairs under your arms trap your body's natural smells. Before people started using things like deodorants, our natural smells were probably very important in our lives. They probably gave other people important signals about us.

The hairs on your skin are some of the best sensors you have. Every hair on your body is connected to a nerve so this increases your sense of touch.

Have you ever felt a tiny insect crawling on you? You were able to sense the insect because it touched some of your sensitive hairs and this gave it away.

You wouldn't survive if you didn't live in a bag of skin!

Skin is very sensitive

There are millions of sensors under your skin which tell you about the world around you. They inform you about what things feel like when you touch them. They also tell you about how hot or cold something is and what the pressure is like on your body. They keep your body in touch with the outside world.

Touch is a mixture of senses

When you touch something, you use all your different sensors to help you get a feel for what the object is like. You can feel all kinds of things but you only use the four basic sensors of heat, cold, pain and pressure to feel with. Different parts of your skin have different numbers of sensors and other structures. Your fingertips have more sensors than any other part of your body. This is why you use them to touch things and to explore the world around you.

Activity

Which of your sensors (heat, cold, pain, pressure) do you use when you:
- kiss someone
- hug someone
- comb your hair
- take a hot shower
- touch a bowl of ice cream
- tread on an upturned drawing pin in bare feet?

FACTFILE

Skin

A 1 cm² patch of skin on the back of your hand contains as many as:
1 oil gland
2 cold sensors
3 m of blood vessels
4 m of nerves
8 hairs
10 heat sensors
20 pressure sensors
80 sweat glands
170 pain sensors.

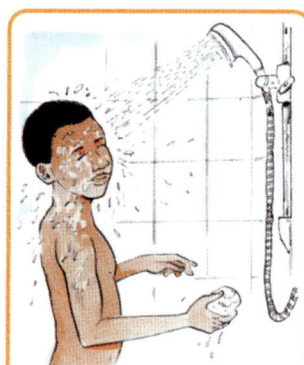

INVESTIGATION: Find out which part of the skin has most touch receptors

Work with a partner.
- Copy the results table. Leave plenty of space in each cell of your table.

Part of skin	Distance apart of pins		
	2 cm	1 cm	0.5 cm
back of hand			
fingertips			
above elbow			

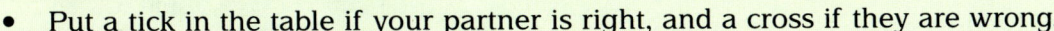

- Use sticky tape to attach two pins exactly 2 cm apart on a school ruler.
- Ask your partner to close their eyes.
- Using the ruler, touch your partner gently on the back of the hand with one or two pins.
- Ask your partner to say how many pins are touching their hand.
- Put a tick in the table if your partner is right, and a cross if they are wrong.
- Repeat this nine more times. You should now have ten ticks or crosses in the first cell of the table (for back of hand, 2 cm).
- Repeat the investigation, but this time touch the skin on your partner's fingertips. Record your results in the table. (You should now have ten ticks or crosses in the next cell down the table.)
- Repeat the investigation, but this time touch the skin on your partner's arm above the elbow. Record your results in the table.
- Now adjust the pins to 1 cm apart and repeat the investigation on each of the three body parts.
- Adjust the pins again, this time to 0.5 cm apart, and repeat the investigation.
- Draw a bar chart of the results.
- Now swap over and let your partner try the complete touch test on you.

1. Why does it become more difficult to tell how many pins are touching the skin as the pins get closer together?
2. Which of the three parts of the body you tested contained most touch receptors?
3. Why do you think this part of the body needs to be so sensitive?

This boy is blind but he can still read by using his sense of touch. His book is written in Braille. Braille is a language used by blind people in which each letter of the alphabet is represented by its own special pattern of small bumps. By feeling the different patterns, the boy can understand what the book is about. He is 'seeing' the words with his fingertips.

Did you know?

A blind person using Braille can read about 3000 words an hour.

Skin – living inside an elastic bag

14 Keeping warm and cool

FACTFILE

History
About 230 years ago, a man called Doctor Blagden did an interesting experiment. Together with some friends, his dog and a large piece of raw meat, he went into a room where the air temperature was 125 °C. Yes; the room's air temperature was 25 °C higher than boiling water. About 45 minutes later, everyone came out (including the dog) in good health, and the piece of meat was cooked and ready to eat!

Heat is lost through the skin by radiation

Every square centimetre of skin has many tiny blood vessels just under the surface. When your body is too hot, these blood vessels get wider, bringing more blood to the surface of your skin. The blood carries lots of heat. When it gets to the skin, the heat radiates from your body to the outside and this cools you down. Your skin works like a radiator because it loses heat by radiation.

If your body gets cold, the opposite happens. The blood vessels get narrower, so not much blood flows through your skin so very little heat is carried there. Instead, heat is kept inside your body and you stay warm. Your brain works like a thermostat in controlling your body temperature, keeping it at about 37 °C.

Skin controls your body temperature in other ways

When it is hot, the **sweat glands** in your skin begin to work. They produce a liquid called sweat which finds its way onto the surface of your skin through tiny holes called pores. The sweaty liquid on your skin evaporates using heat from your body and this cools you down. If it gets colder, your brain tells your sweat glands to stop sweating. Now evaporation stops so you lose less heat from your body and you stay warm.

An African elephant's ears work like two giant radiators. When its body starts to heat up, it flaps them to expose more skin to the outside world. By flapping its ears, an elephant increases the amount of skin available for heat loss by another 20%!

INVESTIGATION: Feel the effect of evaporation

- On a very hot day, find a pair of old socks.
- Dip one in water and then squeeze the water out so the sock is damp.
- Put the dry sock on your right foot and the damp sock on your left foot.
- Sit outside in the sun for a few minutes.
1. How does your right foot feel?
2. How does your left foot feel?

Your left foot feels colder because the heat under the skin of your foot is being used to evaporate the water from the damp sock. This cools your foot down.

Did you know?
Liquid sweat on your skin will evaporate using heat from your body and this will cool you down.

Skin has another trick for trying to control body temperature

Have you ever had 'goose pimples' on your skin? You only get them when you get cold. Your skin tries to warm you up by doing something with the hairs on your skin. It makes the hairs stand upright to try and make a blanket of air round your body. Nothing keeps the body warmer than a blanket of air. However, unlike furry animals, humans don't have much hair so this trick doesn't work very well. All that really happens is that the few hairs on your body make little bumps or pimples on the skin as they stand up. You feel these as goose pimples.

Skin has one more important function

The skin is an important excretory organ. The next time you finish a game of netball or football, give your arm a lick to taste your sweat. Sweat tastes salty because it contains salt dissolved in it. Sweating is a way of getting rid of any extra salt your body doesn't need. Your skin also helps get rid of the waste products your body doesn't want. When you sweat, a waste substance called **urea** is got rid of in your sweat.

Did you know?
You produce about 5 litres of sweat every day, but on very hot days you can sweat double this amount.

Activity
- Think about how skin helps to keep the body cool.
- In no more than 100 words, explain how Doctor Blagden survived such a high temperature.
- If Dr Blagden asked you to accompany him into the room, how would you prepare yourself for such an ordeal?

15

Chest changes and breathing

You are an oxygen guzzler and a carbon dioxide emitter

You are using oxygen and producing carbon dioxide every second of your life, even when you are asleep. Taking oxygen into your body and getting rid of carbon dioxide from your body takes place in your chest. Imagine your chest is like a room. It has walls formed by the **ribs** and rib muscles. It has a floor formed by a big, flat muscle called the **diaphragm**. But the chest is a special room because it has moveable walls. It can change shape and get bigger or smaller by moving the ribs and diaphragm.

A car engine uses petrol or diesel as a fuel. It burns fuel with oxygen to release energy for movement. A car produces waste gases such as carbon monoxide and carbon dioxide.

The chest isn't an empty room. It is full of two big, spongy bags called **lungs** which connect to the outside by a branched tube called the **windpipe** or **trachea**.

The lungs are a pick-up point for oxygen and a drop-off point for carbon dioxide. You suck air into your lungs through your nose and mouth when you breathe in. You push air out of your lungs when you breathe out. Breathing is all to do with muscles.

INVESTIGATION Feel yourself breathing

- Place your hands flat on either side of your chest.
- Now, slowly, take the deepest breath you can.
1. Can you feel your rib muscles gradually lifting your chest upwards?
- Now breathe out very slowly.
2. Can you feel your rib muscles gradually pulling your chest downwards?
- Place your hands flat over your stomach.
- Now, slowly, take another deep breath.
3. Can you feel your diaphragm pushing your stomach outwards as it flattens?
- Now breathe out very slowly.
4. Can you feel your stomach moving inwards as your diaphragm curves up again?

Did you know?

You use food as a fuel. You burn food with oxygen to release energy. The energy drives your life processes. You produce waste carbon dioxide.

Breathing involves muscles

When you breathe in, your rib muscles pull the chest upwards and outwards and your diaphragm muscle flattens across the base of your chest. The space inside your chest now gets bigger and air rushes into your lungs from outside to fill this extra space. When you breathe out, your rib muscles and diaphragm muscle work in the opposite way.

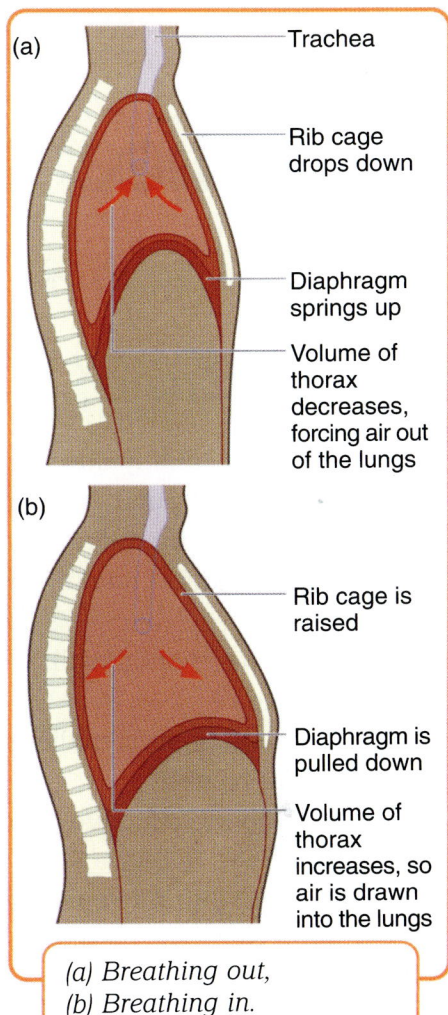

(a) Breathing out, (b) Breathing in.

INVESTIGATION Make a model lung

Work with a partner.

- Ask your teacher to help you cut the bottom off a plastic water bottle.
- Cut the tip off a balloon and stretch it over the cut end of the bottle.
- Push a drinking straw into the mouth of another balloon.
- Hold the balloon tight to the straw with an elastic band.
- Push the balloon on the straw through the neck of the bottle.
- Keep it in place with Plasticine or modelling clay.
- Make sure it is a tight fit with no air gaps.
- Ask your partner to hold the bottle firmly while you gently pull down on the bottom balloon.
- Now gently push the bottom balloon up into the bottle.

1. What happens to the balloon in the bottle when you pull down on the bottom balloon?
2. What happens to the balloon in the bottle when you push the bottom balloon up?
3. Did you find the balloon in the bottle filled and emptied as you pulled and pushed the bottom balloon?
4. What does the straw represent in your body?
5. What does the balloon in the bottle represent in your body?
6. What does the bottom balloon represent in your body?
7. Why did air rush into the balloon when you pulled the bottom balloon down?
8. Why did air rush out of the balloon when you pushed the bottom balloon up?

These students are experimenting with a model lung.

16 The bags you breathe with

> **INVESTIGATION** — **Find out about your breathing rate**
>
> - Sit down quietly and relax for 1 minute.
> - Record the number of breaths you take in 1 minute.
> - Now jump up and down on the same spot for 1 minute.
> - Record again the number of breaths you take in 1 minute.
>
> 1. How many breaths did you take in 1 minute when you were resting?
> 2. How many breaths did you take in 1 minute immediately after exercise?
> 3. What happens to your breathing rate when you do some exercise?
> 4. Why do you think your breathing rate changes when you do exercise?

Lungs are not empty bags

The **respiratory system** (breathing system) is made up of two lungs and the tubes that lead to them from the nose and mouth. The trachea (windpipe) leads from the back of the mouth down to the lungs. When it reaches the lungs, it divides into two smaller tubes. One of these goes into each lung. Once inside the lungs each of these smaller tubes divides into even smaller tubes. These branch again and become smaller and smaller until they are thinner than a hair. Eventually, each tiny tube ends in a group of microscopic bags called **air sacs**. Each group of air sacs is surrounded by a network of tiny blood capillaries. Each lung contains about 300 million air sacs.

The respiratory system has its own air-conditioning device

The cells lining the tubes in your respiratory system make a sticky, slippery liquid called **mucus**. Mucus works like an air conditioner. It filters the air passing through and traps microbes, bits of dust and dirt. It also moistens the air so it can travel more easily along the tubes. Tiny hairs lining the tubes beat the mucus away from your lungs towards your nose and throat so you can swallow it.

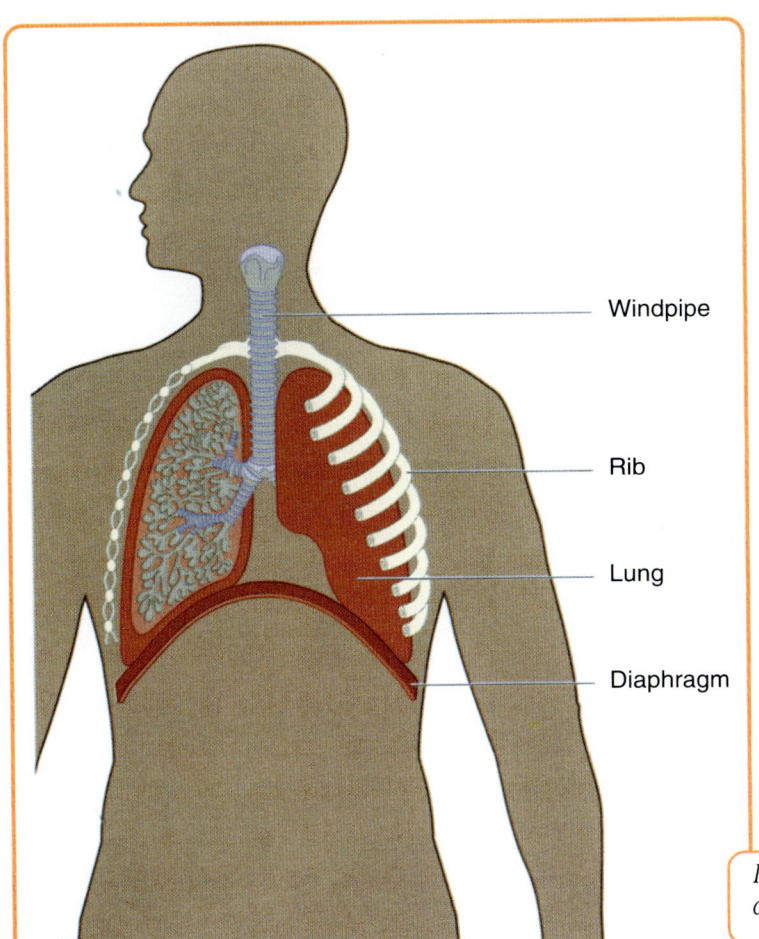

Did you know?
If all the air sacs in your lungs were spread out flat, side by side, they would cover a surface area as big as a tennis court.

In the human respiratory system, each lung is about the size of a football.

The walls of each air sac are very thin

When you breathe in (inhale), the air passes down the trachea and through the branching tubes in the lungs until it arrives at the thin-walled air sacs. The walls of the capillaries surrounding each air sac are only one cell thick, so oxygen doesn't have far to travel to get into the blood from each air sac. Oxygen diffuses from the air sacs into the blood. But the blood in the capillaries contains lots of carbon dioxide. Carbon dioxide diffuses the other way – from the capillaries into the air sacs. When you breathe out (exhale) carbon dioxide passes out of your body.

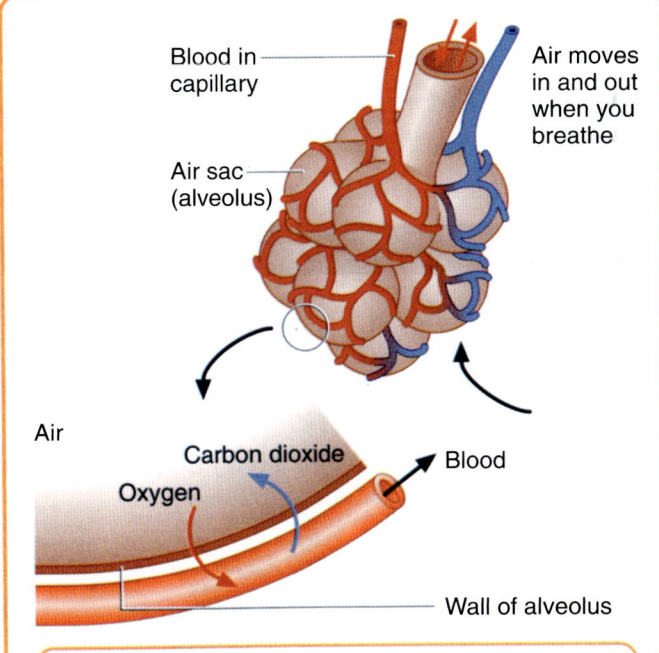

When you breathe in, oxygen diffuses from the air sacs into the surrounding capillaries. Carbon dioxide produced by the body diffuses from the capillaries into the air sacs. This is removed when you breathe out.

INVESTIGATION   Test the air you breathe out

- Breathe out on the back of your hand.

1. What does the air you breathe out feel like?
2. Why does the air you breathe out feel like this?

- Hold a mirror close to your mouth and breathe on its surface.

3. What do you notice on the surface of the mirror?
4. What do you think this substance is?

The air you breathe out contains a lot of water vapour. This is why the surface of the mirror misted over when you breathed on it.

Lime water turns milky if it comes in contact with carbon dioxide.

- Half fill a boiling tube with lime water.
- Gently breathe out and blow some air through a straw into the lime water for 1 minute.

5. What happened to the lime water when you breathed into it?
6. Does the air you breathe out contain carbon dioxide?

When you take a hot shower, you will notice the bathroom mirror often steams up.

The air you breathe out is not the same as the air you breathe in. The table shows the differences.

	Air breathed in	Air breathed out
oxygen	21%	16%
carbon dioxide	0.03%	4%
nitrogen	78%	78%
noble gases	1%	1%
water vapour	variable	always high

Activity

- Imagine you are a molecule of oxygen in the air just in front of your sister's nose. Explain what happens to you from the time your sister breathes you in to the time you end up in your sister's blood.

Energy release and oxygen debt

We need oxygen to help produce the energy we need

When you are resting, you use about 0.15 litres of oxygen every minute to produce the energy needed to stay alive. Your teacher uses about 0.23 litres of oxygen every minute to keep their body alive. A marathon runner uses about 5 litres of oxygen every minute when running in a race. And when an athlete runs a 100 m dash, they need about 7 litres of oxygen to do just 10 seconds' work!

> Why does your teacher use more oxygen than you do when resting?
> Why does a marathon runner need so much oxygen when running a race?
> Why does a 100 m sprinter need so much oxygen for such a short time?

Did you know?

When you are resting, only about 20% of the oxygen in your blood goes to your muscles. When you are exercising, your muscles receive about 80% of the oxygen in your blood.

Oxygen is used to help release the energy

Normally your body contains only about 1 litre of oxygen, so when you exercise you have to find a way of getting more oxygen. You get the extra oxygen you need by breathing more quickly. Your heart also beats faster so you can deliver this extra oxygen to your muscles. So, when you exercise, your oxygen consumption increases, your breathing rate increases and your heartbeat increases to provide your body with the extra oxygen it needs.

Respiration is an oxidation reaction

The chemical reaction which takes place in your cells involving oxygen and the production of energy is called **respiration**. Because this reaction needs oxygen it is called **aerobic** respiration. 'Aerobic' means with air. Chemical reactions which involve oxygen are called **oxidation reactions**. So, aerobic respiration is an oxidation reaction.

The people about to start running this marathon will run just over 42 km before they get to the end of the race. During the race, each of their hearts will beat more than 30 000 times and they will each use about 750 litres of oxygen to release the energy they need for running such a long distance.

Similarly, when a fire burns, oxygen is involved and **combustion** (burning) takes place. So combustion is also an oxidation reaction. A fire burns fuels such as wood or oil. The fuels contain energy and this is released when the fuels react with oxygen. The energy released escapes mainly as heat and light.

Aerobic respiration that takes place in your cells is a kind of extra slow combustion and the fuel involved is the food you eat. The main fuel your body uses is a sugar called **glucose**. In your cells, oxygen reacts with glucose to release energy. Two other by-products of this reaction are carbon dioxide and water. Aerobic respiration can be summarised by a simple equation:

glucose + oxygen → energy + carbon dioxide + water

When you exercise, you get hotter

Have you noticed that when you play football or netball your body gets hotter? Exercise makes you hotter. This is because humans are very inefficient machines. Our bodies are not very good at 'catching' all the energy we release when we respire. In fact we use only about 20% of the energy we produce. The rest (about 80%) escapes as heat and is wasted. Your body becomes hotter when you exercise because most of the energy you produce when your cells respire is wasted as heat.

Sometimes your body works without oxygen for a short time

Sometimes your body needs a quick, extra burst of energy. This happens when you run upstairs or make a jump shot in basketball. In this situation, your lungs can't breathe fast enough to give your muscles the extra oxygen they need to satisfy your increased energy demands. In this case, your body releases the energy it needs without using oxygen. But it can only do this for a short time – 2 minutes at the most. This kind of respiration is called **anaerobic respiration**. 'Anaerobic' means without air.

A sudden demand for energy builds up an oxygen debt

If you run in a 100 m sprint, you complete most of the race without using oxygen. You respire anaerobically. But after the race you 'owe' your body oxygen. At the end of the race, you breathe very fast for several minutes to give your body the oxygen it needed during the race. In this way, you pay back your **oxygen debt**. When the debt is paid back, your breathing returns to normal and you switch back to ordinary aerobic respiration again. This is why an athlete running a 100 m dash needs about 7 litres of oxygen to do just 10 seconds' work! They are repaying their oxygen debt!

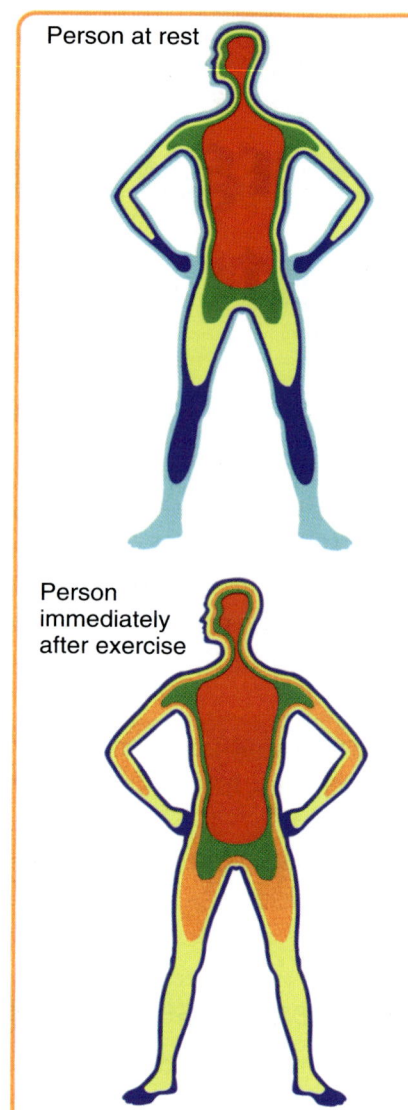

These pictures were taken with a special camera. They are called thermal images. In a thermal image, the cold parts of the body appear as blue areas, the warmer parts as orange areas and the hot parts as red areas. The top image shows a person at rest and the image below shows the same person immediately after exercise. You can see how the person's body has become hotter during exercise.

The perfect pump

Reliable for 70 years or more

Machines such as cars, refrigerators and television sets last for only a few years before they begin to wear out. Then, they have to be replaced. This is true of all man-made machines. But imagine a machine that can work for more than 70 years without breaking down or needing repair!

Your **heart** is just such a machine. It is made of muscle called **cardiac muscle** and is probably the most powerful muscle in your body. It certainly works much harder than any of your other muscles. Your heart is about the size of your fist. It is a bit like a hollow ball with very muscular walls. The muscular walls of the heart continually move in and out (contract and expand) forcing blood around the body day and night.

Your heart beats about 70 times a minute for the whole of your lifetime. So, if you live to be 70 years old (and many people live even longer than this), your heart will beat about 2.5 billion times. In 70 years your heart will pump about 360 million litres of blood around your body. This equals the amount of water needed to give the population of Trinidad and Tobago their morning shower every day for two months!

FACTFILE

The heart

Average work rate: about 70 beats per minute.
Average number of beats per day: about 100 000.
At rest, blood pumped out: about 10 litres per minute.
During hard exercise, blood pumped out: about 45 litres per minute.
Lifetime's volume of blood pumped out: about 360 million litres.
Number of complete circulations of blood: about 1000 per day.
Number of complete circulations of blood in a lifetime: about 25 million.

INVESTIGATION — How hard does your heart work?

This simple experiment will help you get a feel for just how hard your heart works every second of your life. The force needed to squeeze a tennis ball is similar to the force needed to squeeze blood out of your heart.

- Hold a tennis ball in your hand and squeeze it as hard as you can.
- Now time yourself and squeeze the ball 70 times in 1 minute.

1. Does your hand start to hurt as you squeeze?
2. How does your hand feel when 1 minute is up?
3. Could you carry on squeezing the ball for very much longer, or do you think your hand would get too tired?

Squeezing a tennis ball continuously for 1 minute is hard work. Just imagine trying to squeeze the ball 2.5 billion times without stopping!

Valves control blood flow

Your heart is found in the centre of your chest between your lungs. It lies inside the rib cage, just under the breastbone. It is divided into left and right sides by a strong, muscular wall. Each side is divided into two parts or chambers. The top chambers on each side are called **atriums** and the bottom chambers are called **ventricles**. The two sides work together in perfect time, which gives your heart plenty of pumping power. The atriums and ventricles are separated by structures called **valves**. Valves open and close to let the blood flow through your heart in only one direction. Other valves in the big blood vessels leaving the heart stop blood returning to the heart once it has been pumped out.

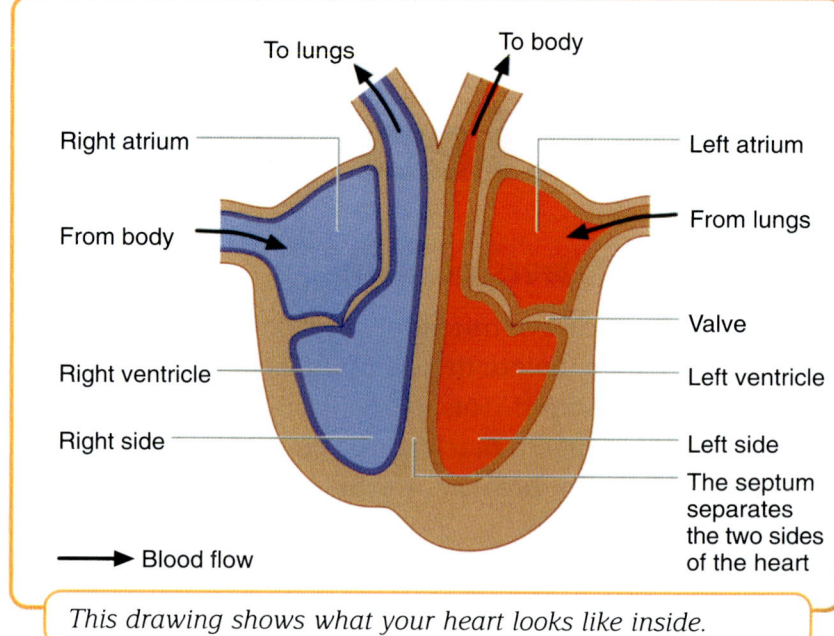

This drawing shows what your heart looks like inside.

The heart is really a double pump

Blood enters the right atrium of the heart from the body. At exactly the same time, blood enters the left atrium from the lungs. The atriums then contract together and pump the blood to the two ventricles. When the ventricles are full of blood, they contract together. The right ventricle pumps blood to the lungs while the left ventricle pumps blood round the rest of the body. Because blood is pumped to the lungs and round the rest of the body at the same time, biologists say that humans (and other mammals) have a **double circulatory system**.

The female heart is naturally stronger than the male heart

On average, women live 5 years longer than men. Now doctors may have solved this age-old puzzle. It is because of pumping power. The average male heart becomes weaker with age. By the age of 70, the pumping power of a man's heart decreases by about 25%. A woman's heart doesn't lose its pumping power. The heart of a 70-year-old woman pumps just as strongly as it did when she was 20. Doctors think this may be why women live longer than men do.

Did you know?

The heart of a mammal lasts for about 1 billion beats before the animal dies.
A human heart is different. It beats about 2.5 billion times in a lifetime.

Pulse rates and fitness

Activity
- Feel the effect of your heart beating by feeling your pulse. The photograph will help you find your pulse point. If you have a problem, ask your teacher for help.

You can make a simple device called a pulsometer to see the effect of your heart at work.

 **Make a pulsometer**

- Make a ball about the size of a pea using Plasticine or modelling clay.
- Push a matchstick into the ball so it is held firmly. You now have a pulsometer.
- Position the pulsometer on your left wrist until it is directly over the area where your pulse beats. You may need to move it about until you find the correct spot.
- Gently push the pulsometer onto your skin so it stays in place.
- Sit quietly and watch what happens.
- Record the number of times your pulsometer moves in 1 minute.
1. Can you see the pulsometer move in time to your heatbeat?
2. How many times did your pulse beat in 1 minute?
3. Compare your pulse rate with those of your classmates.

To feel your pulse find the pulse point in your wrist.

 **Listen to the noises your heart makes**

Make a simple stethoscope and then use it to listen to your heart.
- Ask your teacher to cut the top off a plastic water bottle.
- Fit a piece of rubber tubing over the open end. You have now made a simple stethoscope.
- Take turns with a classmate to listen to each other's heart beating.

If you listen carefully, you should hear two sounds during every beat. You should hear lub-DUB, lub-DUB, lub-DUB. These are the sounds your heart valves make as they open and shut.

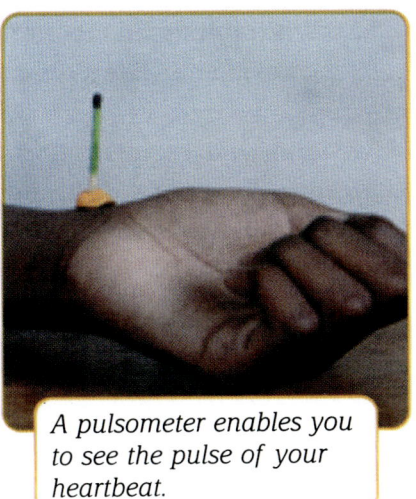

A pulsometer enables you to see the pulse of your heartbeat.

Pulse rates and fitness 51

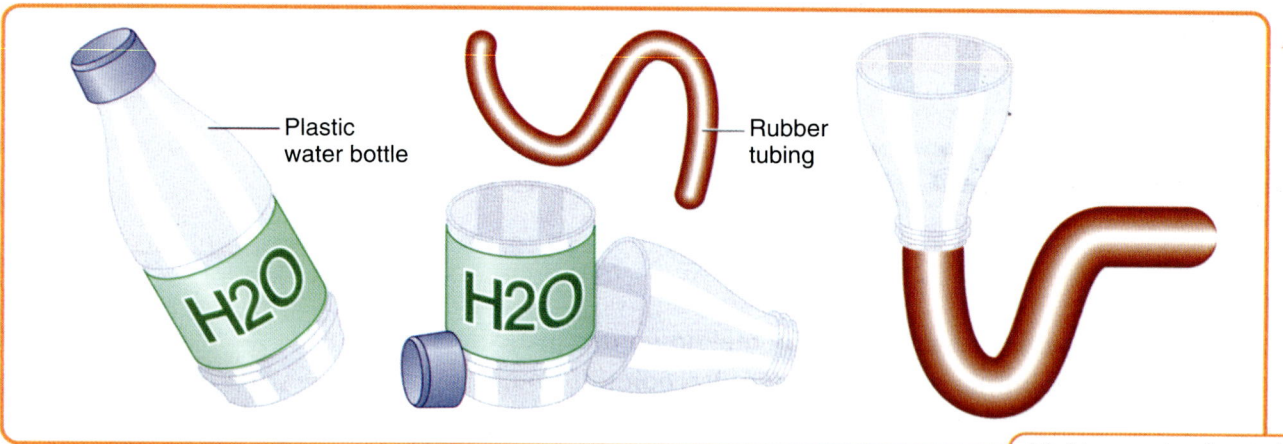

Making a simple stethoscope.

INVESTIGATION Measure your pulse rate before and after exercise

- Lie down and breathe deeply for 1 minute. Your body should now feel relaxed and your heart should be beating at its normal rate.
- Now measure your pulse rate for 1 minute and record the result.
- Do press-ups or jump up and down for 1 minute.
- Record your pulse rate again.

1 What happens to your pulse rate after exercise?
2 Does your heart work harder and faster when you exercise?

When you exercise, your muscles need more food and oxygen. Your heart beats faster to give your muscles the extra food and oxygen they need.

INVESTIGATION Find out how fit you are

Work with a partner. Ask your partner to hold the chair firmly when you step up and down on it.
- Copy out the fitness results table.
- Step up onto a chair and stand with both legs straight. Then step down onto the floor and stand with both legs straight. Step up and down like this for 4 minutes (240 seconds) without stopping. Step up and down at a steady rate. Don't try to go too fast.
- Sit down and rest for 1 minute.
- Now ask your partner to measure your pulse rate for 30 seconds. This is your first pulse reading. Record it in your table.
- Rest for another 30 seconds.

- Now ask your partner to measure your pulse rate for another 30 seconds. This is your second pulse reading. Record it in your table.
- Rest for another 30 seconds.
- Now ask your partner to measure your pulse rate for another 30 seconds. This is your third pulse reading. Record it in your table.
- Now change over and let your partner do the fitness test.
- Use the information in the table to work out your fitness score.
- Compare your score with others in your class. The higher the score, the fitter you are.
- You can also look up your fitness score in the fitness chart below. The chart uses scores that are based on average values calculated for adults.

1. How fit are you?
2. Who are the fittest people in your class?
3. Why do you think some of your classmates are fitter than others?

Fitness results table

Total exercise time = 4 minutes
= 240 seconds

1st pulse reading = ... beats in 30 seconds
2nd pulse reading = ... beats in 30 seconds
3rd pulse reading = ... beats in 30 seconds

Total pulse reading = ... beats
(Add up your three readings.)

Multiply your total pulse reading by 2 to give your Grand pulse reading.

Grand pulse reading = ... beats

$$\text{Fitness score} = \frac{\text{Total exercise time (in seconds)} \times 100}{\text{Grand pulse reading}}$$

= ....

Fitness chart

Fitness score	Fitness level
91 and over	very fit indeed
81–90	very good
71–80	good
61–70	quite good
51–60	poor
under 51	very poor

Darrel Brown is one of Trinidad's most famous athletes. What do you think his score would be if he did the fitness test?

Did you know?

Fitness varies with age: what is outstanding fitness for a 60-year-old is only 'quite good' for a 13-year-old.

Pulse rates and fitness

20 Pressure and lifestyle

Your circulatory system works under pressure

When your heart muscles contract, they increase the pressure on your blood. This pressure is important in helping your body do all the things it has to do. When you feel your pulse, you are feeling this pressure. Your pulse is caused by blood starting and stopping as it rushes through your arteries. When you feel your pulse, you are feeling the arteries stretching and shrinking as blood squirts through them.

High blood pressure is a serious condition

Blood pressure is a measure of how hard the heart has to work to pump blood round the body. When the ventricles contract and they pump blood out of the heart, the pressure is at its highest. When the heart relaxes between pumps, the pressure is at its lowest. However, sometimes things start to go wrong and a person's blood pressure becomes higher than normal. When this happens, the person should see a doctor because they need treatment. High blood pressure is called **hypertension**. It is a very dangerous illness.

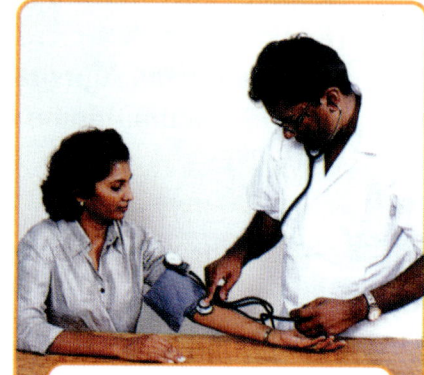

This woman is having her blood pressure taken. The doctor will find out two pressures – the one when the heart is pumping and the one when it is relaxing. The 'pumping pressure' for adults is normally about 120 units and the 'relaxing pressure' is usually about 80 units.

Lifestyle is important in keeping the heart healthy

If looked after properly, your heart will give you good service and last for 70 years or more. However, there are certain rules you should obey to keep it healthy.

Things to do:
- Do regular exercise.
- Maintain regular sleeping patterns.
- Eat a balanced diet.

Things not to do:
- Don't smoke.
- Don't drink alcohol.
- Don't take drugs.
- Don't eat too much salt with your food.
- Don't eat too much fatty food – less fat helps reduce cholesterol levels.
- Try to avoid stress – don't worry too much about things such as schoolwork or exams.

Cardiac arrest!

A healthy heart gives the body a good supply of blood so that all parts get enough food and oxygen. However, sometimes things go wrong with the heart. Some people are born with a faulty heart. Many more people start off with a healthy heart, but later it becomes diseased. Some diseases are caused by infections which can be treated with drugs. Rheumatic heart disease is an example of this.

By far the most common type of heart disease occurs when one or more of the **coronary arteries** (the arteries which supply the heart itself with blood) become blocked and the person has a heart attack. This is called coronary heart disease. When this happens, surgery is required in order to repair the heart by means of a coronary by-pass operation.

During heart surgery, the heart has to be stopped

Before surgery can be performed, the heart has to be by-passed and then stopped and taken out of service so that the surgeon can do the operation. In order to do this, surgeons use a machine called a heart–lung machine. For a short time, the heart and lungs are disconnected from the circulatory system and are replaced by an artificial pump and a machine called an oxygenator. These are connected up to the patient's circulatory system and then switched on to provide the body with blood while the operation is being carried out. During the operation, the heart stops beating. It becomes perfectly still and this allows the surgeon to put the stitches in exactly the right place.

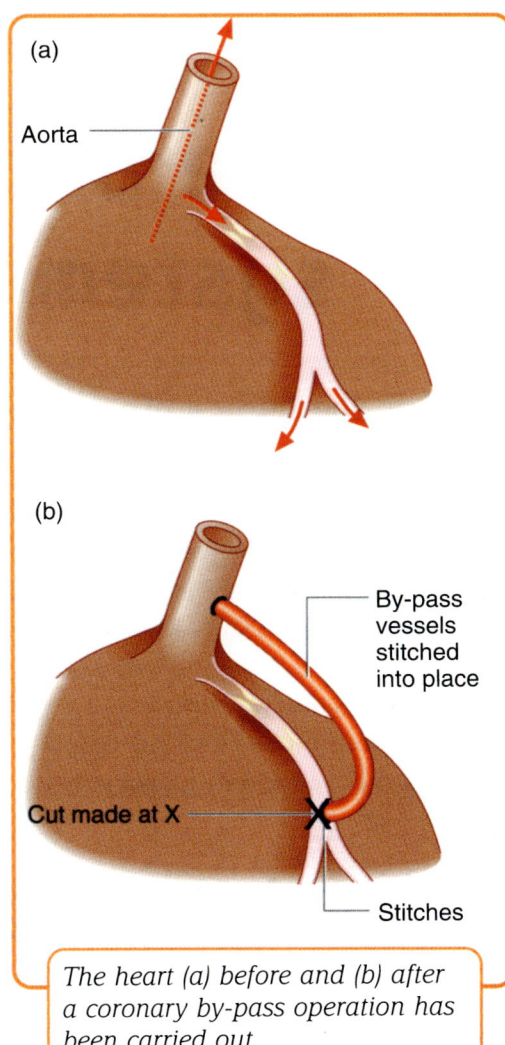

The heart (a) before and (b) after a coronary by-pass operation has been carried out.

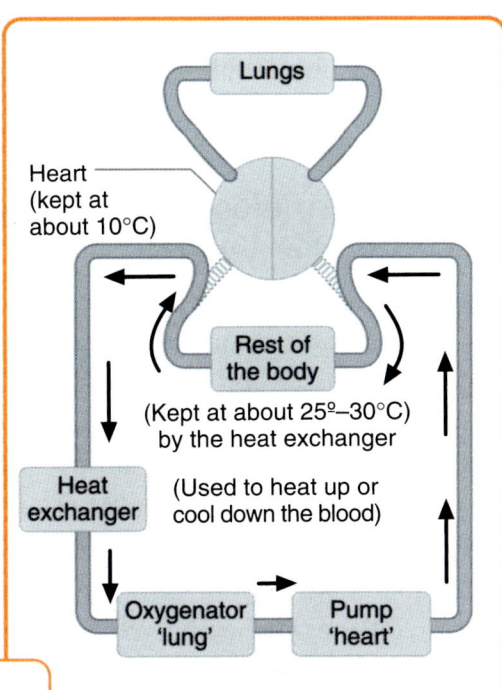

During a major heart operation, the blood circulatory system is kept going by a heart–lung machine.

Pressure and lifestyle

21 The body's transport system

Blood is the body's life support

Humans have a system to carry food and oxygen to all the cells in the body. This system also carries waste products made in the cells to other parts of the body where they are got rid of. Blood travels around the body in special tubes called **blood vessels**. There are three types of blood vessel called **arteries**, **veins** and **capillaries**. The three different types of blood vessel plus the heart make up the body's **circulatory system**.

Blood passes through the heart twice during one complete circulation

Blood is pumped to the lungs from the right side of the heart where it picks up oxygen you have breathed in. Then it returns to the left side from where it is pumped round the body to deliver its oxygen to the cells. Blood that has run out of oxygen returns to the heart to begin another circulation.

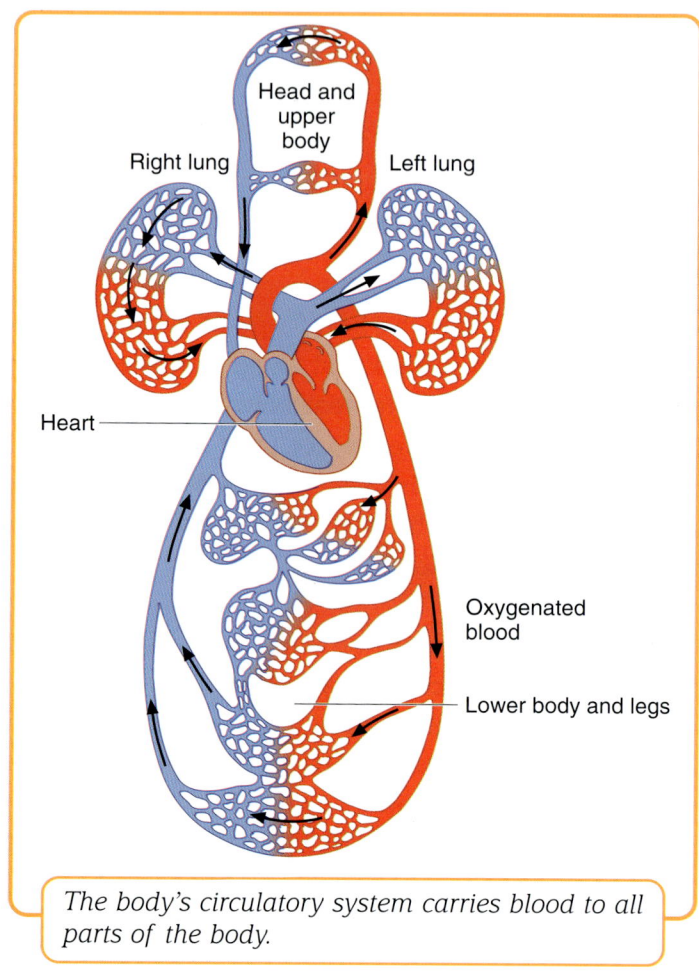

The body's circulatory system carries blood to all parts of the body.

Arteries carry blood from the heart to all parts of the body

Arteries are very strong, muscular tubes with stretchy, elastic walls. Arteries have to be strong and elastic because they have to deal with blood as it is forced into them by the pumping of the heart. Most arteries lie deep inside the body so you can't see or feel them. But some arteries are more easily found. The artery used to measure a person's pulse rate lies just under the skin in the wrist. You tried finding this in Unit 19. There are also other pulse points you can find. You can feel them in your neck, on the sides of your head near your temples, close to your elbow on the inside of your arm and in your groin near your hips.

Veins carry blood back to the heart from all parts of the body

Veins have thin, non-muscular walls. Blood isn't pumped along the veins. Instead, it just flows slowly along them on its way back to the heart. It is easy to see some of your veins because they lie just under the skin.

Activity
- Roll your arm over so you are looking at the palm of your hand.
- Look carefully at the skin between your elbow and your wrist.

Can you see some blue lines running along the length of your arm?

These blue lines are veins.

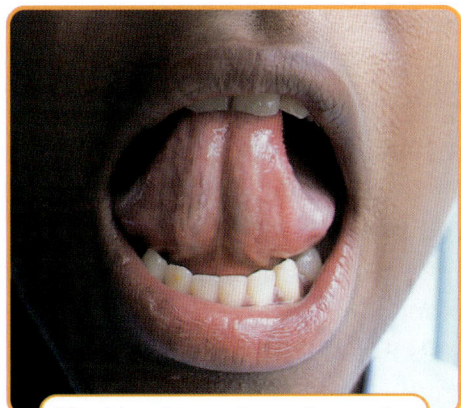

The blood vessels underneath your tongue lie close to the surface so they are easy to see.

Activity
- Hold a mirror in front of your mouth.
- Open your mouth and roll your tongue back so you can see underneath.
1. Can you see some big blue lines?
2. Can you see some big pink lines?

The blue lines are veins. The pink lines are arteries.

Did you know?
If all the blood vessels in your body were laid end to end, they would stretch for a distance of 100 000 km. This is nearly 16 times the distance between Port of Spain and London.

Capillaries are tiny blood vessels

As blood vessels get further and further away from the heart they get smaller and smaller. Eventually, when they get close to the cells, they are microscopic in size. These tiny blood vessels are called capillaries. Many capillaries are narrower than the finest hair on your head. Capillaries are the blood vessels which deliver food and oxygen to the cells and collect waste materials from the cells. No cell in your body is more than a hair's breadth from a capillary!

Activity
- Look at the whites of your eyes in a mirror.
- Now gently pull your bottom eyelid down so you can see the bottom of your eyeball.

Can you see any tiny red lines?

The body's transport system

Blood – the body's taxi service

Blood is a watery liquid

An average adult human has about 5 litres of blood. Blood is mainly water (**plasma**) with billions of cells floating in it. Most of these are **red blood cells** but there are also some **white cells** and small bits of cell material called **platelets**. Plasma makes up about 55% of the blood, with red cells and platelets making up about 44.55% and white cells about 0.45%.

> Is blood a solution, a suspension or an emulsion?
> (If you don't know the answer, look back to the work you did in Year 1.)

This human blood has been allowed to stand for 24 hours. You can see that it has separated into a solid part at the bottom of the tube and a liquid part above. The solid part is made up of blood cells. The liquid part is mainly water and is called plasma.

Red blood cells are tiny oxygen carriers

Just one drop of blood contains about 5 million red blood cells. Each is shaped like a tiny, flat plate. Their job is to pick up oxygen in the lungs and carry it to all parts of the body where they release it. Each red blood cell has a very thin membrane which lets oxygen pass in and out very easily. They are very soft cells so they can squeeze through the narrowest blood vessels.

Red blood cells are not very tough and they have no nucleus. Because of this, they are easily damaged and they don't live very long – normally about 4 months. This means they have to be continually replaced. Your body makes about 2 million new red blood cells every second!

Activity

- Look at the red blood cells in the photograph.
1. Describe the shape of a red blood cell.
2. How does the shape of a red blood cell help it to carry out its main function of absorbing oxygen in the lungs?

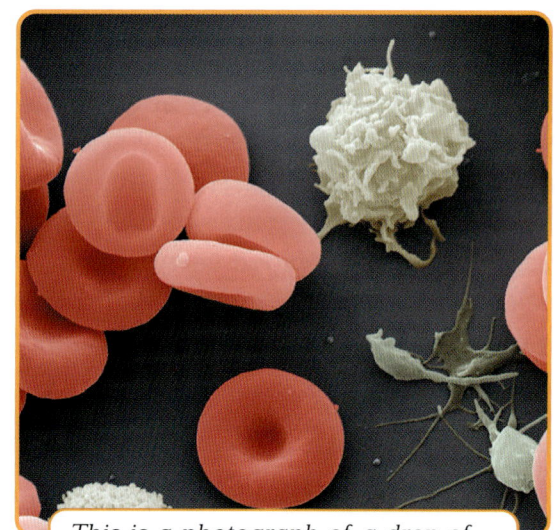

This is a photograph of a drop of human blood magnified about 700 times. You can see red blood cells, white blood cells and platelets.

Red blood cells form an oxygen taxi service for the body

Red blood cells contain a special chemical called **haemoglobin**. Haemoglobin likes oxygen. In fact it can't get enough of it. When blood goes to the lungs, the haemoglobin in the red cells collects oxygen until the cells are full of it. The haemoglobin in the red cells combines with oxygen to make a substance called **oxyhaemoglobin**. The red cells then flow in the blood to all parts of the body. When they reach those parts which need oxygen, the oxyhaemoglobin gives up its oxygen and turns into haemoglobin again. Then the red cells go back to the lungs to get more oxygen.

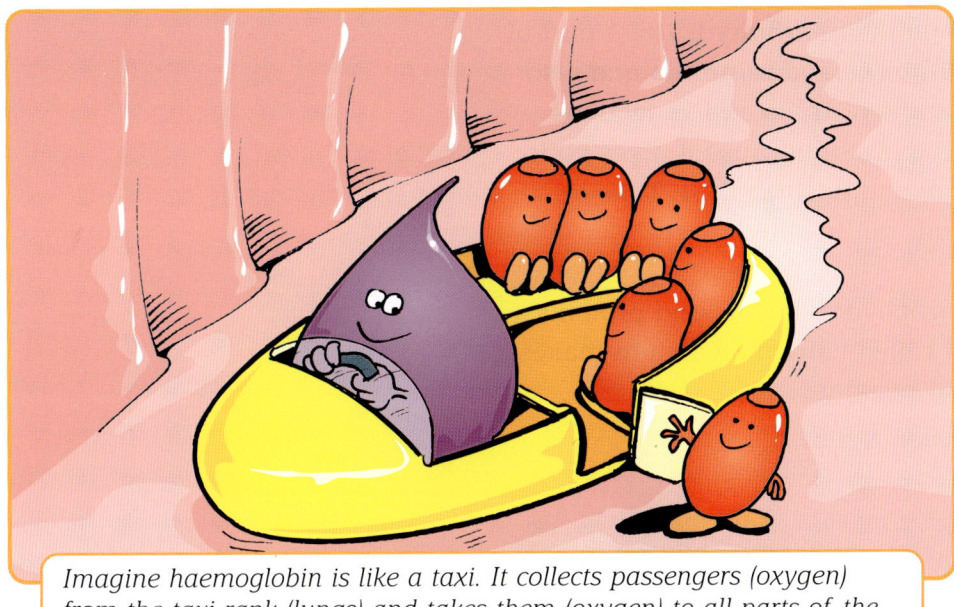

Imagine haemoglobin is like a taxi. It collects passengers (oxygen) from the taxi rank (lungs) and takes them (oxygen) to all parts of the body. When it reaches its destination it drops the passengers (oxygen) off and goes back to collect more passengers (oxygen) from the taxi rank (lungs).

Think back to the work you did on mixtures and compounds in Year 1.

> When haemoglobin combines with oxygen does it form a mixture or a compound?
> Is this an example of a physical or a chemical change?
> Is the change reversible or irreversible?

The blood plasma also carries things

The watery, liquid part of the blood (the plasma) also carries materials around the body. It carries digested food materials to the cells where they are used for repair and to provide energy for all the cells' activities. The plasma also carries waste materials like carbon dioxide from the tissues to parts of the body where they are got rid of.

Did you know?

If all the red blood cells in your body were lined up touching each other, the line would stretch two and a half times round the Earth at the equator.

23 A balanced diet

It is very important to eat a balanced diet

A balanced diet keeps you healthy, helps you grow properly and gives you plenty of energy. It also helps you fight disease. A balanced diet, therefore, contains all the essential nutrients in the right form and amounts to maintain a healthy body.

A balanced diet should have about 5 parts of **carbohydrate**, 1 part of **protein**, 1 part of **fat**, a mixture of **vitamins** and **minerals** and also some **fibre**, or **roughage**. The fibrous bits of fruits and vegetables form roughage in your diet. Fibre is important because it gives your digestive system something to squeeze and push against. This squeezing and pushing helps keep your gut healthy.

Milk contains the right amounts of carbohydrates, fats and proteins. It also contains an important mineral called **calcium**. Calcium makes your bones and teeth grow strong and healthy.

> Why is it especially important for babies and young children to drink lots of milk?

Packaged food should tell you what it contains

Nutritional tables are usually printed on packaged food and cartons of drinks. These tables give information about the amount of proteins, carbohydrates, fats, vitamins, minerals and fibre contained in the particular food or drink. In the case of packaged food, the figures are usually shown in grams (g) or milligrams (mg) per 100 g of the food. In the case of drinks, the figures are in millilitres (ml) per 100 ml of the drink.

The table shows the nutrition information printed on a box of cornflakes. The left-hand column lists the different food substances found in a box of cornflakes. The right-hand column shows how much of each kind of food listed is found in every 100 g of cornflakes.

Nutrition information	
Food material	Amount per 100 g
protein	7.0 g
carbohydrate	
sugar	8.0 g
starch	76.0 g
fat	0.9 g
vitamins	
vitamin B	19.2 mg
minerals	
sodium	0.95 g
iron	7.9 mg
fibre (roughage)	3.0 g

Activity

- Look at the nutrition information in the table.
1. What is the main food component in a box of cornflakes?
2. What is the percentage of protein in cornflakes?
3. How much vitamin B is there in every 100 g of cornflakes?
4. How much fat would there be in a 500 g box of cornflakes?
5. How much fibre would there be in a 500 g box of cornflakes?
6. If you ate nothing but cornflakes, would you be eating a balanced diet?

Activity

- Make a detailed list of the different kinds of food and drink you consume in 1 week. Don't forget to count anything you buy for snacks and drinks between meals.
- Divide the different foods into protein, carbohydrate, fat, vitamin, mineral and fibre-type foods. If you are not sure about a particular food, ask your teacher for help.
1. Do you think you eat a balanced diet?
2. If not, what else should you eat to make your diet balanced?
3. Is there anything in your diet that you shouldn't be eating?

Every food packet or drink carton should display a nutritional table which tells you how much protein, carbohydrate, fat, vitamins, minerals and fibre it contains.

A balanced diet

24 Different diets for different people

Different people need different diets

Everyone should eat a balanced diet, but different people also need different diets. The kind of diet you need depends on how old you are and how active you are. Different people also use different amounts of energy. A girl playing tennis uses more energy than a boy sitting at his desk. A farmer digging his land uses more energy than a woman working in an office. A baby needs more milk than its father needs. A growing girl needs more protein than her mother needs. A pregnant woman needs more calcium than her husband needs.

> Why does a girl playing tennis need more energy than a boy sitting at his desk?
> Why does a farmer digging his land need more energy than a woman working in an office?
> Why does a baby need more milk than its father needs?
> Why does a growing girl need more protein than her mother needs?
> Why does a pregnant woman need more calcium than her husband needs?

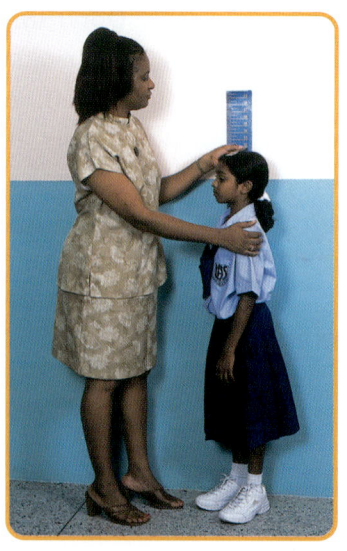
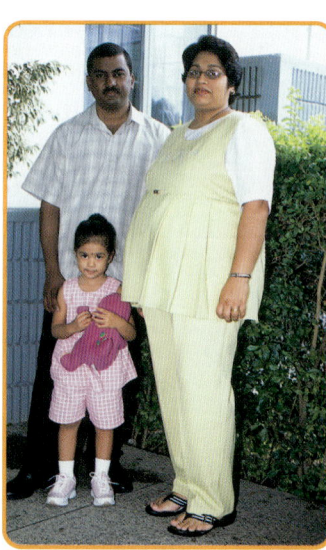

INVESTIGATION: Food for thought at Carnival time

At Carnival time in Port of Spain, Mrs Maharaj works in a stall on the edge of the Queen's Park Savannah. She makes all kinds of tasty fritters including bara, baigani, kachouries, phulouries and sahinas.

- Find out what ingredients you need to make bara, baigani, kachouries phulouries and sahinas.
- Try to find out the nutritional value of each of Mrs Maharaj's fritters.
- Ask your mother to help you make one of these fritters.
- Take your fritter to school and share it with some of your friends.

If your diet consisted only of Mrs Maharaj's fritters and nothing else, would it be a balanced one?

Carnival time in Port of Spain means lots of nice things to eat.

Did you know?

In one day, a baby blue whale drinks enough milk to fill 2500 large glasses!

Activity

- Imagine that a friend is coming to have a meal at your home. Make a list of what you would prepare to give your friend a balanced diet.

Different diets for different people

25 Tests for food

Scientists have developed special tests to identify four of the main kinds of food substances. These tests are called food tests.

INVESTIGATION — Test for the carbohydrate starch

- Put a small amount of starch powder in a test tube and half-fill the tube with water.
- Add a few drops of iodine solution to the test tube.
- Record what happens.

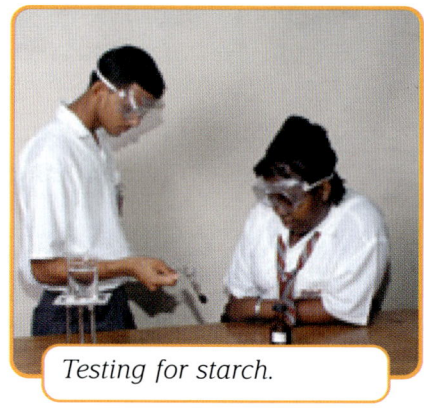

Testing for starch.

When you add iodine solution to starch, the iodine solution turns blue–black. This colour change is a test for the presence of starch.

INVESTIGATION — Test for the carbohydrate glucose

- Dissolve a small amount of glucose sugar in half a test tube of water.
- Now add a few drops of Benedict's solution to the dissolved glucose.
- Gently heat the test tube in a water bath.
- Record what happens.

Testing for glucose.

When you add Benedict's solution to glucose dissolved in water and heat it, the colour of the liquid gradually changes from green to yellow to orange to red, depending how much glucose is present. This colour change is a test for the presence of glucose.

INVESTIGATION — Test for protein

- Gently break a hen's egg and carefully separate the yolk from the white.
- Put some of the white into a test tube.
- Add a few drops of dilute potassium hydroxide or sodium hydroxide solution to the test tube.
- Then add a few drops of dilute copper sulphate solution to the test tube.
- Record what happens.

Testing for protein.

When you add dilute potassium or sodium hydroxide solution and dilute copper sulphate solution to food containing protein, a pink or purplish colour is produced. This colour change is a test for the presence of protein.

INVESTIGATION Test for fat

- Cut a small piece of plain white paper off a sheet of A4.
- Carefully rub a little cooking fat on the paper.
- Let the paper dry for a few minutes.
- Hold the paper against a window and look at the spot where you rubbed the cooking fat.
- Record what you see.

Testing for fat.

When you rub a fatty substance on paper and then hold it to the light, the light will show through. The appearance of a greasy, translucent (see-through) spot is a test for the presence of fat.

INVESTIGATION Test different foods

Your teacher will give you some different foods. Every time you test for a particular food substance, break a bit of the food up as much as possible and then add a little water before testing the sample.

- Test each kind of food separately for starch, glucose, protein and fat.
- Record the presence or absence of a food substance by means of a tick or a cross.
- Summarise your results in the form of a table like the one started below.

Food	Starch	Glucose	Protein	Fat
banana	3	3	5	5

Tests for food 65

26 Biting and grinding

Teeth come in different shapes and sizes. Some teeth are for biting off pieces of food and others are for grinding and chewing the food.

INVESTIGATION   Count your teeth

- Wash your hands before you do this investigation.
- Work with a partner and take turns to look at each other's teeth.
- Count each other's teeth. Count carefully and don't miss any!
- Record the number of teeth you have in your mouth.
- Record the number of teeth your partner has in their mouth.
1. How many teeth do you have?
2. How many teeth does your partner have?
3. Do you have the same number of teeth as your partner?
4. Does your partner have any teeth missing?
5. Do you have any teeth missing?

If you or your partner hasn't lost any, you should each have 28 teeth – 14 in your top jaw and 14 in your bottom jaw.

In your lifetime you only have two sets of teeth. The first set, called **milk teeth**, start to grow when you are a baby. You have 20 milk teeth. By the time you are in fourth year primary, all your milk teeth have fallen out. Then you have your second set of teeth, called **permanent teeth**. You should have 32 teeth in your second set when fully mature.

It's important to look after your second teeth. If you lose any of them, you won't get any more!

INVESTIGATION   Feel your teeth

- Wash your hands before you do this investigation.
- Put a finger in your mouth and feel your teeth.
- Start with your top teeth and then go on to your bottom teeth.
- Feel the shape and size of each tooth.
- Record what each of your teeth feels like.
1. Do all your teeth feel the same?
2. Are all your teeth the same size?
3. Are all your teeth the same shape?
4. What shape are your front teeth?
5. What shape are your back teeth?

Did you know?

An elephant has only four teeth to do all its chewing!

You can learn a lot about teeth by looking at them.

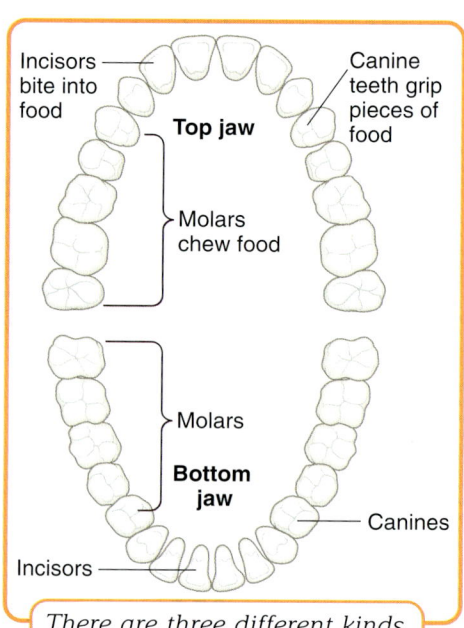

*There are three different kinds of teeth in the human jaw – **canines**, **incisors**, and **molars**.*

66   Biting and grinding

INVESTIGATION — Look for different kinds of teeth

- Look at the drawing of a human jaw.
- Work with a partner and take turns to look in each other's mouth.
- Count how many incisor teeth your partner has.
- Count how many canine teeth your partner has.
- Count how many premolar teeth your partner has.
- Count how many molar teeth your partner has.
- Make a record of the different kinds of teeth you counted.
- Now let your partner count the different teeth you have.

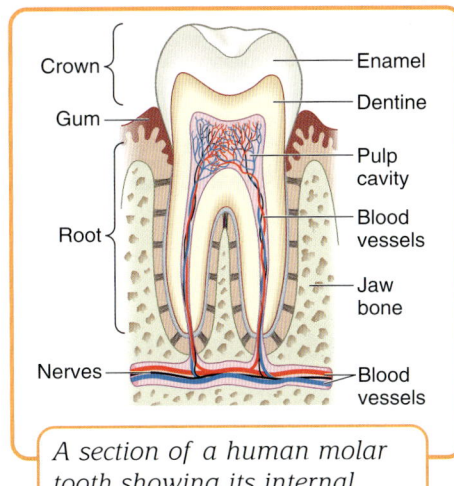

A section of a human molar tooth showing its internal structure.

INVESTIGATION — Feel how you use your teeth

- Feel how you use your teeth when you eat a banana.
- Make a record of how you use your teeth when you eat a banana.
1. Which teeth did you use to bite off pieces of banana?
2. Which teeth did you use to chew the banana?
3. What happened to the banana as you chewed it?
4. Did chewing the banana make it easier to swallow?

You use your front teeth (incisors) to bite off small bits from bigger pieces of food. You use your side teeth (premolars) and back teeth (molars) to grind and chew the small pieces.

What do you think you use your canine teeth for?
Can you think of the name of an animal with big canine teeth?
What do you think this animal uses its canine teeth for?

INVESTIGATION — Try to make your teeth do the wrong job

- Try biting into a mango with your back teeth.
- Try chewing a piece of mango with your front teeth.
- Record what it was like using your teeth in the wrong way.

Was it easy to use your teeth in the wrong way?

The ocelot lives in forests in Trinidad where it hunts birds and small mammals. Why do you think it has large canine teeth?

Biting and grinding

27 Chewing and swallowing

> **INVESTIGATION** Find out the effect of chewing
>
> - Put a piece of bread in your mouth.
> - Taste the bread before chewing it.
> - Now chew the bread for 5 minutes.
> - Record what happened when you chewed the bread.
>
> 1 Did your mouth begin to feel wet and slimy when you chewed?
> 2 What did the bread taste like when you first put it into your mouth?
> 3 What did the bread taste like after you chewed it for 5 minutes?
> 4 What did your tongue do as you chewed the bread?
> 5 What did you do after you finished chewing the bread?
> 6 What did your tongue do when you swallowed the bread?

Digestion of food begins in the mouth

When you eat, your teeth start to break down food into smaller pieces. At the same time, glands in your mouth make a lot of spit called **saliva**. When you chew, you mix this saliva with the food. This is why your mouth feels wet and slimy.

When you chew bread, it mixes with the saliva in your mouth. Saliva contains a chemical which starts to change the chemical structure of the bread. The chemical in saliva that breaks down the bread is an **enzyme** called **salivary amylase**. Salivary amylase breaks down the starch molecules in the bread into smaller sugar molecules called **sucrose**. Because sucrose is a sugar it tastes sweet. After chewing the bread for 5 minutes you can taste the sucrose. This is why the bread begins to taste sweet as you chew it.

The chemical breakdown of bread and other foods is called **digestion**. So, digestion of food begins in the mouth.

INVESTIGATION: Find out what your tongue does

- Chew another piece of banana.
- Feel how your teeth and your tongue work together when you chew.
- When you have finished chewing, swallow the banana.
- Record what happened when you chewed the banana.

1 What does your tongue do when you chew?
2 What does your tongue do when you swallow?

After you have chewed your food, your tongue pushes it to the back of your mouth. When your food gets to the back of your mouth you swallow it.

INVESTIGATION: Find out what happens when you swallow

- Put your fingertips on your throat under your chin.
- Try to find your voice box (larynx).
- Press gently on your voice box and swallow.

What happens to your voice box when you swallow?

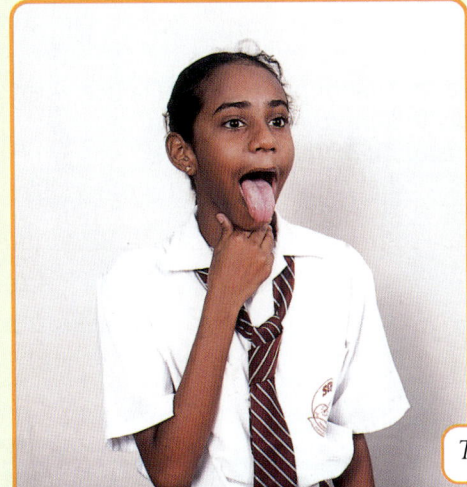

This girl is feeling her voice box.

When you chew, your tongue moves the food around inside your mouth. When you are ready to swallow, your tongue pushes the food into your throat. When you swallow, your voice box moves up to stop any food going into your lungs.

INVESTIGATION: Try the upside down swallowing test

Carry out this investigation under the strict supervision of your teacher. You must be extra careful trying to swallow when you are upside down.

- Turn yourself upside down by doing a headstand.
- Ask a friend to steady you by holding your waist and legs.
- Ask another friend (with clean hands) to feed you with a banana.
- Try chewing and swallowing the banana.
- Repeat the above steps so each of your friends can try the upside down swallowing test.

1 Can you eat a banana when you are upside down?
2 Is it difficult to swallow when you are upside down?

Did you know?

You produce about 0.5 litres of spit, or saliva, every day.

There is no problem for this astronaut eating in space, even though there is no gravity there to help him swallow. Muscle movement (peristalsis) of the astronaut's oesophagus still makes food go to his stomach, even though he is upside down.

Swallowed food gets squeezed along the food pipe

The food pipe is called the **oesophagus**. Its walls are made of muscles, so it behaves like a muscular pipe. Your oesophagus is a squeezer. It uses its muscles to squeeze food and drink from your mouth into your stomach. It squeezes food like you squeeze toothpaste out of a tube. This muscle-squeezing is called **peristalsis**. Normally, gravity helps food drop down your oesophagus into your stomach, but you can also swallow without gravity's help. Your food pipe's muscles can even squeeze against the force of gravity. This is why you can swallow food when you are upside down. You can even swallow a drink of water when standing on your head!

Did you know?

A blue whale's tongue weighs as much as an elephant.

Journey to destruction

FACTFILE

History – a window into the stomach

On 6 June 1822, a man called Alexis St Martin had a terrible accident. He was shot in the abdomen (stomach region). The wound left a hole in his body nearly 2 cm in diameter. But the wound wasn't an ordinary one. The hole went all the way through to the inside of Alexis's stomach. Alexis's doctor, Dr Baumont, treated the wound but couldn't get it to heal up completely. Alexis was left with a hole in his stomach for the rest of his life and he lived until he was 86 years old! Nearly every day for 8 years, Dr Baumont looked through the hole into Alexis's stomach and watched it at work. He was the first man to watch digestion taking place inside a human body.

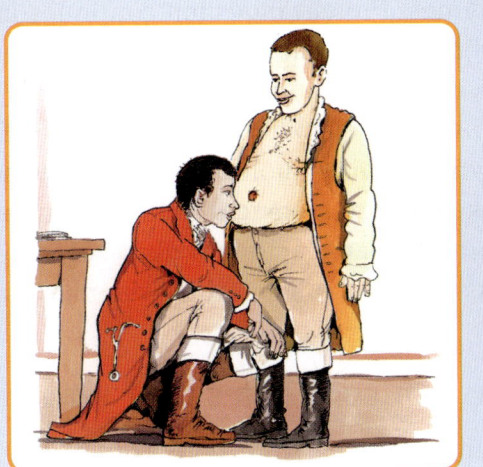

When we eat food, it goes into the digestive system

The digestive system is like a long tube. The tube isn't straight like a pipe. Most of it is neatly folded up. The tube starts in the mouth and ends at the anus. It is made up of different parts. Each part produces its own special digestive juices or enzymes. This is because each part has a different job to do. During digestion, a series of physical and chemical changes take place. These changes break down the food into smaller and smaller bits so it can be absorbed by the body.

The stomach is like a big bag of muscle

Food goes along the oesophagus into the stomach. The stomach works a bit like a food mixer. It churns the food up and mixes it with hydrochloric acid and digestive juices containing enzymes. After a couple of hours in the stomach, your food looks more like soup than solid food. The stomach's digestive enzymes work mainly on proteins, breaking them down into smaller molecules.

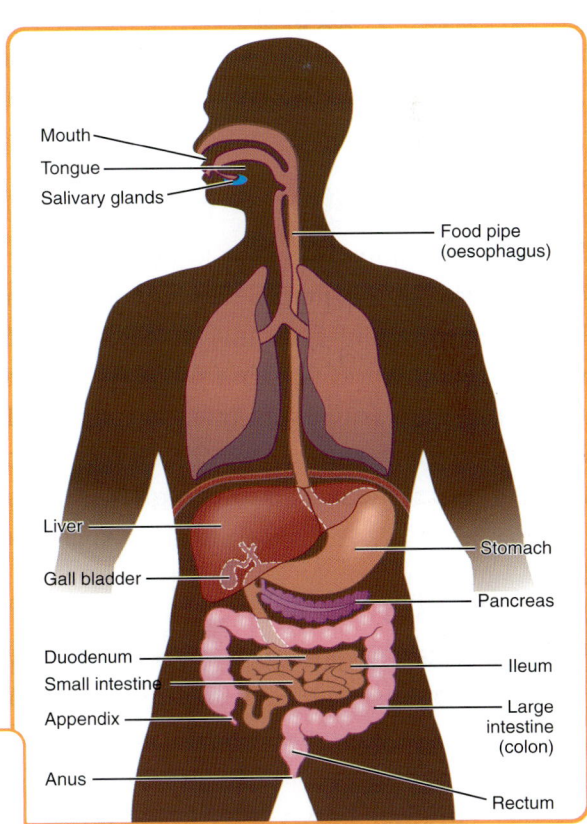

Food begins its 'journey to destruction' in the mouth. As it travels through the different parts of the digestive system it gets completely broken down.

Food is then squirted into the small intestine

It's a strange name for this part of the digestive system because the 'small' intestine is about 7 m long. But even though it is five times longer than your own height, your small intestine is folded up like a packet of sausages so it fits neatly into your abdomen. Here, food is squeezed and mixed up with more juices containing different enzymes. Protein digestion continues in the small intestine. Carbohydrates and fats are digested here as well. The food gradually moves along the small intestine until it is completely broken down into small molecules ready to be used in the body. Proteins are broken down into small molecules called **amino acids**. Carbohydrates are broken down into sugar molecules called **glucose** and fats are broken down into **fatty acid** and **glycerol** molecules. At this stage, the digested food is like a thick 'chemical soup'.

Did you know?
Elephants talk to each other by making stomach rumbles.

You can sometimes hear your digestive system at work

After a big meal, your body sometimes makes funny noises. The rumbles are your digestive juices sloshing around inside you. Your stomach also rumbles when you are hungry. When it does this, it is telling you it needs some food.

The digestive system can make some interesting noises!

Activity
- After your meal tonight, listen to your brother's or sister's stomach to hear if it rumbles. Record how long their stomach rumbles.

The large intestine is a waste disposal expert

Some of the food you eat is too difficult to digest. This kind of food is called fibre, or roughage. Vegetables and fruit contain lots of fibre. You need plenty of fibre in your diet to help keep your digestive system healthy and working properly. All the undigested food from a meal goes into your large intestine. After all the water and minerals have been taken out of it, what's left is got rid of when you go to the toilet. The undigested food you get rid of is called **faeces**, or stools.

Did you know?
An elephant drops about 45 kg of dung (faeces) every day.

Activity
- Imagine you are a piece of beefburger which your brother has just bitten off his lunch snack. Write an account of what happens to you from the time you enter your brother's mouth to the time what's left of you leaves your brother's body later in the day.

Journey to destruction

Food is the stuff of life

There are five main kinds of food materials

The five main types of food are **proteins**, **carbohydrates**, **fats**, **vitamins** and **minerals**. You discovered in Unit 23 that the body also needs fibre, or roughage, which is made up of the food your body can't digest. It is important to eat the right amount of all these types of food if you are going to stay healthy. The body also requires a constant supply of water.

These foods are rich in protein.

Proteins are body-building foods

Proteins are important for growth. Your body also uses proteins to repair itself when it gets damaged. When you cut your leg the wound eventually heals. This is because your body uses proteins to heal the wound. Proteins are also used to help fight disease and, sometimes, as an energy source.

Proteins are found in meat such as beef, goat, lamb and chicken. They are also found in fish, beans, cheese, the white part of eggs, milk, beans, maize and groundnuts.

> What is your favourite kind of meat?
> How often do you eat eggs?
> How do you like your eggs cooked?
> How often do you eat fish?
> If you or your family don't eat meat, which plants or vegetables do you eat in order to get enough proteins in your diet?

Carbohydrates give you energy

You need energy to do all the things you do. You use energy to walk to school and to do your homework. Your heart needs energy to keep beating. You also need energy to breathe, to blow your nose, to sneeze and to blink your eyes. You even need energy when you are asleep.

These foods are rich in carbohydrates.

Food is the stuff of life 73

Carbohydrates are found in foods like bananas, bread, breadfruit, cassava, cowpeas, coconuts, Irish potatoes, maize, plantain, rice, sugar cane, sweet potatoes and yams. The main types of carbohydrate are starch and sugars. Cassava, potatoes and yams are rich in starch. All sweet-tasting fruits like mangoes, melons, oranges, paw-paw and pineapples contain lots of sugar. Sugar is also a carbohydrate.

> Which do you like best, plantain or cassava?
> Do you like to suck a stick of sugar cane?
> Do you like rice or plantain with your meat?
> Do you eat bread every day?
> What is your favourite fruit?

Fatty foods also give you energy and help keep you warm

Foods such as butter, cooking oil, groundnuts, some fish, sunflower seeds and the yolk of eggs contain fatty substances which also give you energy and help keep you warm.

You need vitamins to stay healthy

You only need small amounts of vitamins but they are very important in your diet. Vitamins are protective foods which keep your body healthy and help fight disease. They are found in fresh fruits and vegetables and also in some animal products such as liver and fish.

These foods are rich in fats.

Vitamin A keeps your eyes healthy and helps you see better in the dark. It is found in foods like carrots, paw-paw and mangoes.

Vitamin B is found in foods like liver, brown bread and brown rice. If you don't eat enough vitamin B, you get a disease called beriberi. This disease makes your muscles weak and you can't walk properly.

Vitamin C is found in oranges, lemons and limes. If you don't eat vitamin C you get a disease called scurvy. Scurvy affects your joints and makes your skin dry, your eyes sore and your gums bleed.

These foods contain lots of vitamins.

Food is the stuff of life

Vitamin D is found in foods like butter, cooking oil, eggs, liver and some fish. If you don't eat enough of this vitamin you get a disease called rickets. Your bones don't grow properly and they become weak.

Activity
- Make a table of the main vitamins, the foods they are found in, and why they are important in our diet.

You also need small amounts of minerals

Minerals are very important but you only need in them in very small amounts. They are found in vegetables such as aubergine, calalloo, okra, peppers, spinach, split peas and taro. You need a mineral called iron to keep your blood healthy. If you don't eat enough iron in your diet, you get a disease called anaemia. Iron is found in foods like eggs, green vegetables and liver.

Salt contains a mineral called iodine. **Iodine** is important because it helps your body work at the right speed. If you don't eat enough iodine in your diet, your neck swells up. Doctors call this swelling a goitre.

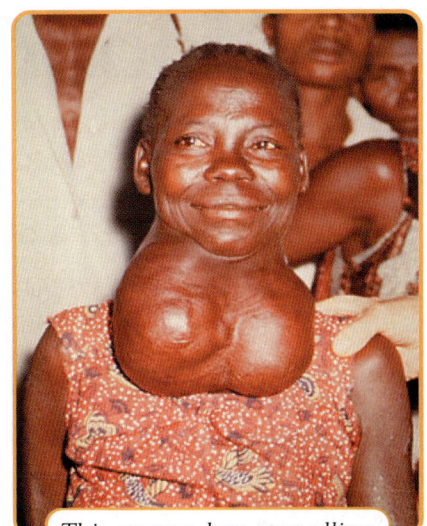

This person has a swelling in their neck called a goitre. It is caused by a lack of iodine in her diet.

Activity
- Look again at the table in Unit 23, showing the nutritional content of a packet of cornflakes.
1. If you ate nothing but cornflakes, would you suffer from goitre?
2. If you ate nothing but cornflakes would you suffer from anaemia?
3. If you ate nothing but cornflakes would you suffer from scurvy?
4. If you ate nothing but cornflakes would you suffer from beriberi?

Did you know?
Gram for gram, a termite contains more protein than an average size fillet steak!

30 What happens to digested food?

> **FACTFILE**
>
> **The small intestine**
> It is about 7 m in length.
> It is about 2 cm in diameter.
> Its lining is covered by about 17 million villi.
> Its total internal surface is about 300 m².
> It produces at least eight different enzymes.
> Food takes about 8 hours to pass through it.

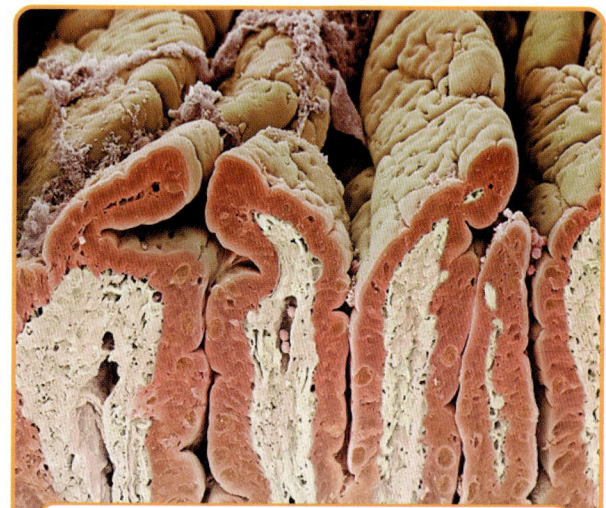

This is a photograph of the inside of the small intestine magnified 200 times. It shows the lining covered in millions of tiny projections called villi. Every square centimetre of small intestine contains about 4000 villi. They provide a large surface for absorbing digested food.

The wall of the small intestine absorbs digested food

The wall of the small intestine has millions of tiny finger-like structures called **villi** (singular, **villus**) sticking out into the digested food. The cells forming the outer covering of each of these villi show another example of cells having a special shape for specialised work. They are

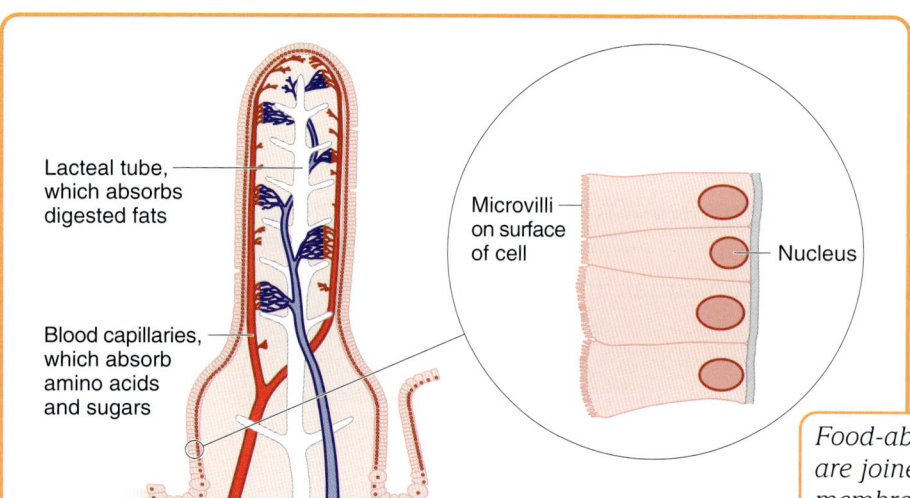

Food-absorbing cells on the outside of each villus are joined together at the sides but the membrane on the top surface of each is crinkled up into microscopic folds. This folding gives each cell a large surface area for absorbing food.

shaped like tiny columns. The membrane on the top surface of each cell, next to the digested food, is crinkled up into lots of microscopic folds. This folded membrane increases each cell's surface for absorbing digested food. Digested food enters each villus by passing through the folded membranes of its outer cells.

There are lots of tiny blood capillaries inside each villus

Once digested proteins and carbohydrates have entered a villus, they pass into the blood capillaries inside. They are then taken in the blood to the liver.

But digested fats don't go into the blood system like other digested food. Instead, they pass into a central tube in each villus called a **lacteal tube**. From there, they go into another body system called the **lymphatic system**.

Activity

Your teacher will show you a piece of liver from a cow.
- Gently feel the piece of liver.
- Look at the liver after your teacher has cut it open with a knife.
1. What did the cow's liver feel like when you touched it?
2. What did the cow's liver look like when your teacher cut it open?
3. Did you see lots of blood inside the liver?

The liver is the body's chemical laboratory

Your liver is one of the biggest and most important organs in your body. It carries out a delicate chemical balancing act all the time. It continually receives information about your body's food needs. For example, if your cells need sugar, your liver allows glucose absorbed by the small intestine to go to them so they can use it straight away. But if you have an excess of sugar in your blood, your liver changes the glucose absorbed by the small intestine into another substance called glycogen. It then stores glycogen until your cells need more glucose. When this happens, your liver changes some of the glycogen back into glucose and sends it to the cells that need it.

> Is the chemical reaction that changes excess glucose into glycogen a reversible or a non-reversible reaction?

Your liver also looks after your body's protein needs. The problem with proteins is that you cannot store them. Any excess amino acids from digested proteins have to be got rid of. Your liver does this by changing the unwanted amino acids into a substance called **urea**. This is then excreted from the body in the form of urine when you go to the toilet.

Is the chemical reaction that changes excess amino acids into urea a reversible or a non-reversible reaction?

It is very important to take care of your liver

Drinking too much alcohol damages the liver. Malaria can also weaken it. A disease called hepatitis also attacks the liver.

Did you know?

If all the folds and crinkles of the wall of the small intestine were flattened out, they would cover an area of about 300 m^2.

Activity

- Imagine you are a banana. Write down all the things that happen to you from the time you are peeled to when you get to the liver.

Activity

- Read the paragraph below. Think about it.
  Winston and Charlene had an argument. Winston says that once he has swallowed food it is part of him because it is inside his body. But Charlene disagrees. She says that food is not part of Winston's body until it has been digested and absorbed into his blood.
1. Who do you think is right, Winston or Charlene?
2. Give reasons for your answer.

78 What happens to digested food?

Getting rid of metabolic waste

Your body is working all the time, even when you are asleep

All the activity taking place in your cells produces lots of waste materials which scientists call **metabolic waste**. If these waste materials were allowed to stay in the body, they would soon poison the body's cells and you would quickly die. This means these waste materials have to be got rid of. Your body **excretes** them. **Excretion** is the removal from the body of waste materials produced by chemical (metabolic) reactions taking place in the cells.

The table shows the main waste materials excreted by humans.

Waste material	Where it is made	How it is made	Where it is excreted
carbon dioxide	in all living cells	by respiration	from lungs
nitrogenous waste products, e.g. urea	in liver	by deamination	from kidneys in urine
bile pigments	in liver and spleen	from haemoglobin	in bile which flows into duodenum and out of body in faeces

Activity

- Read the paragraph below. Think about it.
  Winston and Charlene had another argument. Winston says that when he goes to the toilet and gets rid of undigested foods this is excretion. But Charlene disagrees. She says getting rid of solids in the toilet isn't excretion because undigested food has not been produced by the metabolic reactions taking place in Winston's cells.
1. Who do you think is right, Winston or Charlene?
2. Give reasons for your answer.

Kidneys are waste disposal experts

Your lungs remove carbon dioxide and water when you breathe out. When you sweat, your skin removes small amounts of salt, water and an important excretory product called urea. But your body's main waste removers are your kidneys.

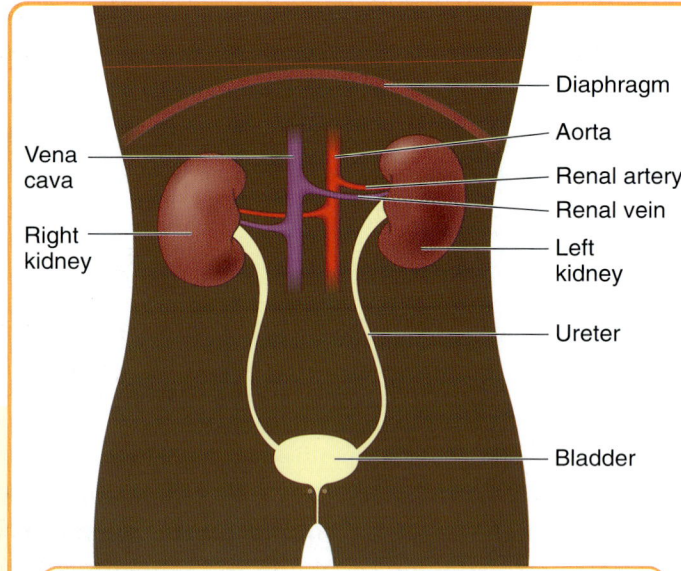

Activity

Your teacher will give you a lamb's kidney from the supermarket.
- Cut the kidney in half as shown in the photograph.
- Look carefully at one of the cut surfaces.
- Record the colour of the inside of the kidney.
- Use a hand lens to help you see more details of the structure.
- Find the lighter coloured bands towards the edge of the kidney.
- Take a needle and try to lift up one of these.
1. Why is the inside of the kidney red in colour?
2. Did you see some of the tiny tubes in the kidney?
3. Did you see some larger tubes when you used the needle?

Your two kidneys are found on either side of your backbone in the middle of your back. They are protected by your lowest pair of ribs. They each rest in a large cushion of fat which also protects them from being damaged. They connect by two tubes to your bladder.

The kidney is red because it is full of blood vessels. The tiny tubes you saw are the filter tubes. The larger white-coloured tubes are the tubes which drain urine away from the kidney.

FACTFILE

Kidneys

Each kidney contains about 1 million tiny filter tubes.
Each kidney filters about 90 litres of blood every day.
An adult human produces about 1.5 litres of urine every day.
Urine is about 95% water.
Urine contains about 5% urea.
An adult bladder holds about 1 litre of urine.

More about kidneys

Each kidney is about the size of a small orange

Each of your kidneys is made up of tiny filter tubes and blood vessels. If you straightened out all the filter tubes in one of your kidneys and arranged them end to end, they would stretch from Port of Spain to San Fernando! Blood passes through your kidneys all the time. It is brought to each kidney by an artery called the **renal artery** and taken away by a vein called the **renal vein**. As blood passes through the kidneys, it is filtered and cleaned up. The waste materials it carries are taken out and removed from the body.

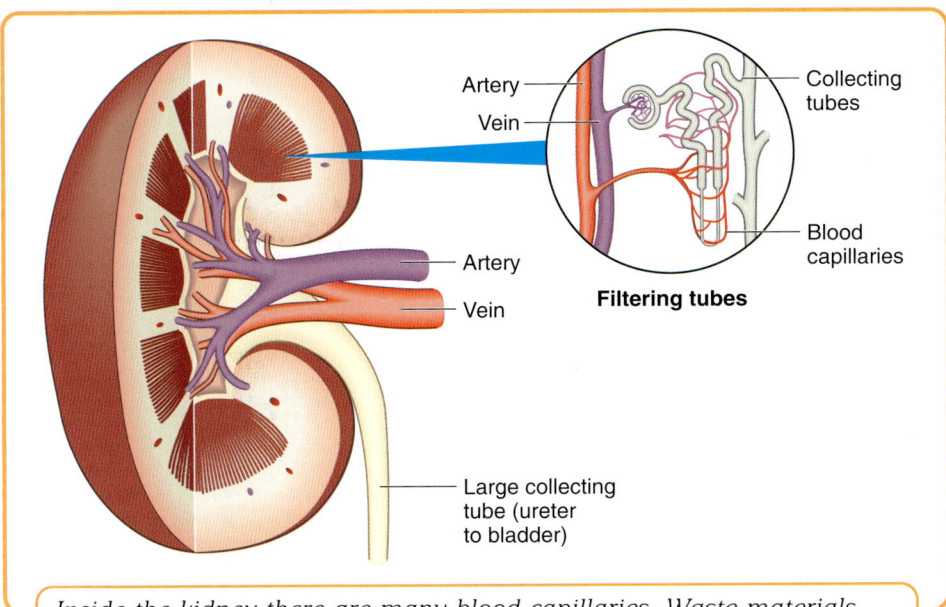

Inside the kidney there are many blood capillaries. Waste materials pass out of the blood into the kidney. They then leave the kidney in the form of urine and pass down a tube into the bladder and out of the body.

The waste liquid produced by kidneys is called urine

The kidneys produce a liquid called **urine**. Urine is mainly water with a waste substance called **urea** dissolved in it. Urea is produced by your liver from the excess amino acids which your body didn't want after the digestion of proteins. The process of producing urea is called **deamination**. Urine leaves your kidneys and goes to the bladder where it is stored until you are able to go to the toilet. Your bladder has a special way of telling you when it is full so it's not difficult for you to get your timing right!

Did you know?

Fresh urine is very clean and it has no bacteria in it. Some South American Indians use it as a mouthwash and some people even used to sip it as a refreshing drink!

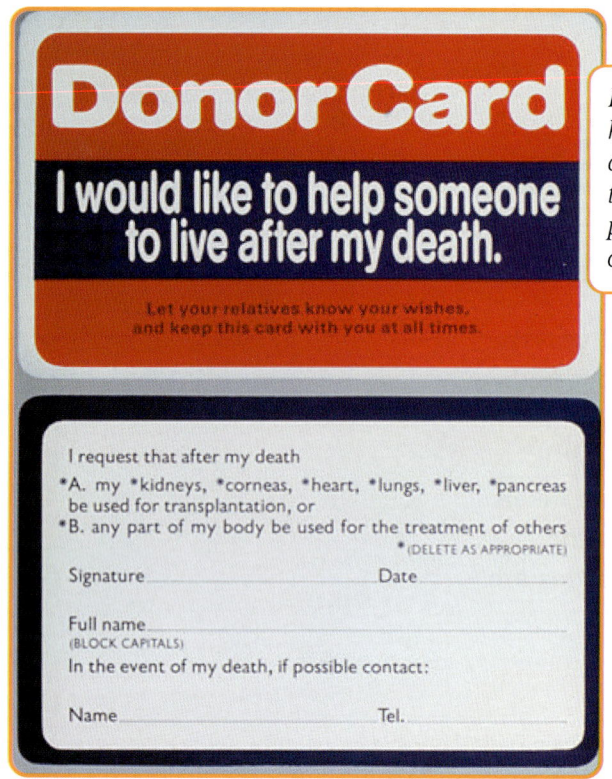

If a person's kidneys become diseased, doctors sometimes do a kidney transplant operation. The patient is given a kidney from another person. The donor is someone who has given permission to use their kidneys after they have died. Doctors know they have permission to use a dead person's kidneys because the donor carries a card like the one on the right.

Kidneys control the amount of water in the body

Apart from getting rid of urea, kidneys also help control the amount of water and salts in the body. If you have too much water in your body, your kidneys take the excess out of your blood as it passes through them and get rid of it. If you have too little water in your body, your kidneys take less water out of your blood as it passes through them. In this way your kidneys help control the water balance in your body.

The amount of urine varies

The amount of urine you produce depends on how much liquid you drink and how hot or how cold it is. If you drink lots of liquid you will produce more urine. If you drink a small amount of liquid you will produce less urine. In very hot weather, you sweat a lot and your body loses water. When this happens, your kidneys try to conserve water in your body and so you produce small amounts of urine. In colder conditions you sweat less so your body loses less water. When this happens there is less need to conserve water in your body so your kidneys produce more urine.

Why do you urinate more when you go to a party and drink lots of fizzy drinks?

Creating new life

The process of creating new life is called reproduction

How well a species survives depends on how well it is able to adapt to changes in its surroundings. Any animal or plant has a much better chance of coping with change if it inherits its genetic make-up from two parents. This is why most living organisms have males and females. New life is created at the cellular level. Males provide single cells called **sperm** and females provide single cells called eggs, or **ova** (singular, **ovum**). Each sperm and ovum contains half the genes of the male or female that produced it. When a sperm fertilises an egg, the two lots of genes are combined and genetic material gets mixed up. In this way, future generations inherit different characteristics which may help the species to survive.

Approximately half the people in the world are male and the other half female.

Sexual maturity is reached at puberty

The time when boys and girls approach sexual maturity is called **adolescence**. At this stage, boys start producing sperm and girls begin to **ovulate** (produce eggs). During adolescence, certain things develop related to sexual maturity. These are called **secondary sexual characteristics**. In boys, hair starts to grow on the face, under the arms and around the pubic region. Their voice begins to break and their muscles start to develop. In girls, pubic hair begins to grow, the breasts start to develop and the pelvic girdle (hips) becomes broader. During adolescence, both boys and girls begin to want more independence and they become more interested in each other. All these changes are brought about by chemicals called **hormones**. The main male hormone is **testosterone** and the main female hormone is **oestrogen**. The point at which sexual maturity is reached is called **puberty**. Girls often reach puberty several years earlier than boys.

Sperm cells are produced in the testes

A male human has two **testes** (singular, **testis**) which produce sperm cells. The testes hang down in two baggy sacs called the **scrotum**. The scrotum hangs outside the body. Sperm stay cool in the outside air surrounding the scrotum. They would soon die if they were kept inside the body because it would be too warm for them.

Sperm are passed to the outside through a structure called the **penis**. Sperm reach the penis by travelling along two tubes called **sperm ducts**. Sperm ducts leave the testes and open into a tube called the **urethra**. The urethra runs down the centre of the penis. As sperm travel down the sperm ducts, they are mixed with a fluid from the prostate gland. The mixture of sperms and fluid is called **semen**.

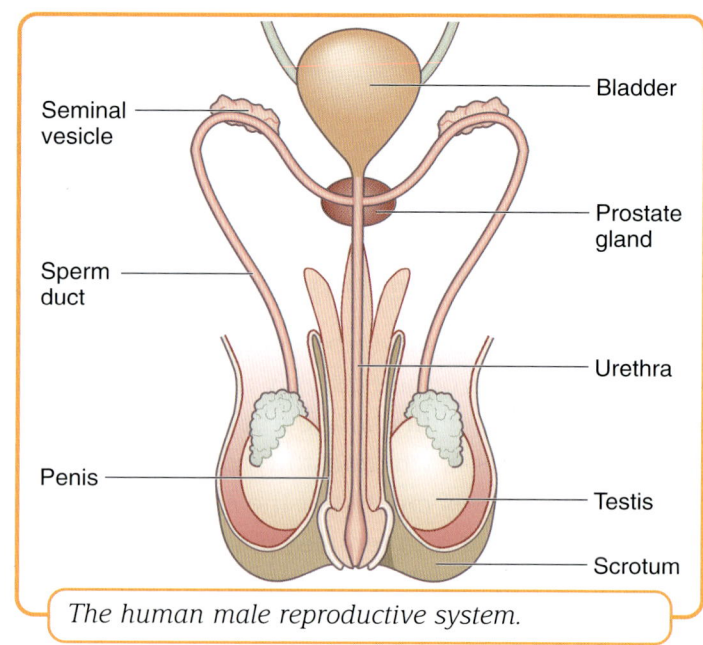

The human male reproductive system.

Ova are produced in the ovaries

At birth, a baby girl already has hundreds of ova stored in two organs called **ovaries**. When she reaches 8 or 9 years of age, a girl starts the long process of becoming an adult. At puberty, she starts to release her ova, one every month, and she will do this for the next 40 years or more. The process of releasing an ovum from an ovary is called **ovulation**. When the ovum is released, it passes into one of the **Fallopian tubes**. The two Fallopian tubes lead into a large, pear-shaped, muscular organ called the womb, or **uterus**.

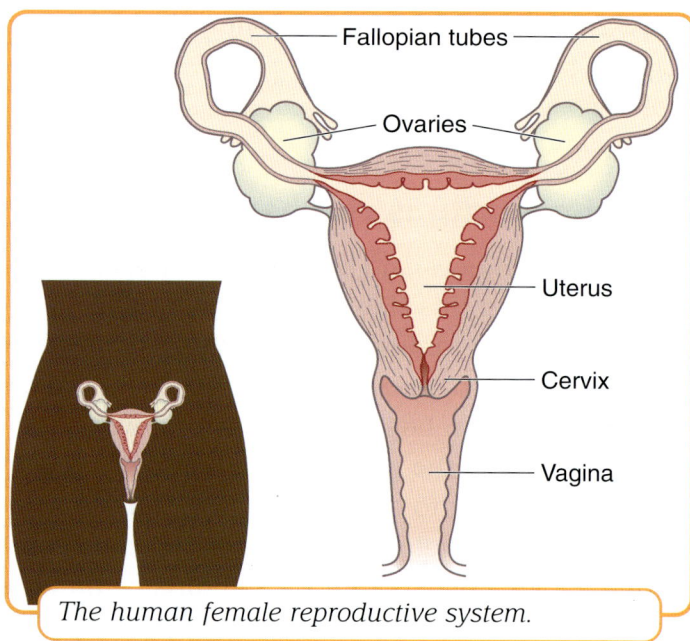

The human female reproductive system.

A human sperm cell is specialised for 'swimming'. An ovum contains 'food' for the developing embryo.

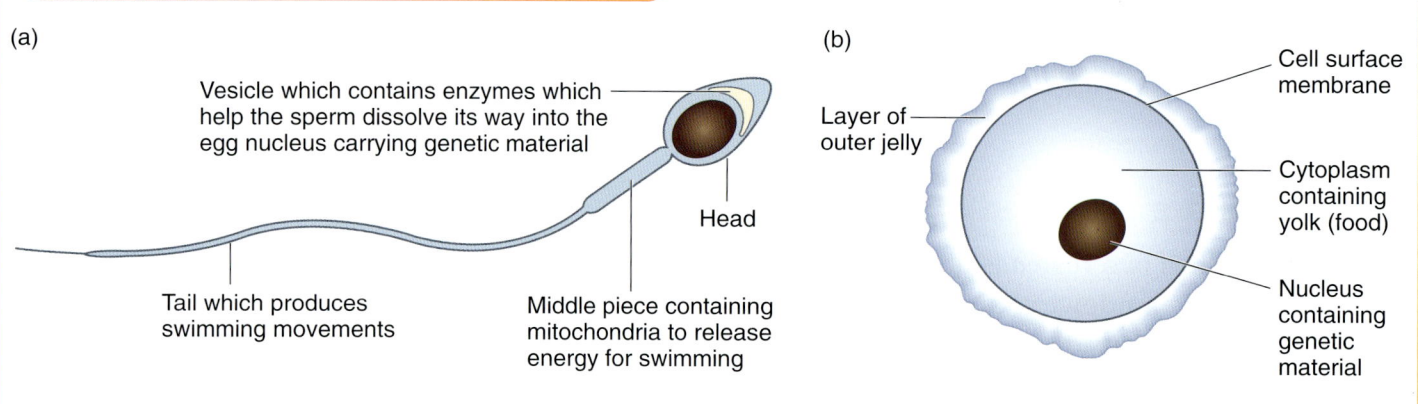

84   Creating new life

Fertilisation and beyond

Fertilisation takes place inside the female

If fertilisation is to take place, the male penis has to be inserted into the female vagina. This happens during sexual intercourse. The penis becomes stiff so it can enter the female more easily. Once inside the female, muscles inside the penis contract and millions of sperm cells are squirted into the female's vagina. This squirting is called ejaculation. Sperm use their tiny tails to swim into the Fallopian tubes. If they meet an ovum coming down, fertilisation takes place. But only one sperm is actually involved in the process of fertilisation.

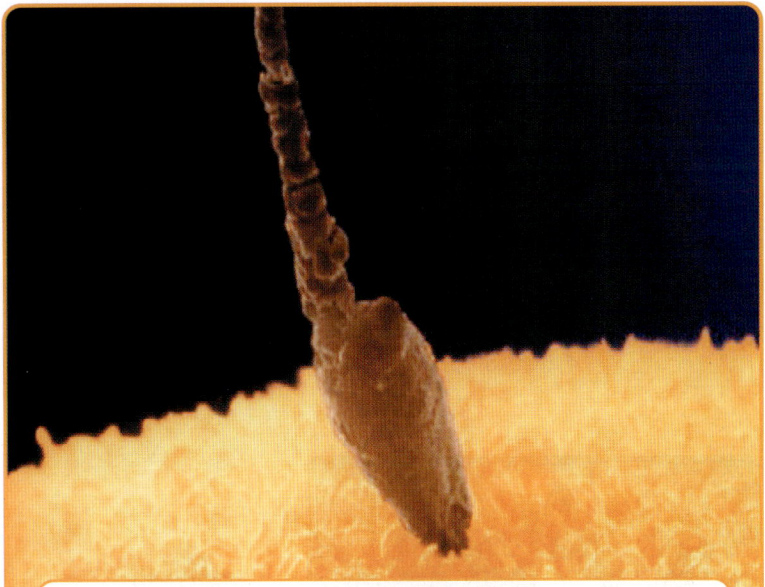

In this photograph, a sperm cell is about to fertilise an ovum. Sperm cells are some of the smallest cells in the human body. It would take about 100 000 to cover the full stop at the end of this sentence. Ova are some of the biggest cells in the human body. An ovum is just about visible to the naked eye.

Why do you think a male produces so many sperm if only one is needed for fertilisation of an egg?

Cell division eventually produces a new human

After fertilisation has taken place, the new cell quickly starts to divide as it makes its way to the uterus. When it reaches the uterus, it attaches to the wall and continues to divide. It will stay there for the next 9 months. For the first 2 months of its development, the future baby is called an **embryo**. For the last 7 months, it is called a **foetus**. When a female is carrying a baby, she is said to be pregnant.

Gradually, as more cell division takes place, new cells such as bone and blood cells are formed. Then, as more cell division takes place, cells of the same kind group together to form tissues such as nerve tissue or muscle tissue. Different tissues gradually make up organs such as the heart and the liver. About 3 months after fertilisation, all a baby's organs are formed. They will develop further over the next few months. Eventually, different organs group together to form systems, such as the digestive system. After about 9 months, a new human is produced. When the baby is ready to be born, it is pushed out of the uterus, through the cervix and out through the vagina. This process is called birth.

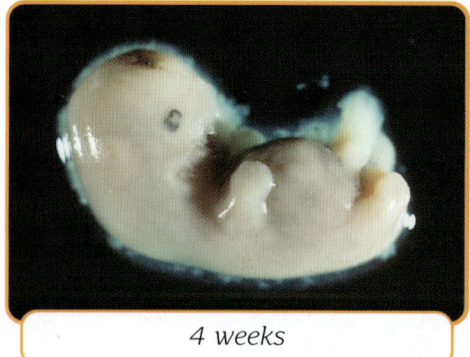
4 weeks

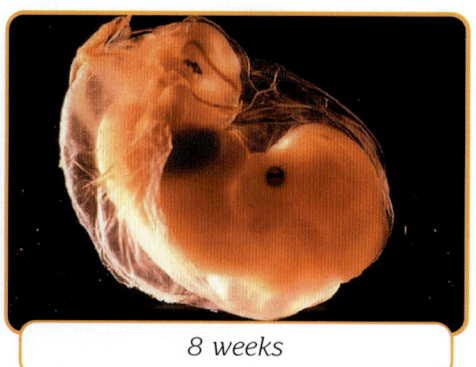
8 weeks

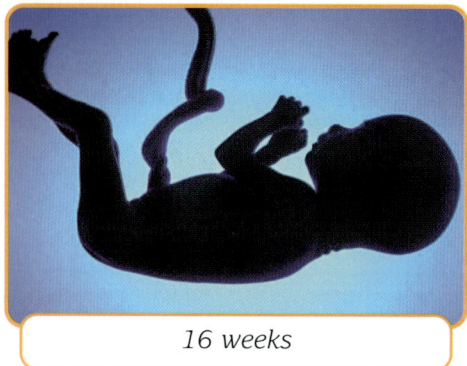
16 weeks

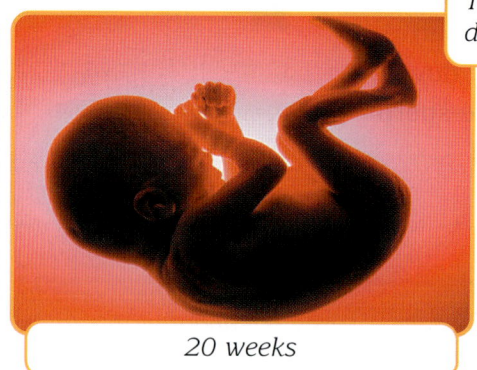
20 weeks

These photographs show a human baby developing inside its mother.

Did you know?

During sexual intercourse in humans, about 500 million sperm cells enter a female.

Activity

- Look at the photographs and record at what stages you can first see the baby's eyes, nose, ears, arms, mouth, fingers and fingernails.

Activity

- Imagine you are an ovum. Write a short account of what happens to you from the time you leave an ovary to the time you attach to the uterus wall.

86 Fertilisation and beyond

Reproduction technology

> **FACTFILE**
>
> ### History
> On 25 July 1978, a baby girl called Louise Brown was born. Her birth made history because she became living proof that fertilisation could take place outside the female body. In Louise's case, one of her father's sperm fertilised an egg from her mother in the laboratory. She became known as the first 'test tube baby'.

Since Louise Brown's birth, many thousands of babies have been produced in the same way. The process is called In Vitro Fertilisation, (IVF) for short. IVF involves collecting eggs from a woman's ovary and putting them, together with sperm from her male partner, in a dish. If one of the sperm fertilises one of the eggs, the embryo is then placed back in the woman's uterus and she becomes pregnant.

Louise Brown was the first 'test tube baby'.

IVF helps childless couples to have children

Some married couples have difficulty in having children. There are lots of reasons for this. The female may not produce eggs easily, or the male may have what doctors call a 'low sperm count'. IVF is designed to help such couples have a family. Fertilisation is always a bit of a chancy business anyway. IVF increases the chances of an egg becoming fertilised by a sperm and a new baby being brought into the world.

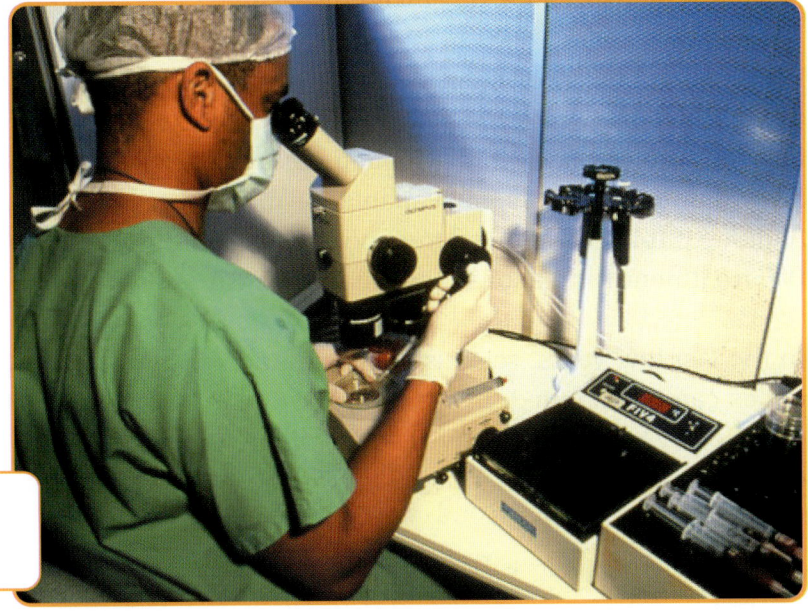

This scientist is adding sperm cells to some egg cells as part of IVF treatment to help a couple have a baby.

You are what your genes are

In Year 1, you discovered that a fertilised egg cell contains a development plan. The plan is contained in a special chemical called **DNA** and is made up of a series of chemical instructions in the form of a special code called the **genetic code**. This code controls everything about you. The code is made up of **genes**. Your genetic code contains about 40 000 genes.

Some diseases are caused by 'faulty' genes

In the past 25 years, scientists have discovered more about human genes and how they work. They can now identify specific genes controlling specific characteristics. These include the genes responsible for certain diseases. Doctors can now help couples by detecting certain diseases at the embryo stage. The development of IVF treatment means an embryo can now be checked to find out if it has any gene faults before being placed in a woman's uterus.

> Do you think embryos should be checked for 'bad' genes?
> When do you think checks on an embryo's genes should be allowed?

Some diseases are linked to the sex of a baby

Haemophilia is a disease where a person's blood is not able to clot. If you suffer with haemophilia, even the tiniest scratch can cause you to bleed to death. But haemophilia is a disease that affects only males. It is what scientists call a sex-linked disease.

If there is a history of haemophilia in either partner's family, do you think it is a good idea to check embryos to make sure that no male embryos are put back in the female partner after IVF treatment? Should embryo checks be available for medical reasons only? Should couples be allowed to choose what kind of embryo is used in IVF treatment for reasons other than medical ones?

In the last few years, scientists have learned a lot about how human genes can be changed. In the future, we may be able to 'cure' genetic diseases by replacing faulty sections of DNA with healthy DNA. This could be carried out on an egg, a sperm or a tiny embryo.

Perhaps one day parents will design their own babies

Scientists can now genetically modify our food crops. Perhaps one day they will use similar techniques to genetically modify humans. It may even be possible to change an embryo's genes so that it will have all the characteristics its parents want it to have. The parents may not even supply their own reproductive cells. Instead, the sperm and eggs used may come from donors who sell their reproductive cells for use in IVF treatment. This will allow parents to choose not only their baby's sex, but also how tall it will eventually grow, the colour of its eyes, the colour of its hair, the shape of its nose, how intelligent it will become, how artistic or musical it will be, how athletic it will be and all kinds of other characteristics as well.

How far can we go in controlling reproduction?

Recent developments in reproduction technology raise all kinds of moral and ethical questions. For example:

> Should couples be able to order a 'designer baby' in the same way they order clothes from a catalogue?
> Should couples be able to click on a website and buy a donor egg from a glamorous model or request sperm from a highly intelligent male donor?
> Should couples be allowed to buy sperm and eggs from two Olympic champions in order to create a baby who will become a winning athlete at some future Olympic Games?
> And if couples are unhappy with their order, should a designer baby come with a money-back guarantee?
> What if the baby grows up to be unattractive, does badly at school or is not very athletic? Should he or she be sent back because they are not what its parents ordered?

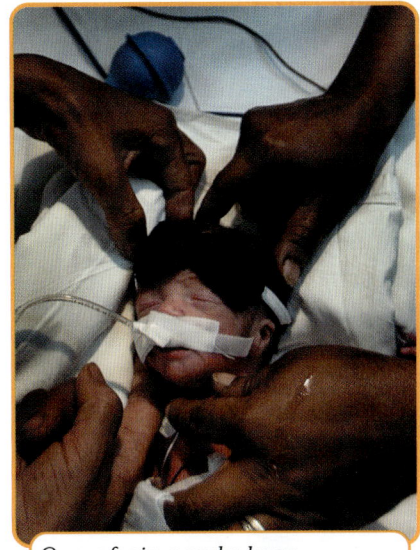

One of six newly born Dominican sextuplets. Fertility treatments and multiple births are increasingly frequent in this Caribbean nation.

Activity

- Imagine you are a doctor working in a fertility hospital and a young married couple come to see you because they want to start a family and are having difficulty. The couple tell you that they want to 'design' their own baby. Write a list of all the things you would say to the couple to try and convince them that the creation of a designer baby is both unethical and morally wrong.

36 Skin and bones hold you together

Skin helps hold your body in shape

Adult human skin weighs about 3.6 kg and covers an area of about 19 000 cm². Skin is the largest organ in your body. It stretches over your body and holds everything inside you in place. Skin stops your body from being floppy. But because skin is elastic, it can stretch when your body changes shape. Your body changes shape when you move.

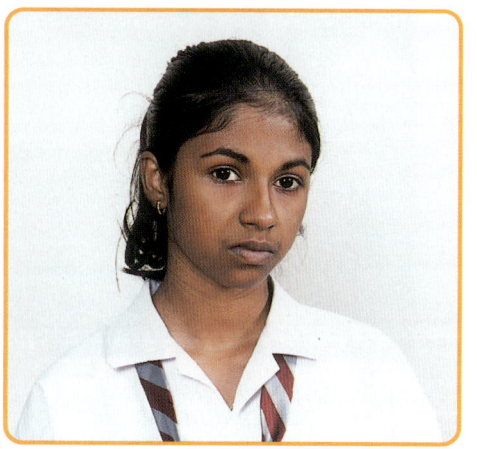

If this girl's face wasn't covered in skin, she wouldn't be able to smile like this because her face would be floppy and uncontrollable.

Your skeleton also holds you in shape

Inside their body humans have a **skeleton** made of bones. Your skeleton is a very flexible framework which supports your body and also helps it keep its shape. Your skeleton also helps you to move.

Activity
- Draw a picture of what your body would look like if you didn't have any skin or bones to hold it in shape.

Feeling your bones tells you a lot about them

Although most of your bones are hidden deep inside your body, you can still feel some of them. Try and find the bones labelled in the drawing of the skeleton.

Activity

- Feel the bones in your head (skull), back (backbone), chest (rib cage), breastbone, collar bone, shoulder blade, elbow, hip, knee, arm, thigh bone, shin bone, wrist and ankle.
1 Are all the bones in the skeleton the same shape?
2 Are all the bones in the skeleton the same size?
3 What connects your skull to your pelvis (hips)?
4 What is the longest bone in your body? (Remember your backbone is made up of more than one bone so this doesn't count.)
5 Which part of the skeleton looks like a round box?
6 What is the name of this bony box?
7 Which part of the skeleton looks like a bony cage?
8 What is the name of this bony cage?

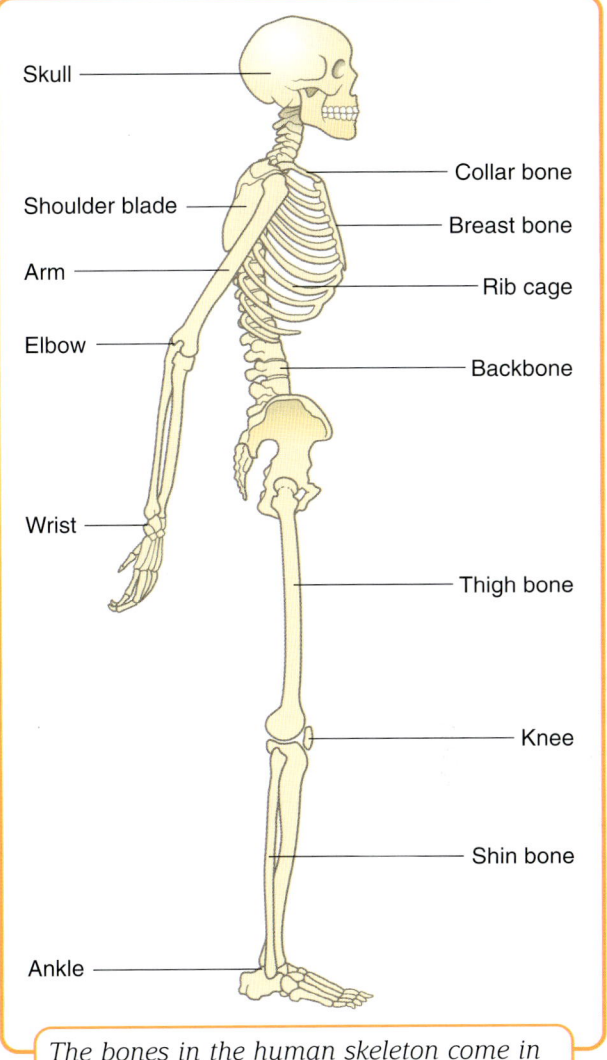

The bones in the human skeleton come in different shapes and sizes.

Many of your bones are hollow

Even though your bones are very strong, many of them are hollow in the middle. Hollow structures are very strong for their weight. If an elephant's leg bones were solid in the middle, they would be so heavy that the elephant would not be able to stand up and walk around. It would be the same for you.

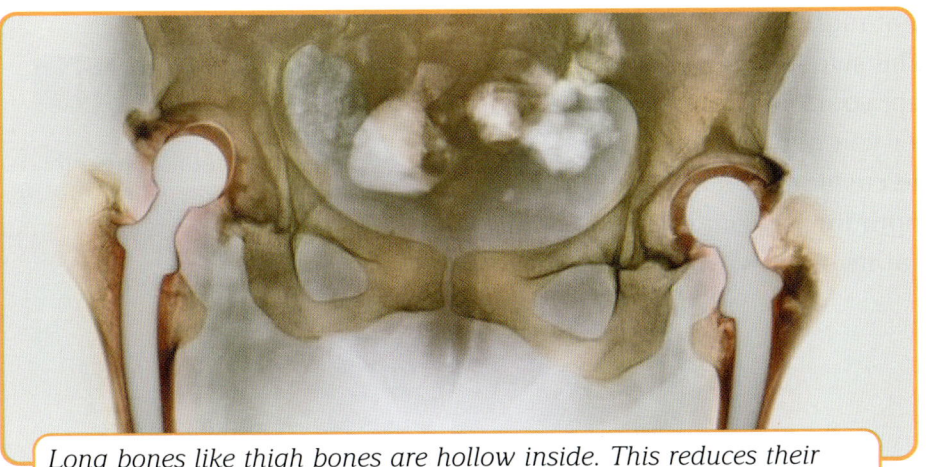

Long bones like thigh bones are hollow inside. This reduces their weight without reducing their strength.

Skin and bones hold you together

Your skeleton supports and protects

Your skeleton supports your body and allows you to move. It also protects the soft, delicate parts of your body. Your skull protects your brain. Your rib cage protects your heart and lungs. The bones which form your backbone protect your main spinal nerve, which is called the **spinal column**.

Some of your bones also have additional functions. Red blood cells are made in the ribs, vertebrae and some limb bones. Bones also manufacture some of your white blood cells.

 **INVESTIGATION** — Try the shrinking–stretching test

- Ask one of your parents to measure your height very carefully as soon as you get up in the morning.
- Record your height in centimetres.
- Re-measure your height when you come home from school later the same day.

Did you find any difference in the two heights?

Believe it or not, but you are not the same height all day

Your backbone is made up of about 25 smaller bones called **vertebrae**. Each vertebra is separated from the next by a cushion of soft, spongy cartilage. When you sleep at night, water collects in the cartilage cushions and they swell up. The swollen cushions push the vertebrae apart. So when you are asleep, your backbone is at its longest and you are at your tallest. After you get up, your weight gradually squeezes the water out of the cushions of cartilage. Now your backbone gradually shrinks in length throughout the day. So, just before going to bed, your backbone is at its shortest and you are at your shortest.

Did you know?

A giraffe's neck is about ten times longer than your neck. But a giraffe still has only seven bones in its neck, just like you!

Bones, big and small

Bone is living tissue

You have lots of bones inside you. At first, you might think bones are hard, non-living things. But although bones look non-life-like, they are alive. Like all parts of your body, bones need oxygen to stay alive and food for growth. When they get damaged or worn, your body repairs them. So bones are living, just like other parts of your body.

Bone is very strong material

Bone is one of the strongest materials known. A block of bone as small as 25 cm^3 can support 9 tonnes – more than the weight of a fully-grown African elephant.

With every step you take, you put just over 1 tonne on every square centimetre of your femur (thigh bone).

> **FACTFILE**
>
> **Bones**
>
> 30% of bone is living tissue, cells, blood and blood vessels.
> 45% of bone is made of mineral salts.
> 25% of bone is water.
> Bone is very strong for its weight.
> Half your bones are in your hands and feet.

Soft bones become hard bones

When you were born, your bones were very soft. They were made mainly of a substance called **cartilage**. You can get an idea of what cartilage is like because some parts of your body are still made of cartilage. The tip of your nose is soft and rubbery. Your ears feel the same. Noses and ears are made of cartilage. However, soon after birth, most of your bones begin to get harder. They become harder because mineral salts gradually build up in them. The main type of mineral salt that builds up in your bones is calcium phosphate. Calcium phosphate is found in milk.

Why do babies need plenty of milk to drink?

Athletes like this put lots of stress on their bones and muscles. Their bones respond to this by growing bigger in those parts where they feel the most stress.

INVESTIGATION Tie a knot in a bone

- Ask your teacher to put 125 cm³ of dilute hydrochloric acid into a beaker.
- Carefully put a leg bone from a chicken in the acid and leave for 24 hours.
- Carefully remove the bone from the beaker using forceps. Be careful not to get any acid on your hands.
- Carefully wash the bone in cold water to remove all the acid.
- Now try tying a knot in the bone.

1 What did the chicken bone feel like after 24 hours in the acid?

The acid gradually removed the calcium phosphate from the bone. This left the soft cartilage in place. Cartilage is very rubbery so the bone was no longer hard. It was easy to bend it into all kinds of shapes. You can even tie a knot in it.

2 Could you tie a knot in the chicken bone?

Different bones for different jobs

Bones aren't all the same. Some bones are long and thin. The bones in your arms, legs, fingers and toes are like this. Other bones are short and fat. The bones found in your wrists and ankles are like this. You also have flat bones. Your shoulder blade and hipbone are shaped like this. Some bones have very strange shapes. The bones which make up your backbone have all kinds of bits sticking out of them. Your rib bones are thin and curved and some of the bones in your skull are flat and curved.

Bones also vary in size. The biggest bone in your body is your thigh bone in the upper part of your leg. The smallest bone in your body is found inside your ear. It is less than 1 mm long.

Did you know?

When you were born, your body had more than 300 bones. When you become an adult, your body will have only 206 bones.

What do you think happens to the 'lost' bones when you become fully-grown?

Moving parts – joints

You can move your body in lots of different ways

You can bend, stretch, straighten, twist and turn. You can sit down and stand up. You can bend and straighten your arms and legs. You can swing your arms and legs round in a circle. You can grip with your fingers, and some people can even grip with their toes!

You are able to make all these movements because your skeleton has joints. Joints allow your bones to move. This is why you are so flexible. Bones forming a joint are held together by tough strands of elastic material called **ligaments**.

You can move your body in lots of different ways

Activity

- Try moving your head in as many ways as you can.
- Try walking around the classroom without bending your knees.
- Try touching your toes without bending at your hips.
- Try touching your lips without bending your arm.
- Try sitting down without bending at your hips.

1. How many different ways can you move your head?
2. Is it easy to walk without bending your knees?
3. Is it easy to touch your toes without bending at your hips?
4. Is it easy to touch your lips without bending your arm?
5. What other parts of your body have to bend so you can sit down?

Activity

- Feel your body from head to toe and try to count all the joints in it. Remember that your backbone has about 25 joints in it. Don't forget to count all the joints in your fingers and toes!
- Record the number of joints you counted.

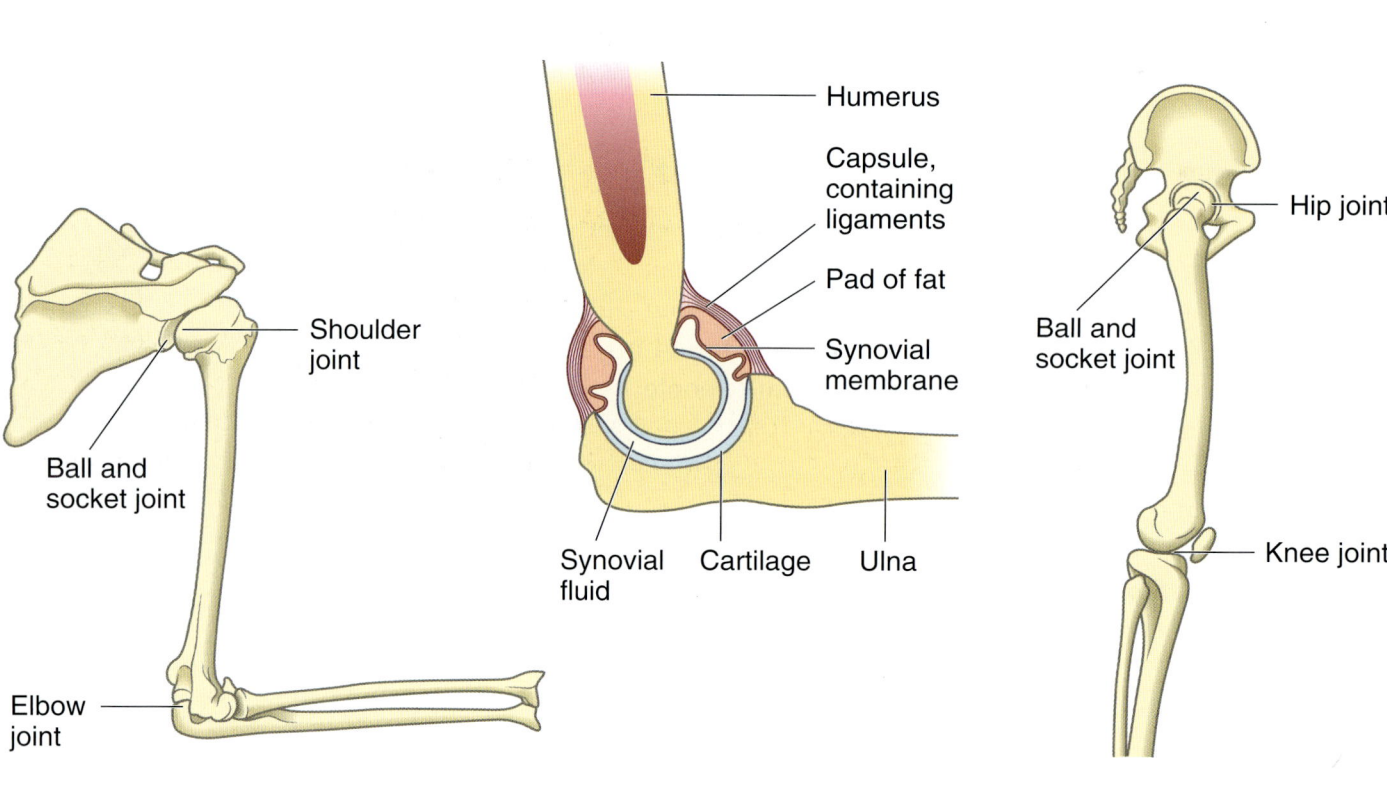

You have different kinds of joint in each arm and leg.

- Now look at the drawings of the joints shown here.
1. How many joints do you have in each arm?
2. What are the names of the joints in your arm?
3. How many joints do you have in each leg?
4. What are the names of the joints in your leg?

Activity
- Feel the joints in your arms and legs when you move them.
1. In how many directions can you move your shoulder joint?
2. In how many directions can you move your hip joint?
3. In how many directions can you move your elbow joint?
4. In how many directions can you move your knee joint?
5. What would happen if your knee joint could move in the same way as your hip joint?

Did you know?

People of the Doma tribe in Zimbabwe and the Kalanga tribe in Botswana have 'lobster-claw feet'. They have only two toes on each foot. Their toes are so strong that the people use them to take the tops off Coca-Cola bottles!

You have hinge joints at each elbow and knee

Your elbow and knee joints are called hinge joints. Hinge joints work like the hinge on a door. A hinge joint lets you move bones in only one direction.

This hinge allows movement in only one direction.

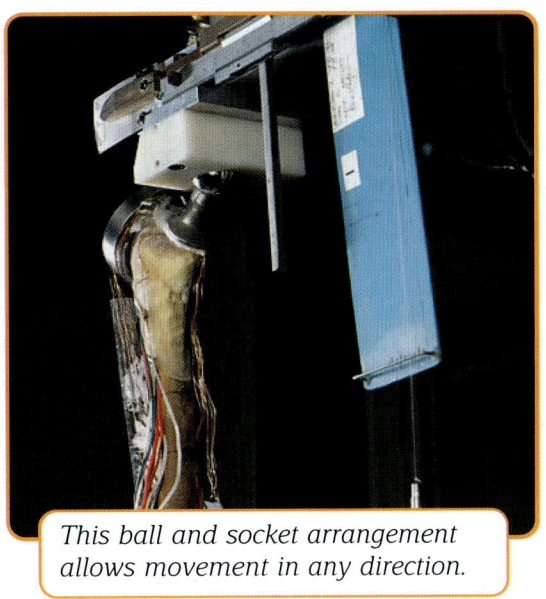

This ball and socket arrangement allows movement in any direction.

Your elbow joint lets you move your arm only up and down. Your knee joint lets you move your leg only backwards and forwards.

You have ball and socket joints in your shoulders and hips

Your shoulder and hip joints are called **ball and socket** joints. A ball and socket joint lets you move bones round in a circle.

Joints take a lot of wear and tear

A layer of slippery cartilage around the end of each bone in a joint helps keep the bones from wearing away. Joints are also well oiled to make them work smoothly and stop them wearing away. But sometimes joints do become badly worn and then a person suffers with arthritis.

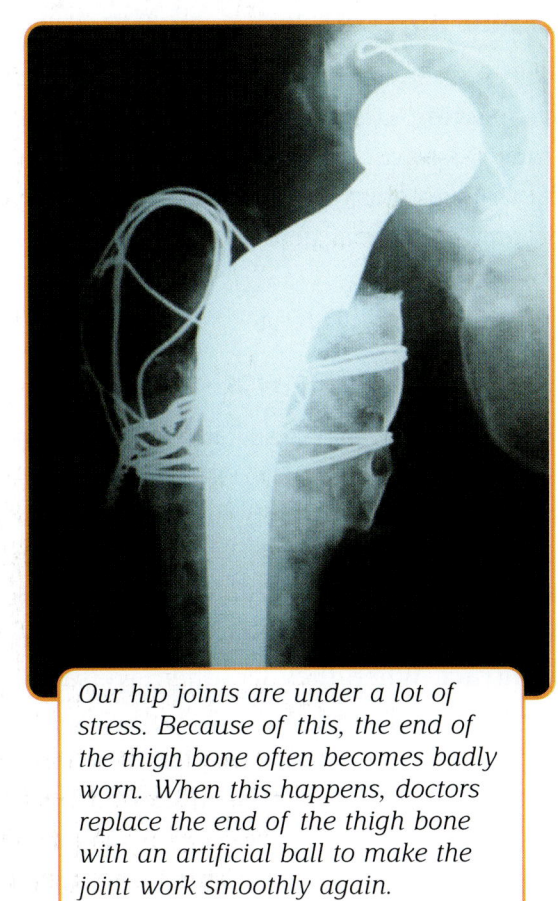

Our hip joints are under a lot of stress. Because of this, the end of the thigh bone often becomes badly worn. When this happens, doctors replace the end of the thigh bone with an artificial ball to make the joint work smoothly again.

Moving parts – joints 97

39 Muscle power

Muscles help you to move

Think of all the movements your body can make can make. You can crawl, walk, hop, jump, skip, swim, roll over, curl up and even do a somersault. You can blink your eyes, move your lips, swallow, sneeze, cough, sing and talk. You can do all these things because you have muscles.

You use 37 different muscles just to say one word. Your heart beats because of muscles. Your lungs use muscles to help you breathe. Even your food moves through your body because of muscles.

Think how difficult life would be without muscles!

Did you know?
Muscles can be made bigger by lifting heavy weights.
This will make the muscles stronger and more powerful.

Some muscles work all the time

The muscles which keep your heart beating can work for over 100 years without stopping. You keep breathing because your chest muscles never stop working. Your gut muscles never take a rest. They even keep going when you are asleep if you have eaten a big meal before you go to bed.

A muscle never works by itself

Muscles work in teams. Sometimes there are only two muscles in a team. Other teams have lots of muscles working together. Muscles often work by pulling and moving bones. When bones move, your body moves. Muscles can shorten and they can lengthen. When they shorten, we say they **contract**. When they lengthen, we say they **relax**.

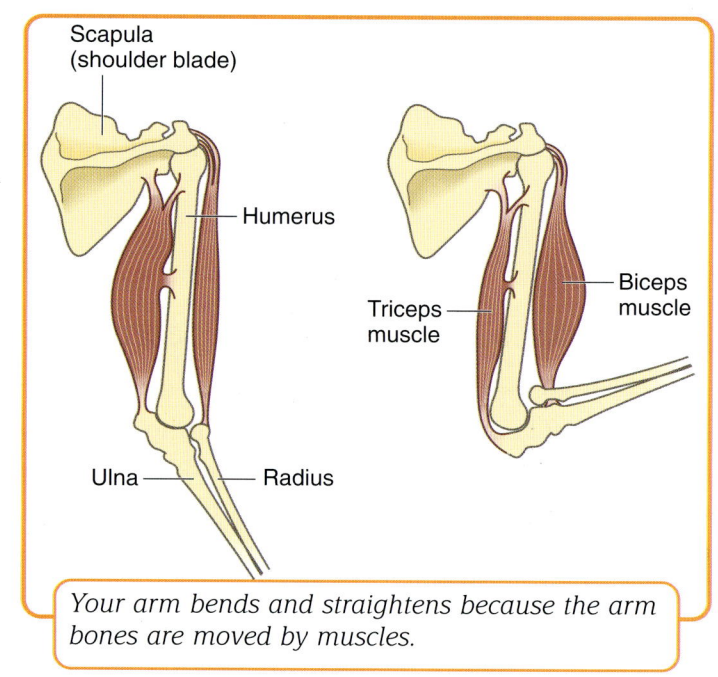

Your arm bends and straightens because the arm bones are moved by muscles.

Activity

- Look at the diagram of the arm and then find your own biceps and triceps muscles.
- Bend your arm and feel what happens to your biceps.
- Now straighten your arm and feel what happens to your triceps.

1. What happens to your biceps when you bend your arm?
2. What happens to your triceps when you bend your arm?
3. Did you find that your biceps contracted when you bent your arm?
4. Did you find that your triceps contracted when you straightened your arm?
5. What happens to your arm when your biceps contracts?
6. What happens to your arm when your triceps contracts?

- Now bend and straighten your arm several times.

7. What happens to your triceps when your biceps contracts?
8. What happens to your biceps when your triceps contracts?

Your biceps and triceps muscles work opposite to each other. When one shortens (contracts) the other lengthens (relaxes). When your arm muscles contract and relax they move the bones in your arm. Muscles move bones because they are attached to them by strong strands of tough material called **ligaments**.

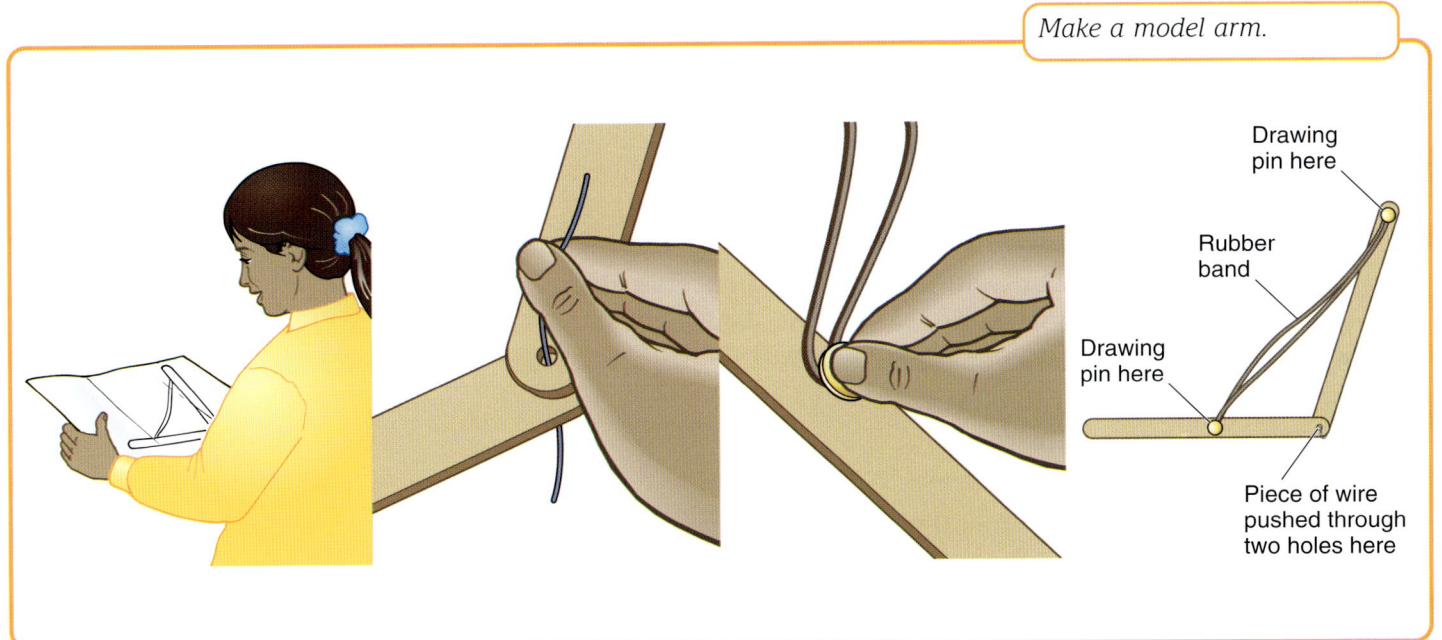

Make a model arm.

Activity

- Look at the drawings showing you how to make a model arm.
- Push the wire through the holes in the two pieces of wood and tie it.
- Pin the two rubber bands to the front and back of the pieces of wood.
- Your model is now like your real arm with its bones, elbow joint and muscles.

1. What do you have in your real arm instead of the two pieces of wood?
2. What do you have in your real arm instead of the holes and the wire?
3. What do have in your real arm instead of the rubber bands?

There are 639 muscles in your body. They make up nearly half your body weight.

A caterpillar has as many as 2000 muscles.

Activity

- Bend and straighten your model arm.
- Bend and straighten your real arm.

1. What happens to the two rubber bands when you bend your model arm?
2. What happens to the two rubber bands when you straighten your model arm?
3. Do your own muscles work like the rubber bands in your model arm?

Activity

You have muscles you have probably forgotten about or didn't even know you had. Work with a partner and observe each other closely. Try the following exercises on your face.

- Try to open and close your nostrils.
- Try to wrinkle your forehead.
- Try to waggle your ears.
- Try to open and close one eye.
- Try to raise your mouth at the corners.
- Try to turn your mouth down at the corners.

How many facial movements were you able to make?

Muscle power

The science of moving

Activity
- Take a step forwards with your right foot.
- Now take a step forwards with your left foot.
- Walk round the classroom and feel what happens to your feet.
1. What happens to your left foot when you step forwards with your right foot?
2. What happens to your right foot when you step forwards with your left foot?
3. What happens to your feet when you walk round the classroom?

Did you find that when you stepped forwards with your right foot, your left foot pushed against the ground?
Did you find that when you stepped forwards with your left foot, your right foot pushed against the ground?

Activity
- Try taking a step forwards with your right foot without pushing backwards with your left foot.
- Try taking a step forwards with your left foot without pushing backwards with your right foot.

Could you step forwards without pushing backwards at the same time?

When an animal walks on land, it pushes backwards against the ground and moves forwards.

When an animal swims in water, it pushes backwards against the water and moves forwards.

When an animal flies in air, it pushes backwards against the air and moves forwards.

The cheetah is the fastest animal on land. It can run at more than 70 km per hour. Does the cheetah's body remain the same shape when it runs or does it change shape?

There are three rules of movement

When an animal pushes backwards against its surroundings it creates a force. The force that moves an animal forwards is equal to the force pushing backwards against its surroundings. Every time an animal moves, its body changes shape.

When we move, we also obey the three rules of movement

In the activities above, you found you pushed backwards against the floor when you walked. In doing this you created a force. If you watched your friends walking, you would have noticed that their body changed shape when they moved. Yours did the same.

Walking wheels

Animals have structures to make them move. A cat has legs, a fish has fins and a bird has wings. A human is like a cat. We have legs, but only two of them.

Machines like bicycles, cars, ships and aeroplanes have parts that turn round to make them move. Bicycles and cars have wheels, while ships and aeroplanes have propellers. Although jet aeroplanes don't have propellers, they have similar devices in their engines to make them move.

Animals don't have wheels or propellers to make them move. Instead, they push themselves along by means of rods or levers which move up and down or from side to side. But even these rods or levers work a bit like a wheel.

The spokes of a wheel are a bit like legs

The wheel with six spokes in the diagram on the right is a bit like an animal with six legs. As the wheel turns round, only one boot at a time pushes against the ground. After it has pushed backwards, the boot moves on and the next boot repeats the action. Each boot in turn pushes backwards and the wheel moves forwards.

The wheel with two spokes works differently. It's a 'walking' wheel with two 'legs'. Imagine each spoke has a device at the centre of the wheel which lets it swing backward and forwards. This model now works like a pair of human legs. After the boot on one spoke has pushed backwards, the second spoke swings forwards and its boot pushes backwards against the ground. Then the first spoke swings forwards to repeat the action and the wheel keeps moving forwards.

Next time you go for a walk, try to imagine your legs are working like a two-spoked bicycle wheel!

Activity
- Think of the two-spoked wheel as a model of a human.
1 What do the spokes represent in your body?
2 What do the boots represents in your body?
3 What does the device that allows the spokes to swing backwards and forwards represent in your body?

Remember, in your body your 'spokes' are moved by muscles.

Activity
- Imagine you are sitting in the middle of a frozen pond with no clothes on apart from your shoes. The ice covering the pond is frictionless so it's impossible to walk on it. (If you have forgotten what friction is, try to remember the work you did in Year 1, or ask your teacher.)

What do you have to do to get to the edge of the pond?

Diseases

Apart from injuries, anything which stops all or part of your body working properly is called a **disease**.

Diseases can be classified into **infectious**, **deficiency**, **lifestyle**, **socially transmitted** and **hereditary** (genetically linked) types. Some diseases are also caused by the environment.

Pathogens cause infectious diseases

In Year 1, you learned that infectious diseases are caused by harmful pathogens called bacteria and viruses which produce waste products called toxins. These toxins gradually poison our cells. Other pathogens attack and destroy our cells. This is why pathogens make us feel ill when they are present in our bodies.

Diseases are also caused by other types of pathogens such as single-celled animals (protozoa), fungi and parasitic worms of different kinds. Malaria is caused by a microscopic animal called plasmodium. The disease is one of the biggest killers and more than 500 million people are affected worldwide every year.

Infectious diseases are difficult to avoid

Infectious diseases spread in crowded situations such as towns and cities. They spread very quickly where hygiene is bad, where sewage services are poor or where water supplies are contaminated.

Infectious diseases are easily spread in conditions like this.

Pathogens pass from one living thing to another. They can be spread in air, water and by touch. They can also be carried by other animals.

When an infectious disease spreads quickly through a population it is called an epidemic. Infectious diseases which spread quickly include cholera, food poisoning, influenza, measles and tuberculosis.

When a fly feeds on faeces or rotten matter, the pathogens in the faeces stick to the fly's feet and hairy body. When the fly lands on food, the pathogens are spread to the food. If you eat infected food, the pathogens are transferred to your body and you become ill.

Activity
- Make a list of all the infectious diseases you can think of.
- For each disease in your list, state the symptoms and explain how it can be controlled or prevented.

A lack of chemicals in the diet causes deficiency diseases

If our diet lacks particular substances or chemicals, we can develop specific diseases called deficiency diseases. Anaemia is an example of a common deficiency disease of the blood. It occurs because there is not enough iron in the diet. People who are anaemic are always tired and they have very little energy. Other deficiency diseases occur when there are insufficient vitamins or minerals in the diet. Deficiency diseases can be prevented or controlled by improving the diet so it includes all the nutrients needed for a healthy life.

Some diseases occur because of our lifestyle

The way we live is a big factor in causing specific diseases. Eating the wrong diet, not doing enough exercise, smoking and drinking too much alcohol are all examples of how lifestyle affects our health. You will learn more about lifestyle and health in Unit 42.

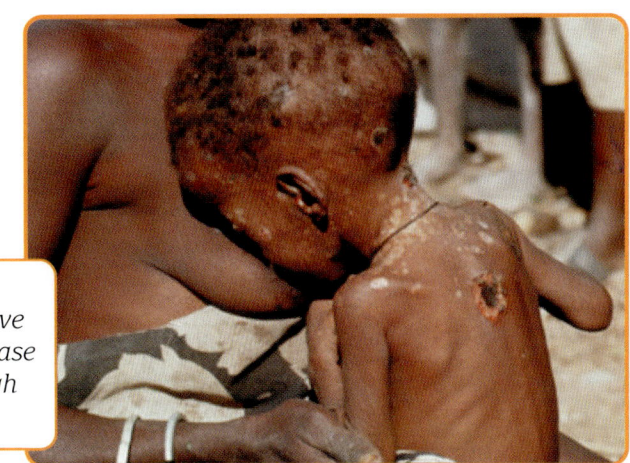

In many African countries, young children suffer a deficiency disease called kwashiorkor. This develops when children don't have enough protein in their diet. Marasmus is another deficiency disease in Third World countries. It occurs when people don't have enough food to eat.

Socially transmitted diseases occur because of the way we behave

Socially transmitted diseases involve some kind of pathogen whose rapid spread through the community is increased because of the way we behave. Sexually transmitted diseases such as syphilis, gonorrhoea and AIDS are examples of socially transmitted diseases. In many countries, these diseases are on the increase.

The HIV virus, which leads to AIDS, is especially important. Twenty years ago, AIDS was not a major killer in Trinidad and Tobago. Now it is one of the top five killer diseases and it is likely to become even more important. There are nearly 450 000 people in the Caribbean living with the HIV virus. More than 80 000 Caribbean children have been orphaned because of the disease. In Trinidad and Tobago, more than 17 000 people suffer with AIDS. In the next few years, AIDS could become the biggest single killer disease in Trinidad and Tobago.

Some diseases are linked to our genes

Diseases affected by genes are called genetically linked diseases. Faulty genes cause diseases such as haemophilia and sickle cell anaemia. Scientists now think that faulty genes also cause some forms of cancer. The sickle cell disease is caused by a gene which leads to damaged haemoglobin in the red blood cells. When they are damaged, these cells cannot carry oxygen as efficiently as normal red blood cells, so someone suffering with sickle cell anaemia becomes very ill. About one in every ten people in the Caribbean carries the sickle cell gene. If two people with the sickle cell gene have children, the chances are that one in four of them will inherit the sickle cell disease. Couples with the sickle cell gene should talk to their doctor
or medical counsellor before deciding whether to have children.

Old age brings its own specific diseases

As we get older, certain diseases begin to develop. Diseases such as arthritis, Alzheimer's and Parkinson's disease tend to occur in old age.

Industrial wastes also cause specific diseases such as lead poisoning and lung diseases such as silicosis.

Finished drawing by Alzheimer's patient. With the right care a great deal can be done to help the old and sick.

Living the right lifestyle

The kind of life you lead affects your health

Lifestyle diseases are becoming more important in all countries throughout the world. These diseases develop because of the kind of life people lead. Several factors combine to cause these diseases.

One of the most important diseases related to lifestyle is **obesity**. Obesity is when someone is overweight. The things which cause obesity include too much junk food, a poor diet in general and lack of exercise. Obesity can lead to a number of other serious diseases such as hypertension (high blood pressure), heart attacks, diseases of the circulatory system, diabetes and some types of cancer. All of these are important health issues in many countries.

Other activities such as smoking cause lung diseases like bronchitis and lung cancer.

Drinking too much alcohol damages the liver, and eating too much salt also causes hypertension.

Obesity has now become one of the most important diseases in the world today. In the Caribbean, there is a higher frequency of obesity among adult women than men, but it is also beginning to affect teenagers, young children and even babies.

Poor people are at the highest risk of becoming obese

Many poor people are at risk of becoming obese because they cannot afford to eat a balanced diet. There is also a growing number of working mothers who find it difficult to find time to prepare healthy and nutritious family meals. In this situation, children become dependent on fast foods, which are fattening and cause obesity. Anyone who eats too many fast food meals is in danger of becoming obese.

Did you know?

Doctors estimate that the cost of dealing with obesity is about 5% of the total cost of health care in many countries.

Everyone needs some body fat

A lot of people think they are overweight even though they are not. Just because you don't measure up to the supermodels in magazines it doesn't mean you are bigger than you should be! In fact everybody should have some body fat. The average man should expect his body fat to be 10–18% of his body weight. The figure for women is higher. In fact, 18–25% of a woman's body weight should be fat.

Your Body Mass Index (BMI) is an important indicator

You can find out if someone is overweight by measuring something called their Body Mass Index (BMI). In order to do this you need to make two measurements and then do a simple piece of arithmetic.

If you measure a person's weight in kilograms and divide it by the square of their height in metres you will find out their BMI. For example, if the person's height is 1.82 m, the square of this $1.82 \times 1.82 = 3.3124$. If the person's weight is 70.5 kg, then their BMI is 70.5 divided by 3.3124, which is 21.28.

> **Did you know?**
> In developing countries, there are about 250 million obese adults.

INVESTIGATION — Work out your BMI

Work with a partner.
- Ask your partner to measure your height in metres.
- Find the square of your height. To do this, multiply your height by itself (if your height is 1.60 m, multiply 1.60 by 1.60).
- Now use a set of bathroom scales to measure your weight in kilograms.
- Divide your weight by the square of your height to work out your BMI.
- Record your result.
- Now repeat this investigation using your partner's measurements.

1. What is your Body Mass Index?
2. What is your partner's Body Mass Index?

The higher the BMI figure, the more overweight a person is. But, like any of these types of measurement it is only an indication, and other things such as body type and shape are important as well.

The table shows some BMI values. Remember that BMI is just a guide. It does not apply to old people, pregnant women or very muscular athletes. It can also vary quite a lot for growing children and teenagers.

> **Did you know?**
> In Barbados, 22% of the population suffer from hypertension.

BMI for adults (age 20 and over)	Approximate BMI for 13-year-olds	Comment	Disease risk and health implications
below 18.5	below 15.5	underweight	
18.5 to 24.9	15.5 to 22.4	ideal weight	none
25 to 29.9	22.5 to 25.4	overweight	high; double the risk of high blood pressure and heart disease, 14 times more likely to get diabetes
30 and over	25.5 and over	obese	very high; 4 times the risk of heart disease and high blood pressure, 30 times more likely to suffer with diabetes, 4 times more likely to get arthritis

Activity
- Look at the data in the second column of the BMI table.
1. Are you over underweight, overweight or is your weight ideal?
2. What about your partner?
3. Does your body weight indicate that you have any health risks?

The BMI test is only a guide

You are young and healthy so your BMI is probably well below 22.5 and you are not overweight. However, if the BMI-test shows that you are overweight, you should think about doing something about it for the sake of your health. This test is meant as only a guide. If you are worried about your weight, you should talk to your doctor.

Remember that obesity can cause diabetes, heart disease, cancer and high blood pressure. If your BMI is above 30, you should definitely act straightaway. Also remember if you need to lower your BMI do it gently. Don't starve yourself or over-strain your body with strenuous exercise. Read about how to lose weight the healthy way and take your doctor's advice.

A healthy lifestyle, including regular exercise and a balanced diet, helps prevent obesity and keeps you fit and healthy.

Activity
- Imagine you are a doctor and an adult patient comes to see you because they are worried about their weight.
1. What would you do first to find out if they have a weight problem?
2. If their BMI is 28, what advice would you give them?

Living the right lifestyle

43 The cost of being unhealthy

Everyone becomes ill from time to time

Most of us get sick occasionally. We may be ill for a short time before we get better. We may miss a few days of school or work, but we usually recover quite quickly. We may buy some suitable medicine to make us feel better. We may even visit the doctor if things don't clear up quickly. However, before too long, we usually feel well enough to go back to school or work and life returns to normal.

Sometimes people have to go to hospital

An illness may become much more serious and then a person may need to go into hospital for treatment. People get very worried when they have to spend time in hospital. They worry about the nature of their illness, whether there will be enough doctors and nurses to look after them and whether the hospital will have enough of the right kinds of medicine to treat them. If you go into hospital your parents may worry about the cost of treatment, and whether their medical insurance will cover all the bills. If one or other of your parents has to spend time in hospital, they may worry about what's happening at home, whether you are getting regular meals and whether you have enough clean clothes to wear. The personal cost of being ill can be very high and it may not just be money that worries people when they are sick. Their worries are often to do with everyday family matters and money.

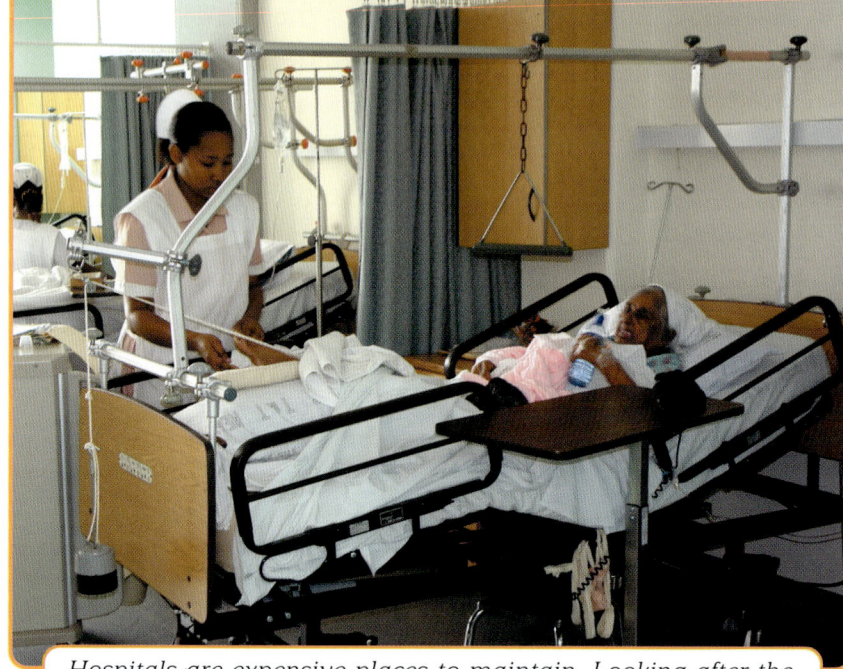
Hospitals are expensive places to maintain. Looking after the nation's health is very costly to governments.

The cost of being unhealthy is expensive

Even though the individual cost of being ill can be high, the cost of poor health to the nation is always much higher. Every Caribbean government spends millions of dollars every year on the nation's health.

Looking after patients in hospital costs a lot of money

The longer a patient has to stay in hospital, the more money it costs. In Jamaica, in 1998, heart disease was the leading cause of deaths in government hospitals. It accounted for 25% of all deaths. That year, on average, a patient with heart disease stayed in hospital for 11 days. Patients with diabetes had an average length of stay of 15 days. Heart disease accounted for over 67 000 days of in-patient care and diabetes accounted for 55 000 days of in-patient care.

Activity

- Read the paragraph above.
1. What was the main cause of death in government hospitals in Jamaica in 1998?
2. What was the total length of stay in government hospitals for all heart patients added together?
3. What was the total length of stay in government hospitals for all diabetic patients added together?
4. What was the total number of patients who were treated in hospital for heart disease?
5. What was the total number of patients who were treated in hospital for diabetes?
6. What action could the government of Jamaica take to reduce the cost of hospital care for patients suffering with heart disease and diabetes?

Did you know?

Physical fitness protects against high blood pressure, high cholesterol, heart disease, stroke and diabetes, as well as all risk factors for Alzheimers and other forms of dementia.

The table shows the main causes of death in Trinidad and Tobago in 1998.

Cause of death	Number of deaths	Percentage of total deaths
Cancer	1268	13.2%
Cardiovascular	1080	11.2%
Diabetes	1217	12.6%
Heart disease	2447	25.4%
HIV/AIDS	439	4.6%
Total main causes	6451	67.0%
Total number of deaths	9635	

In this table:
'Heart disease' means heart attacks.
'Cardiovascular' means other types of heart disease and diseases of the arteries.
'Total main causes' means the total number of deaths caused by the five main killer diseases.
'Total number of deaths' means the total number of people who died from all causes in Trinidad and Tobago during the year.

Activity

- Look at the table and read the caption carefully.
- Use the data in the column headed 'Number of deaths' to construct a bar chart.
- List the diseases in order of the number of deaths.
1. Which disease caused the most deaths?
2. Which disease caused the fewest deaths?
3. What percentage of all deaths was caused by the five main killer diseases?
4. Name two other diseases or factors which could have contributed to the total number of deaths.

Activity

- Imagine you are a doctor working in Scarborough, in Tobago. One day, just before the start of the main tourist season in November, a patient comes to see you. You examine him and discover his main symptoms are very bad diarrhoea, dehydration and general weakness. You suspect the patient is suffering from cholera. Your suspicions are increased when the patient tells you he and his family have just returned from a holiday in Belize. You remember that Belize has just suffered an outbreak of cholera.
1. What would you do to establish that the person was suffering from cholera?
2. If your diagnosis proved to be correct, who would you inform?
3. What action would you advise the Trinidad and Tobago Ministry of Health to take to control the spread of the disease?
4. If the news of your discovery is reported overseas, what effect might it have on Tobago's tourist industry that year?

Activity

- Design a poster which the Ministry of Health could use to inform the general public about the dangers of cholera, the symptoms to look out for and what action people should take if they think they may be infected with the disease.

Solutions and solubility 44

Temperature, surface area and solubility

In Year 1 you learned something about solutions, solutes, solvents and solubility. You learned that:
- Some substances dissolve more easily than others.
- The solubility of a substance depends on the nature of the solvent.
- When a substance dissolves there is no loss of mass.

A solution can become saturated

In Year 1 you learned that the maximum amount of sodium chloride which will dissolve in 100 g of water is 36 g. This is true, but only for a specific temperature. We should have said that this is true only when the temperature of the solvent (water) is 20 °C.

The amount of solute that dissolves in a given volume of solvent has an upper limit depending on temperature. When this upper limit is reached, the solution is said to be saturated. Until this upper limit is reached, the solution is said to be unsaturated.

The solubility of most solids increases with temperature

Have you noticed that sugar dissolves more easily in a cup of hot coffee but it dissolves less easily if the coffee has cooled down?

The best way to show how solubility changes with temperature is to make a line graph. The graph shows the solubility curves for three different substances – potassium chloride, copper(II) sulphate and lead nitrate.

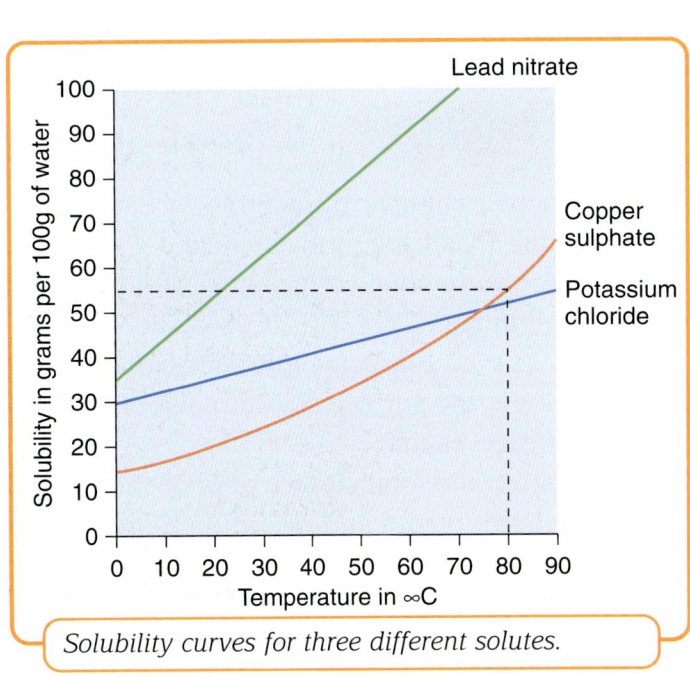

Solubility curves for three different solutes.

Temperature, surface area and solubility 113

Activity

- Study the graph showing three solubility curves.
  1. What units are used to measure solubility?
  2. Why is it important to plot solubility curves over a range of temperature?
  3. What is the advantage of having the three curves on the same graph?
  4. What happens to the solubility of each substance as the temperature increases?
  5. Which substance is least soluble at 10 °C?
  6. Which substance is most soluble at 50 °C?
  7. At what temperature are the solubilities of copper(II) sulphate and potassium chloride the same?
  8. How much more soluble is lead nitrate than potassium chloride at 60 °C?
  9. Is copper(II) sulphate always less soluble than potassium chloride?
  10. What would happen if you cooled a saturated solution of copper(II) sulphate from 70 °C to 10 °C?

Activity

- Look again at the graph showing the three solubility curves.
- Look again at the information about the solubility of sodium chloride.
  1. How does the solubility of sodium chloride at 20 °C compare to that of potassium chloride at 20 °C?
  2. Is sodium chloride more soluble or less soluble than copper(II) sulphate at 20 °C?
  3. Is sodium chloride more soluble or less soluble than lead nitrate at 20 °C?

Find the surface areas of different solids

Your teacher will give you a lump of Plasticine.
- Use the Plasticine to make a cube with a volume of $1\,cm^3$.
- Work out the total surface area of your $1\,cm^3$ of Plasticine and record the figure in cm^2.
- Now cut the Plasticine into four equal-size pieces.
- Work out the surface area of each of the four pieces of Plasticine and record the figure in cm^2.
- Work out the total surface area of the Plasticine when it is cut into four equal-size pieces and record the figure in cm^2.

Does the total surface area of the Plasticine change when it is cut into four equal-size pieces?

INVESTIGATION: Find out how surface area affects solubility

- Pour 250 ml of water into each of two beakers and label them A and B.
- Gently heat both beakers until the water starts to boil.
- While the water is coming to the boil, take two same-size jelly cubes.
- Leave one cube as it is but cut the other cube into four equal-size pieces.
- As soon as the water in each beaker starts to boil, turn off both Bunsen burners.
- Using a spoon, carefully put the large cube of jelly into one of the beakers.
- Use the spoon to put the four smaller pieces of jelly into the other beaker.
- Observe the two beakers and record what happens to the jelly in each beaker.

1. In which beaker did the jelly dissolve more quickly?
2. Which beaker contained the bigger surface area of jelly?
3. Does the amount of surface area of a solute in contact with a solvent affect its solubility?

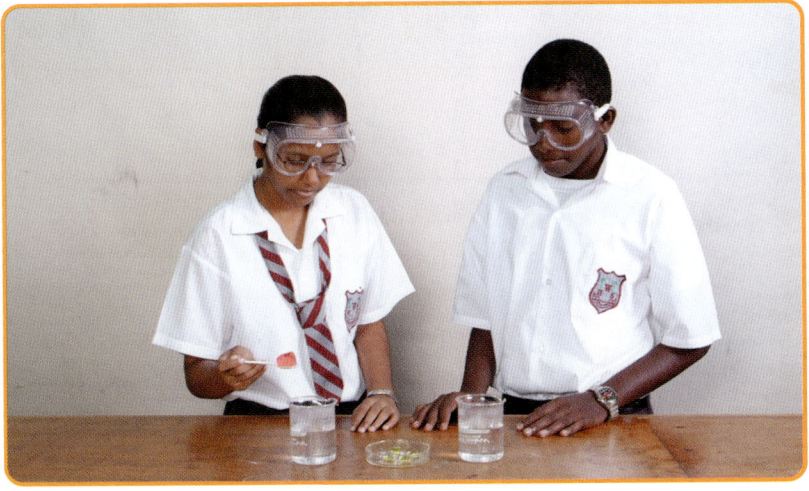

Activity

- In no more than 100 words, explain why the amount of surface area of a solute in contact with a solvent affects the solubility of the solute.

Temperature, surface area and solubility

Water – the wonder solvent

We are all made of water

Water is one of the most unusual substances on Earth. It can freeze you or burn (scald) you depending on its state. However, in its liquid state it is essential for life. The bodies of living organisms are mainly made up of water. A sweet potato is nearly 80% water and a melon is more than 95% water. Even humans are 65% water, which makes our bodies more liquid than solid. All the chemical reactions in living organisms take place in water. Water is the most important solvent for life on Earth.

The Earth is sometimes called the 'blue planet'. This is because two-thirds of its surface is covered by water which makes it look blue when seen from space. The Earth's water acts like a gigantic solvent dissolving billions of tonnes of different solutes.

Water has a chemical name

One molecule of water contains two atoms of hydrogen and one atom of oxygen. When another element combines with oxygen, chemists call the compound an **oxide**. The chemical formula for water is H_2O.

> Can you write down the correct chemical name for water?

In order to answer the above question, think how carbon dioxide gets its name.

Water is rarely found in its pure state

Water is such a good solvent that it is hard to find it in its pure form. It usually has other substances dissolved in it. On average, 1 litre of sea water contains about 35 g of solutes. In other words, 3.5% of sea water is made up of dissolved solutes of various kinds. Sea water contains 73 of the 92 naturally occurring elements found in the Earth's crust. The most common of these are sodium and chlorine which make up 85% of the elements found in sea water. On average, 1 litre of sea water contains about 25 g of sodium chloride or common salt.

FACTFILE

Water

It has no taste or smell.
It is the most common substance on the Earth's surface.
It is a compound of hydrogen and oxygen.
It can be a liquid, solid or gas, depending on temperature.
Liquid water is 800 times denser than air.
It has the ability to dissolve more substances than any other liquid.

Fresh water is different from sea water

Fresh water found in rivers and lakes contains fewer dissolved substances than sea water. Fresh water is a much weaker solution than sea water. Scientists also use the word '**salinity**' to describe the concentration of dissolved solutes in water. Salinity is really a measure of 'saltiness'. Sea water has a high salinity.

We use two terms to describe the strength of a solution. A strong solution is called a **concentrated** solution. A weak solution is called a **dilute** solution.

> How would you describe the salinity of fresh water?
> Is sea water a concentrated or a dilute solution?
> Is fresh water a concentrated or a dilute solution?

Did you know?
Two-thirds of the Earth's liquid fresh water flows between the banks of the Amazon River.

The Dead Sea is a salt water lake lying nearly 400 m below sea level. It is fed by the Jordan River which gradually brings more and more dissolved solutes to add to the lake's salinity. Much of the lake's water evaporates because of the hot, dry climate. This helps to increase the salinity of the water. This is why the Dead Sea is one of the world's saltiest lakes.

Some seas are more salty than others

Not all seas have the same amount of solutes dissolved in them. For example, the North Sea, which separates the British Isles from the European mainland, is less salty than the Caribbean Sea. The Dead Sea, situated between Israel and Jordan, is really a lake. It is a very unusual lake because it contains some of the saltiest water on Earth. Its water makes a very concentrated solution. The stronger a solution is, the more dense it is. So the Caribbean Sea is more dense than the North Sea. The Dead Sea contains some of the densest water on the planet. It is so dense that a swimmer can just lie on their back and float in it without fear of sinking.

> Do you remember, from Year 1, that one of the things alchemists did was to try and find a universal solvent?
> What would a universal solvent do?
> Do you think water is a universal solvent?

Did you know?
Over 43 billion tonnes of salts are thought to be dissolved in the Dead Sea.

Dissolved gases and life in water

Water is a solvent for important gases

Water not only acts as a solvent for a wide variety of solids, it also acts as a solvent for important gases such as oxygen and carbon dioxide.

Some **aquatic animals** (animals living in water) still get oxygen from the air. These animals, like manatees, whales, seals and turtles, can swim under water for long periods because they are good at holding their breath. However, they always come back to the surface to take in air when they need to breathe. Other aquatic animals spend their whole lives under water.

A Caribbean reef is home to a wide variety of living organisms. All the organisms in this picture live permanently under water. The water in which they live has oxygen dissolved in it. Most aquatic animals are specially designed to extract this oxygen to carry out their life processes.

Living permanently under water requires special breathing apparatus

Many aquatic animals have special breathing organs called **gills** designed to extract dissolved oxygen from the surrounding water. Sometimes these gills are easy to see because they are on the outside of the animal's body. However, many aquatic animals have internal gills.

This strange looking aquatic animal from Mexico is called an axolotl. It uses its large, feathery external gills to absorb dissolved oxygen from the water in which it lives.

Fish have internal gills for gaseous exchange

A fish continually draws water into its body through its mouth and passes it out of its body through its gills. Gills are very thin structures with a rich blood supply. As water passes through the gills, the oxygen dissolved in it diffuses into the blood flowing through the gills and enters the fish's body. Blood flowing through the gills also contains a high concentration of dissolved carbon dioxide produced by chemical reactions taking place in the fish's body. This diffuses the other way and leaves the fish's blood to enter the surrounding water. So gills act as a site for a two-way **gaseous exchange** to take place.

Underwater plants also make use of dissolved oxygen. They absorb it into their tissues and use it during respiration. Like animals, they also produce carbon dioxide which diffuses out of their leaves and dissolves in the surrounding water.

When industrial waste is discharged into rivers or lakes, it pollutes the water. The waste material removes oxygen from the water. Any aquatic organisms are killed because there is no dissolved oxygen left to breathe.

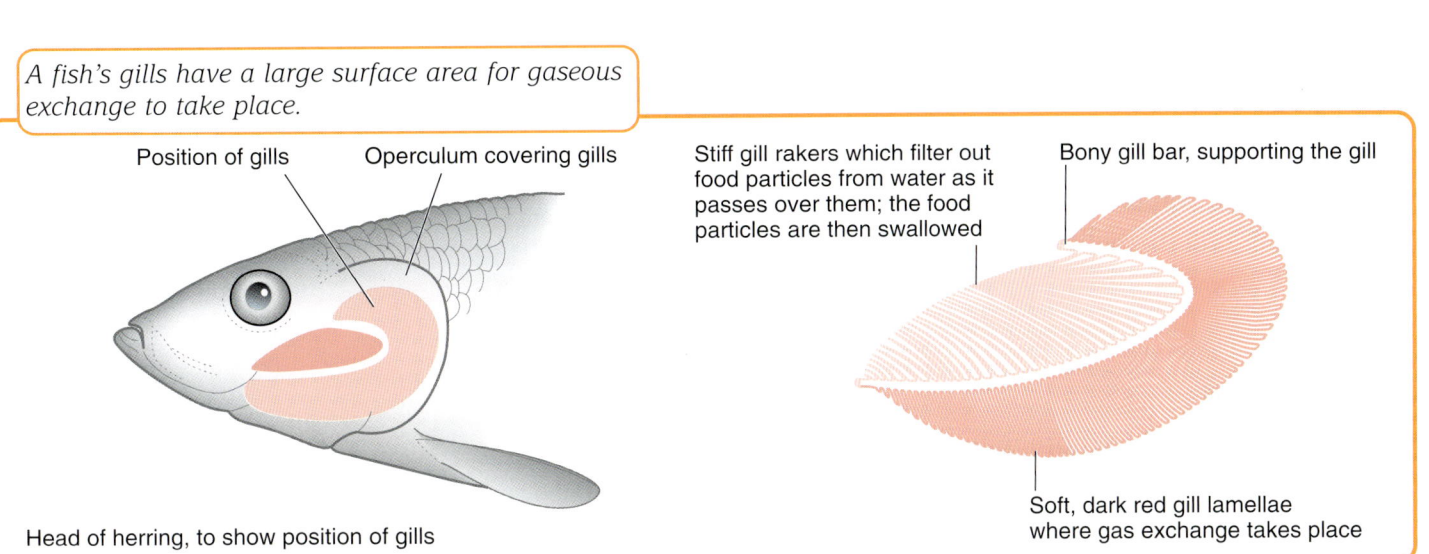

A fish's gills have a large surface area for gaseous exchange to take place.

Position of gills

Operculum covering gills

Stiff gill rakers which filter out food particles from water as it passes over them; the food particles are then swallowed

Bony gill bar, supporting the gill

Soft, dark red gill lamellae where gas exchange takes place

Head of herring, to show position of gills

Dissolved gases and life in water

The crab that lives out of water

The robber crab is a huge crab which lives in the Indian and Pacific Oceans. Like all crabs, it has gills for breathing. However, it is a special crab because it lives most of its life out of water. Its favourite food is coconuts. It even climbs to the top of the tallest palms to get a tasty dinner! The robber crab can live out of water because it carries its own supply of dissolved oxygen with it. It keeps its gills soaked in sea water. This water contains the dissolved oxygen the crab needs. The crab renews its oxygen supply by washing its gills in sea water every day.

Gases dissolve differently compared to solids

You have already discovered that most solid solutes become more soluble in water as the temperature rises. In the case of gases, the opposite is true. The table shows the solubilities of some gases at different temperatures.

Gas	Solubility (cm^3 per 100 cm^3 of water)			
	0 °C	20 °C	40 °C	60 °C
nitrogen	2.4	1.6	1.3	1.0
oxygen	4.8	3.3	2.5	1.9
carbon dioxide	171	92.3	56.6	36.0

Activity

- Look at the table of solubilities.
- Draw three line graphs to show simple solubility curves for nitrogen, oxygen and carbon dioxide.
1. Which gas is most soluble at 0 °C?
2. Which gas is least soluble at 60 °C?
3. How much more soluble is oxygen at 0 °C than at 40 °C?
4. Do gases become more soluble or less soluble as the temperature rises?
5. When you heat water, dissolved nitrogen and oxygen bubble off. Will the bubbles contain more nitrogen or more oxygen?

Did you know?

A bull sperm whale can hold its breath for nearly 2 hours in a deep dive.

Activity

- Explain in no more than 100 words why the Caribbean Sea contains less dissolved oxygen than the Southern Ocean around Antarctica.

Solutes cause problems for life in water

A fish living in the middle of the Caribbean Sea is in danger of dying through lack of water. It's true! If you think back to Year 1 when you learned about the movement (diffusion) of particles in and out of cells, you will remember that particles always diffuse from where they are in high concentration to where they are in low concentration. Water particles are no different – they behave in the same way.

> Can you remember the special term used to describe the diffusion of water particles?

In the case of water, you can describe particle diffusion in another way. In Unit 45, you learned the word 'salinity'.

> Can you describe the movement of water particles in terms of salinity?

Living in water has its problems

Fish living in the sea (marine fish) face the problem of drying out. A marine fish's blood has a lower concentration of solutes than the surrounding sea water. Therefore, its blood has a lower salinity than the surrounding sea water. This difference in salinity causes water to move continually out of a marine fish's body. This water loss takes place mainly through the fish's gills. So it's true! A fish living in the sea is in danger of drying out, even though it is surrounded by water! Marine fish solve their dehydration problem by drinking lots of sea water. This helps to replace the water lost by osmosis. But a marine fish also has to get rid of all the extra salt it 'drinks'. It does this by passing the extra salt out into the surrounding sea through its gills. So a marine fish's gills have two functions. They allow gaseous exchange to take place and they also remove extra salt from the fish's blood.

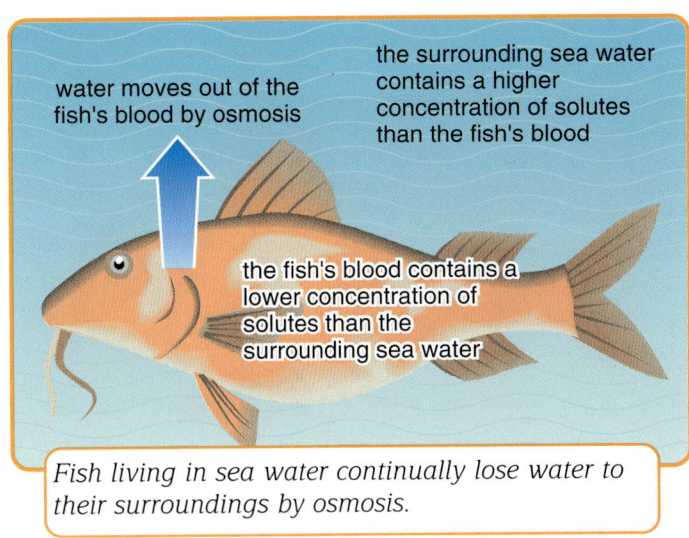

Fish living in sea water continually lose water to their surroundings by osmosis.

Fish living in fresh water face a different osmotic problem from their sea-going relatives. In their case, they live in water which has a lower salinity than their own blood. So water is continually moving into their body, and they face the problem of 'bursting'. But fish living in fresh water don't burst because they get rid of the excess water in their body by continually producing large volumes of very dilute urine.

The process by which animals and plants control the level of solutes in their bodies is called **osmoregulation**.

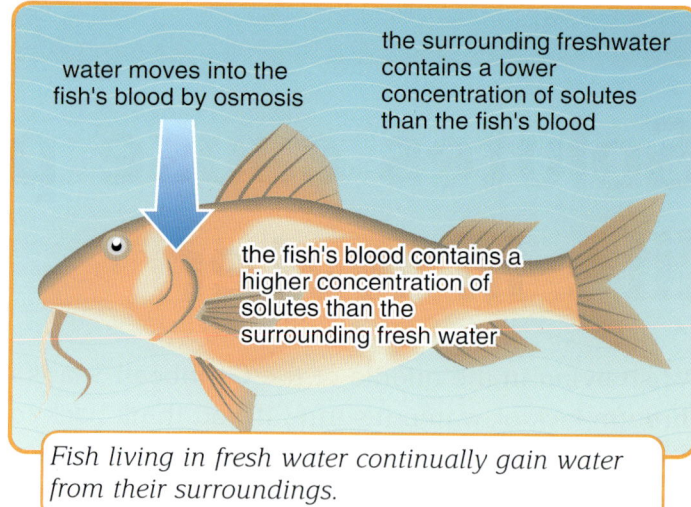

Fish living in fresh water continually gain water from their surroundings.

Turtles cry salty tears

The green turtle is one of the most common turtles in the Caribbean. Adults feed mainly on turtle grass which they graze with their horny mouths. As they eat, these turtles also consume lots of smaller animals living on the turtle grass. Because the plants and animals in their diet are salty, green turtles continually take in lots of extra dissolved salt. This high intake of salt causes an osmotic problem. Green turtles solve their osmotic problem in a very interesting way. They have special glands next to their eyes which take the extra salt out of their blood. If you see a green turtle 'crying', it's not really shedding tears. It is getting rid of the extra salt it eats in order to control its blood's solute concentration. Its 'tears' contain a strong solute concentration which is much higher than that of the surrounding sea water.

Green turtles 'cry' very salty tears.

A kangaroo rat.

Did you know?

The kangaroo rat doesn't live in water. It doesn't even drink water. It is a most unusual animal. It can live its whole life without ever taking one sip of water.

Carbonic acid and caves

INVESTIGATION: Add a dilute acid to a carbonate

- Put a small lump of calcium carbonate in a test tube.
- Add about 5 cm³ of dilute acid – vinegar or lemon juice will do.
- Observe what happens.

What did you observe taking place in the test tube?

Carbonates fizz when dilute acids are added to them because carbon dioxide is given off.

Carbonate compounds react with a dilute acid to produce water, carbon dioxide and a soluble product called a salt which goes into solution. This can be summarised as:

carbonate + acid → salt + water + carbon dioxide

Rain water is slightly acidic when it lands on Earth

A similar reaction to the one above takes place in Nature. When rain falls, it dissolves carbon dioxide and other gases present in air on its way to the ground. By the time it reaches the ground, rain water has become a weak acid called **carbonic acid**.

Rocks called limestone are made of calcium carbonate. A common name for calcium carbonate is chalk. There are large areas of limestone in all the bigger Caribbean islands, and the Bahamas and the Cayman Islands are made up almost entirely of limestone. In the Caribbean, much of the limestone has been produced over millions of years by the tiny animals that produce coral. If you go snorkelling over a coral reef, you are swimming over large formations of calcium carbonate.

Harrison's Cave is a famous tourist site in Barbados

At Welchman's Gully, in Barbados, carbonic acid in rain water has gradually reacted with the limestone rock over thousands of years and gradually dissolved it. This reaction has slowly created a large,

Did you know?

The biggest underground cave is the Sarawak Chamber in Gunung Mulu National Park, in Sarawak. It is 700 m long, has an average width of 300 m and its height is never less than 70 m. It is so big that 40 Boeing 747 jumbo jets could fit into it all at the same time.

underground cave system called Harrison's Cave. Harrison's Cave is the result of carbonic acid reacting with calcium carbonate. This process can be summarised by the equation:

$$\underline{\text{calcium carbonate}} + \underline{\text{carbon dioxide}} + \underline{\text{water}} \rightleftharpoons \underline{\text{calcium hydrogencarbonate}}$$
$$\underline{CaCO_3(s)} + \underline{CO_2(g)} + \underline{H_2O(l)} \rightleftharpoons \underline{Ca(HCO_3)_2(aq)}$$

(carbonic acid in rain water)

Calcium hydrogencarbonate is soluble in water and is washed away as the water flows over and through the limestone. This process is called **chemical weathering**.

Stalactites and stalagmites are made of calcium carbonate

The reaction between calcium carbonate and carbonic acid is reversible – it can go backwards as well as forwards. This means that dissolved calcium hydrogencarbonate can change back into solid calcium carbonate.

$$Ca(HCO_3)_2(aq) \rightleftharpoons CaCO_3(s) + CO_2(g) + H_2O(l)$$

Over thousands of years, this reverse reaction has taken place in the water seeping through the roof of Harrison's Cave and dripping onto the floor. As the water drips, some of the solid calcium carbonate has been left behind on the roof of the cave and more has been deposited on the floor of the cave where drips have landed. Over very long periods of time, the excess water has evaporated and solid calcium carbonate has gradually collected on the roof and the floor of the cave to form structures called stalactites (on the ceiling) and stalagmites (on the ground). This is an on-going process that is still taking place today.

Harrison's Cave, in Barbados, is the island's top tourist attraction. Visitors go on a 1.5 km underground ride through a series of artificially lit smaller caves full of dripping stalactites and 'forests' of spiky stalagmites.

Activity
- Imagine the Barbados Tourist Board has asked you to write an article giving tourists a simple, scientific explanation of what they see when they visit Harrison's Cave. Your article is needed for a new brochure to be handed to tourists when they arrive at the Cave.
- Here's a hint to help you with your brochure – people often get confused between stalactites and stalagmites. They can't remember which is which. Try and make up a simple rule to remind tourists how to tell the difference between a stalactite and a stalagmite. Don't forget to include your rule in your article.

Did you know?
Stalactites and stalagmites grow very slowly. It takes about 100 years to add 1 cm³ of calcium carbonate to a stalactite or stalagmite.

How solutes affect our tap water

Some water is hard and some is soft

In Unit 48 you discovered that carbon dioxide dissolves in rain water to form a weak acid called carbonic acid. You also discovered that carbonic acid reacts with limestone (calcium carbonate) to produce carbon dioxide and a soluble substance called calcium hydrogencarbonate.

Domestic water supplied to houses in limestone areas contains a number of different solutes including calcium hydrogencarbonate. This compound is not removed at water treatment plants and so it finds its way into our tap water. Calcium hydrogencarbonate has an important effect on household water supplies. It makes the water '**hard**'. This kind of hardness is called **temporary hardness**.

Other compounds, including calcium sulphate and magnesium sulphate, also make water hard. This kind of hardness is called **permanent hardness**.

Water that doesn't come from limestone areas is not 'hard'. It is '**soft**'. The dissolved solutes that cause hardness are not present in soft water.

The amount of hardness in water affects the way the water behaves. We can tell how hard or soft water is by finding out how well it forms a lather with soap.

INVESTIGATION: Experiment with water hardness

You are going to compare lather formation in hard water and distilled water.
- Take two boiling tubes and half-fill one with distilled water and half-fill the other with hard water.
- Use a bulb pipette to add drops of soap solution, one by one, to the distilled water. After each drop, put a cork in the boiling tube and shake its contents thoroughly.

- Keep adding drops of the soap solution and shaking until you have a good soapy lather.
- Record how many drops you added.
- Now repeat using the boiling tube of hard water.
- Leave both tubes for 2 minutes and observe them again.

1. How many drops of soap solution did you add to the distilled water?
2. How many drops did you add to the hard water?

The extra number of drops you added to the hard water is a measure of its hardness.

3. Which tube showed the best lather?
4. In which tube did the lather last the longest?
5. Which sample of water was harder?
6. Why do you think this is?
7. How would you describe distilled water?

These two test tubes show the results of an investigation to demonstrate how lather formation is affected by hardness in water.

Activity

- Bring a sample of your home tap water to school to test it for hardness.
- Carry out the lather test, as in the previous investigation.

1. Is your house water hard or soft?
2. Did your result agree with those of your classmates?
3. Did the class results of this activity show a variation in water hardness depending where your classmates live?

Temporary hard water can cause other problems

Apart from lather problems, temporary hard water is a nuisance in other ways in the home. It causes problems in the bathroom and the kitchen. When you have a bath, the soap reacts with solutes such as calcium hydrogencarbonate in hard water to form a messy scum. If you live in a limestone area, you will have noticed a ring of scum around the bath tub after you let the water out.

How does hard water affect washing the dishes at home after dinner?
How does hard water affect washing clothes at home?

Over time, temporary hard water also makes a mess of your electric kettle. When you boil temporary hard water, the calcium hydrogencarbonate is changed back into calcium carbonate. This is insoluble in water and collects on the heating element as something called **lime scale** or 'fur'. You can see this in the photograph. The same thing happens if you use temporary hard water in a steam iron.

How would you explain to your mother why her electric kettle gets lime scale?
In terms of energy, how would you explain to your mother that lime scale affects an electric kettle's efficiency?
What would you advise your mother to do to get rid of the lime scale in her kettle?

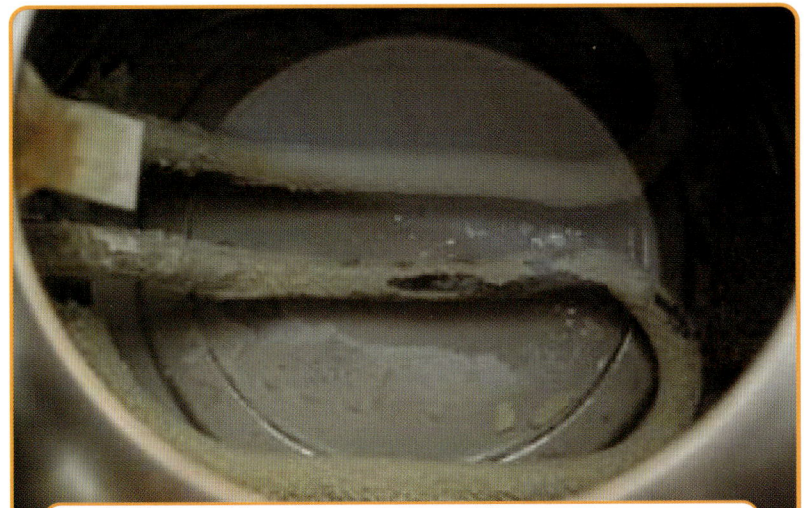

When temporary hard water boils in a kettle, its calcium hydrogencarbonate is changed into calcium carbonate which is insoluble. It collects on the heating element as a chalky deposit called lime scale.

Did you know?

In an ion exchange tank, hard water containing calcium and magnesium compounds is passed through a special material called zeolite. As the hard water passes through the zeolite, its calcium and magnesium ions change places with the sodium ions in the zeolite. The water coming out of the bottom of the tank is now soft because it has lost all its calcium and magnesium ions.

50 Acid rain is the result of soluble gases

Burning fossil fuels causes acid rain

Fossil fuels such as coal, natural gas and oil contain sulphur. When these fuels are burned in power stations and factories, they release sulphur into the air where it combines with oxygen to form a gas called **sulphur dioxide**. Sulphur dioxide is carried high into the air where it dissolves in the water droplets in clouds which form rain. When sulphur dioxide dissolves in water droplets it forms an acid called **sulphuric acid**.

Car exhausts also cause acid rain

Car exhaust fumes contain gases produced from the combustion of gasoline. These include oxides of nitrogen. Like sulphur dioxide, these oxides go into the air and dissolve in water droplets in clouds. This time the acid formed is called **nitric acid**. Rain water with dissolved sulphur dioxide and oxides of nitrogen is more acidic than ordinary rain water. It is called **acid rain**. Acid rain has become an important pollutant in some industrial countries. When it falls, acid rain corrodes metals, damages stone buildings and kills trees.

These trees have been killed by acid rain falling on them over a period of time.

What is the solvent in acid rain?
What are the solutes in acid rain?

Activity
- Carry out an investigation to find out if acid rain is a problem in the area where you live.

Aeroplanes are as much to blame for acid rain as power stations, factories and cars. Their jet engines produce a number of gases from the fuel they use, which help make acid rain.

Activity
- Look at the photograph showing the carved figure and read the caption.
1. What is the chemical name for the rock from which the figure is carved?
2. How would you describe the figure?

3 Why do you think the figure looks like it does?
4 Can you explain where the missing bits of the statue went?
5 Why do you think the figure needs to be replaced?
6 What is the process called that has made the figure look like it does?

This figure is made of limestone. It has been on the building for a long time.

Modern technology is helping to reduce acid rain

Many power stations and factories are beginning to use new technology to remove the sulphur dioxide from the wastes they release into the air. This means less sulphur dioxide will go into the air and less acid rain will be produced.

Car manufacturers are also developing new kinds of engines which produce fewer harmful gases. This new technology will make acid rain less of a problem in the next 50 years.

Oil companies are producing new kinds of gasoline which contain less sulphur. This means less sulphur dioxide goes into the atmosphere in car and aeroplane emissions.

Catalytic converters make car exhaust fumes less harmful

Another dangerous gas produced by car engines is called **carbon monoxide**. In many countries, new cars are required to have a device called a **catalytic converter** in their exhaust systems. A catalytic converter contains substances called **catalysts**. These catalysts speed up the chemical reactions which make the oxides of nitrogen and carbon monoxide in exhaust fumes react together to produce nitrogen and carbon dioxide.

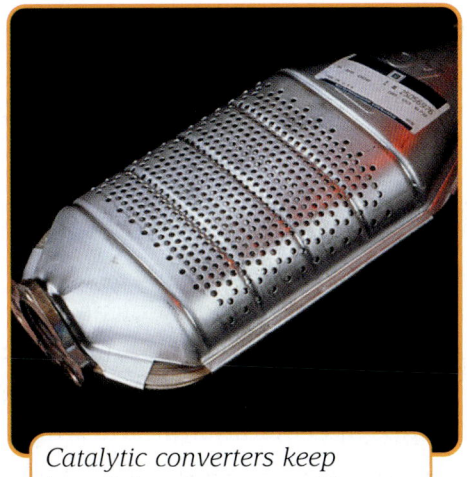
Catalytic converters keep harmful carbon monoxide out of the atmosphere.

Activity
- Imagine you are the Minister for the Environment for Trinidad and Tobago and that you have been invited to an international conference on acid rain. Prepare a short speech to explain to other delegates your ideas for reducing the problem of acid rain.

Ground water – an important solvent

Ground water is important for the environment

When rain water reaches the Earth's surface, much of it seeps into the soil and becomes **ground water**. Ground water plays a very important role in the environment. In many parts of the world it provides over one-third of all drinking water. It also finds its way into lakes and maintains the flow of rivers.

Ground water works like a gigantic solvent

As it slowly seeps through soil and rocks, ground water dissolves many of the minerals it comes in contact with. You already know (from Unit 48) about the effect of carbonic acid in ground water on limestone rocks. Ground water acts as a solvent for many minerals in other types of rock. It also dissolves some of the compounds made by human activity that get into the soil. These include degreasers, petroleum compounds, pesticides, certain industrial by-products and pollutants such as nitrates, chlorides and heavy metals.

Harmful products get into ground water

Chemicals produced by the petroleum industry escape from underground storage tanks and pollute ground water. They can cause cancer, even when they are present in low concentrations. Waste metal compounds from mining activity, landfill sites and other waste dumps also get into ground water and contaminate it. Metal and plastic compounds from fabric cleaning and electronic and aircraft manufacturing are often discharged and pollute ground water. When metals such as lead get into ground water, they are harmful to health because they collect in the body and affect the nervous system. Pipes, fittings, solder, and the connections of some household plumbing systems also contain lead which contaminates drinking water. Children and pregnant women are most at risk from this kind of pollution.

Fluoride compounds are essential for maintaining healthy teeth and strong bones. They occur naturally, dissolved in ground water, but some governments put small traces of extra fluorine in domestic water supplies to prevent tooth decay. However, high concentrations of fluorine have an opposite effect on health. Excess amounts can cause yellowing of the teeth, damage to the spinal cord and other serious conditions.

Sewage can affect the quality of ground water

Untreated or poorly treated sewage is a major source of pollution of ground water and surface water in developing countries. Sewage uses up large amounts of oxygen and this upsets the ecological balance of rivers, lakes and wetlands when it seeps into them. Sewage also carries microbes that spread disease.

Nitrates cause special problems

Fertilisers from agricultural activities and manure from livestock increase the level of nitrates in the ground water they get into. When these dissolved substances seep into ponds, lakes and wetlands, they make the water very rich in nutrients. This encourages the growth of algae which use up all the oxygen in the water. Now the waterways become stagnant and this kills any wildlife living there. In many Caribbean islands, this process (called **eutrophication**) even affects coastal areas.

The presence of nitrates can affect health

Nitrates from agricultural activities also find their way into drinking water. Sometimes, they reach concentrations far above the safety levels recommended. Good agricultural practices can help in reducing the amount of nitrates in the soil and thereby lower their content in the water we drink. Excess nitrates in our water cause health problems. Healthy human adults can take in fairly large amounts of nitrates without affecting their health. However, young babies are poisoned by high nitrate concentrations. Sheep and horses are also affected by high concentrations of nitrates, and dairy cows show reduced milk production.

Water contaminated with nitrates can be treated so that it meets drinking standards. Treatments are expensive, however, and include processes such as reverse osmosis, deionisation, and distillation. Boiling, softening, or disinfecting will not reduce the water's nitrate content.

Wells with high nitrate levels should be inspected for sources of contamination. Common sources of nitrates include septic systems, animal manure, decaying organic matter, and commercial nitrogen fertilisers.

Aluminium is very poisonous to wildlife

You learned about acid rain in Unit 50. As it soaks into the ground, acid rain dissolves aluminium compounds and washes them out of the soil. When the ground water containing aluminium compounds runs into rivers and lakes, it poisons the water and kills fish and other aquatic animals. The extra aluminium in the water stops the gills of fish from working properly. When this happens, fish can't absorb oxygen from the water so they suffocate. In some parts of the world, rivers and lakes now contain very few fish because of the effect of the dissolved aluminium compounds.

These fish have been killed by acid rain.

Activity
- Try to find out where the water piped to your home by Trinidad and Tobago's Water and Sewerage Authority (WASA) comes from.

Did you know?

A person living in New York uses about 680 litres of water a day. An average Kenyan uses just 4 litres daily.

In the last century, the Earth's human population increased three times but the world's water consumption increased six times.

Today, 20% of the world's population does not have access to safe drinking water.

Solutes and solvents in everyday life

Many simple activities at home are to do with making solutions

A lot of the activities which take place in the home are to do with dissolving, solubility and making solutions. This is especially true of activities carried out in the kitchen and the bathroom. When you make a cup of instant coffee, you make a solution of coffee with hot water. The same is true when you make a cup of tea. If you use a teabag, not all the tea dissolves in the boiling water so you are left with some which you throw away in the used bag. If you put sugar in your tea or coffee, you are making use of the fact that the sugar will dissolve in the water and this will sweeten your drink.

Lots of headache and other tablets are soluble in water.

Activity

Darlene made herself a cup of instant coffee by adding hot water to three spoonfuls of coffee granules in a mug. Then her mother asked her to go to the shop and Darlene didn't have time to drink her coffee. The next day, when Darlene looked at her mug of cold coffee, she noticed some solid coffee in the bottom of the mug.
- Use the ideas of solute, solvent, solubility and saturated solutions to explain what happened to the coffee in Darlene's mug.

Activity

- Write down what you would say to your mother to explain what happens when she adds salt to something she is cooking.

Does anyone in your family use nail polish?
Do you think nail polish is likely to contain water as a solvent?
What should be an important property of the solvent present in nail polish?

Many women use nail polish to make their hands and feet look more attractive. Nail polish contains coloured dyes in a solvent that evaporates quickly.

Activity
- Ask your mother or older sister if you can look at her nail polish remover. If nobody in your family uses nail polish, go to the supermarket and look at the labels on some bottles of nail polish remover on the shelves.
- Write down the name of the solvent or solvents in nail polish remover.

An alcohol called ethanol is used as a solvent for nice-smelling oils in perfumes. When this model sprays perfume on herself, the ethanol quickly evaporates from her warm skin, leaving behind the nice-smelling oils.

It's a sticky world

If we didn't have glues and adhesives, our world would fall apart. This book would certainly disintegrate because its pages are stuck to the spine with strong glue. Without adhesives, the soles on your shoes would come off, the chair you are sitting on would collapse, and the desk you are working at would fall to pieces.

All glues start off runny and sticky and then become solid. When they become solid, they hold two objects (or two surfaces) together. Materials called **solvent glues** work in this way. Solvent glues have a solid (solute) dissolved in a solvent. The solvent is a special kind which evaporates easily and quickly when it is exposed to air. This kind of solvent is called a **volatile** solvent. When the solvent evaporates, the solid is left behind and this holds the objects or surfaces together.

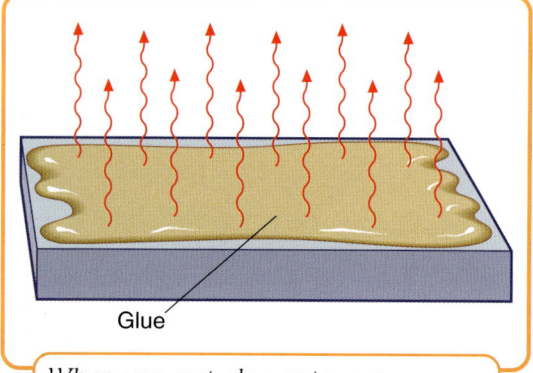

When you put glue onto one surface, the solvent starts to evaporate.

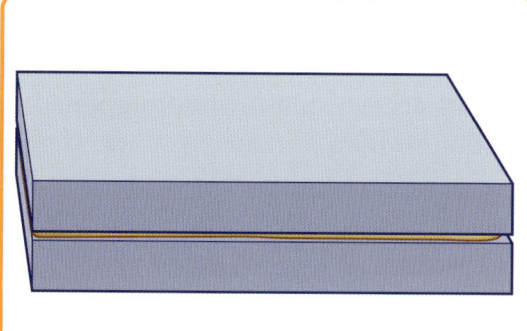

When the solvent has evaporated, a layer of solid is left behind which holds the surfaces together.

This girl has used glue to mend a puncture in her bicycle tyre. The glue used to mend punctures contains rubber (the solute) dissolved in a special solvent. The solvent is a volatile one which begins to evaporate very quickly as soon as the glue is spread over the puncture.

Activity

- Look at the photographs of the boy sticking a stamp on an envelope and read the caption.
1. Where is the solute in this example of sticking a stamp on an envelope?
2. Where is the solvent in this example of sticking a stamp on an envelope?
3. In not more than 100 words, write an explanation of what happens in terms of solutes, solvents and solutions when you stick a stamp on an envelope.

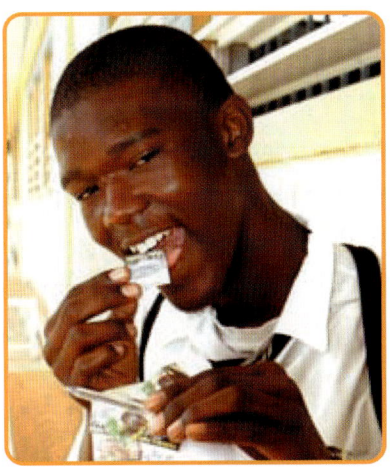

When you stick a stamp on an envelope, you are using a solvent glue.

Activity

- Try to find out the name of a solvent you would use to clean paint brushes.
- Try to find out what solvent could be used to clean oily hands.
- Look at the photograph of the pool and read the caption.

In the case of sterilising a swimming pool, what is the solvent and what is the solute?

Domestic water supplies and swimming pools are sterilised by dissolving small amounts of chlorine in the water.

Solutes and solvents in everyday life

53 Getting things clean

Washing is all about making solutions

When water is used for washing, it dissolves dirt. But water isn't able to dissolve all kinds of dirt. For example, it cannot dissolve oily or greasy dirt. Things called **soaps** and **detergents** are needed to get rid of oily or greasy dirt. Soaps are natural products, made from fats or plant oils. But soaps form a messy scum in hard water, as you saw in Unit 49. Detergents are synthetic products, made from chemicals. They can be used effectively in all types of water.

These days, soap powders and soaps are made from oils extracted from plants like the oil palm tree mixed with potassium hydroxide solution.

FACTFILE

History of soap

People used to make soap by boiling fat from the animals they killed for food combined with the ash from their fires. This is how the Romans made soap more than 2000 years ago. The soap the Romans made wasn't very nice – it smelled terrible – but it did help keep them clean. These days, soap is made with more pleasant smelling oils such as palm oil. The oil is boiled with potassium hydroxide solution. Just to make sure modern soap smells even more pleasant, nice-smelling chemicals are also added.

Detergents are made up of special kinds of molecules

A detergent has a special way of dealing with oily and greasy dirt. Detergent molecules are made of two parts. They have a head and a tail. The tail 'hates' or 'fears' water. When something 'hates' water, it is said to be **hydrophobic**. The head of the detergent molecules 'likes' water. When something likes water it is said to be **hydrophilic**. To help you remember which is which, the 'lic' in hydrophi**lic** is a bit like '**lik**e', and the 'ph' in '**ph**obia' sounds like the 'f' in '**f**ear'. (Also, the word 'phobia' means 'fear'.)

The hydrophobic tails of the detergent molecules are attracted to the oil. The hydrophilic heads are attracted to the water so the detergent molecules arrange themselves with their tails buried in the oil and their heads in the water. The heads push each other away and as they move apart they pull the oil into a spherical droplet. The oil droplet, surrounded by detergent molecules, floats off into the water. When you wash a greasy dish in washing-up liquid, the grease comes off the plate into the water and forms an emulsion.

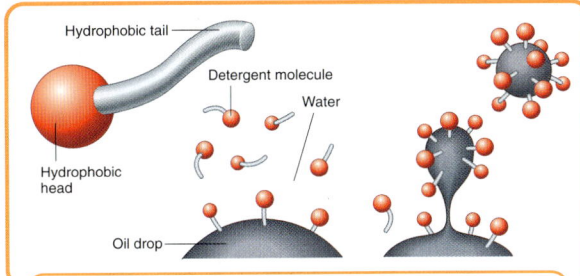

This shows how a detergent molecule dissolves oil.

Water isn't the only solvent for cleaning

We use water and detergents to do our washing because water is cheap and there is plenty of it. But sometimes putting clothes in the washing machine or the kitchen sink and cleaning them with detergent and water is not the best way to remove stains. Many items of clothing carry a label warning you not to wash them at home. It may say 'Dry clean only'. You should never try to wash an item of clothing with detergent and water if the label tells you to 'Dry clean only'.

Activity
- Ask your mother if you can check all the clothes at home to find out which carry a dry cleaning label.
- Make a list of the different items of clothes which need dry cleaning when they are dirty.

Dry cleaning requires special solvents

Dry cleaning establishments use special solvents to get rid of dirt and stains. They use solvents called **organic solvents**. These solvents have no water in them so they are called **non-aqueous solvents**. Non-aqueous solvents dissolve grease and oil stains more easily than water does. But they are much more expensive than water. Because they are so expensive, non-aqueous solvents are distilled and re-used instead of being thrown away like water from a washing machine.

Many items of clothing have a label on the inside lining that tells you to have them dry cleaned when they become dirty.

Is dry cleaning really a 'dry' process?
Gasoline dissolves grease and oil but it is never used in dry cleaning. Can you explain why?

Activity
- Imagine you are the manager of your local dry cleaning establishment. List four factors you would need to consider when deciding what type of solvent or solvents to use on your customers' clothes and other household items.

Ironing a garment that has been dry cleaned.

Getting things clean 137

54 Separating solvents from solutes

In Year 1 you discovered a way of separating a solute from its solvent. You used **evaporation** to drive off the water (the solvent) from a solution of sugar (the solute). This left the sugar behind in the bottom of the beaker, so you collected the solute. But you 'lost' the water (the solvent). The molecules of water disappeared into the surrounding air. If we want to improve this kind of separation, we need to find a way to collect the water (the solvent) as well.

It is often important to be able to separate and collect water from a solution. For example, if you want a sample of pure water, you need to be able to separate it from any impurities it may contain. Pure water is useful for lots of scientific experiments and research. It is also widely used in industry, and sometimes in the home. The correct name for pure water is distilled water.

> What would be the advantage of using distilled water in your electric kettle if the domestic supply to your house was hard water? What would be the advantage of using distilled water in a steam iron if the domestic supply to your house was hard water?

When you take a hot shower, you may have noticed that the bathroom mirror often steams up. The hot steam from the shower hits the cold surface of the mirror. The cold surface of the mirror cools the steam and changes it back into water. This process is called **condensation**. A substance formed by condensation is called a **condensate**. We can use condensation to obtain a pure solvent, such as water, from a solution.

INVESTIGATION Try to 'catch' steam

- Put a large spoon in a refrigerator for about 30 minutes.
- Gently heat an evaporating dish half-full of salt solution until steam appears.
- Now hold the cold spoon (curved surface down) directly over the dish.
- Record your observations.

1. Why did you put the spoon in a refrigerator before starting the investigation?
2. What happens to the steam when it hits the surface of the spoon?

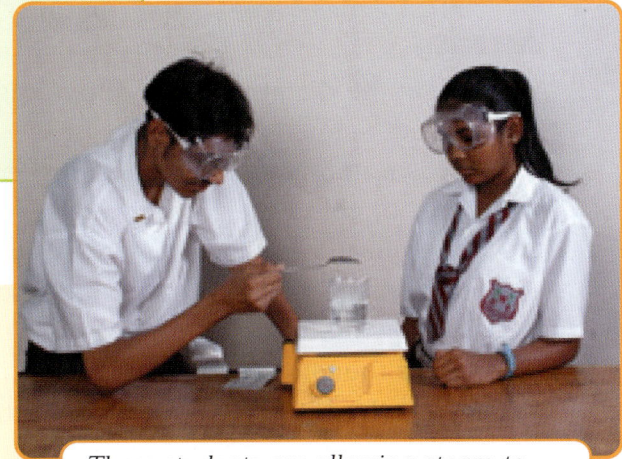

These students are allowing steam to condense on the surface of a cold spoon.

Activity

- Copy and complete the following statement using these words. You will need to use two of the words twice.

condensed   cooling   evaporates   gas   liquid   steam

When a salt solution is heated, the water .... as .... The water changes state from a .... to a .... The steam can be .... back into pure water by .... it down. The steam changes state from a .... back into a ....

In the investigation above, you didn't really collect the water. It just condensed on the surface of the spoon. But there is a piece of scientific apparatus, called a **condenser**, which does allow you to collect the water.

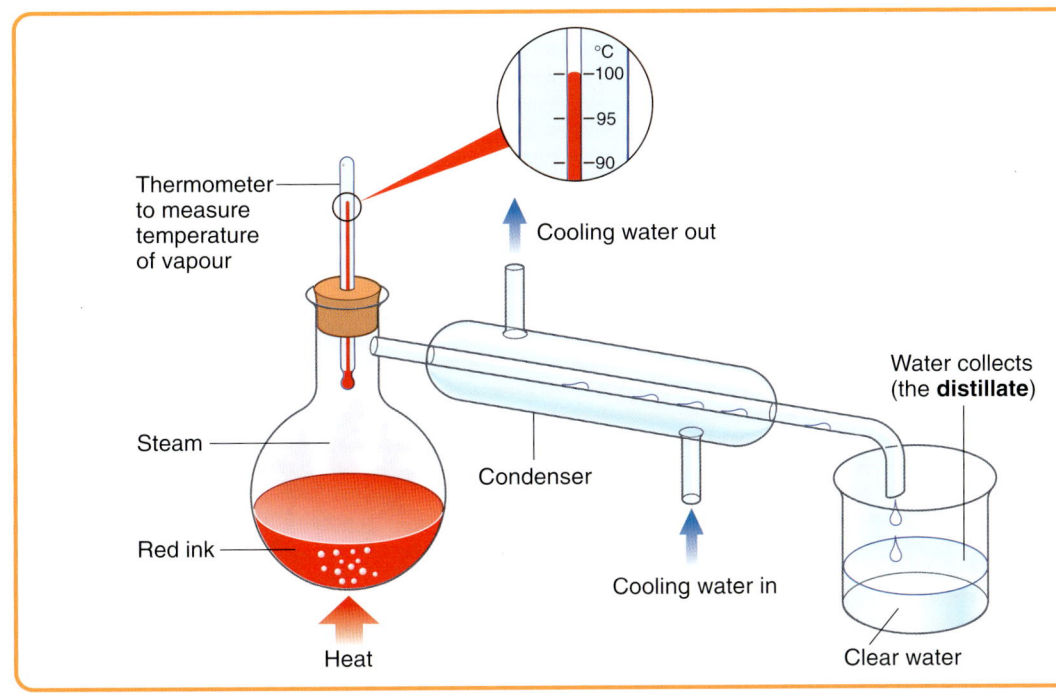

This piece of apparatus is used to produce distilled water.

Separating solvents from solutes 139

Activity

- Look at the diagram of the apparatus used to produce distilled water.
1. Why is it important for the condenser to have a continual supply of cold water?
2. Will the water leaving the condenser be warmer or cooler than the water entering the condenser?
3. Why do you need a thermometer in this experiment?
4. What is the temperature reading on the thermometer?
5. What is the significance of heating the solution of red ink to this temperature?

The process of separating and collecting a solvent, such as water, in this way is called **distillation**. A substance produced by distillation is called a distillate.

During this example of distillation, water (the solvent) is separated from red ink (the solute) and collected. The solute (the red ink) is also collected because it remains behind in the flask.

> Why is distillation an improvement on evaporation as a means of separating a solvent from its solute?

Activity

- Imagine you don't have a proper condenser like the one in the diagram. Design an experiment using less complicated apparatus to produce a sample of distilled water from a salt solution.

Activity

- Imagine you have been shipwrecked on a desert island where there is no fresh water to drink but plenty of driftwood on the beach. Just before you escaped from the sinking ship, you managed to fill a sack with a small saucepan, an extra large metal pan lid, a large dish and a box of matches. Explain, in not more than 100 words, how you could obtain a small, but steady, supply of fresh water to drink until you are rescued by a passing boat.
- Don't forget to include a diagram with your explanation to show how you would get fresh water.

140 Separating solvents from solutes

Separating a mixture of solutes

Some solutions contain a mixture of different solutes. Scientists use a technique called **chromatography** to separate this kind of mixture. Chromatography means 'making a coloured picture'. The kind of 'picture' made by chromatography is called a **chromatogram**.

You can use chromatography to separate a mixture of different coloured inks.

INVESTIGATION — Find out what colours are present in black ink

- Cut a strip of filter paper 15 cm long by 3 cm wide.
- Put a small spot of black ink about 3 cm from one end of the strip.
- Attach the other end of the strip to a glass rod with a bulldog clip.
- Pour water in a beaker to a depth of 2 cm.
- Now hang the strip above the beaker so the water just touches the end. Make sure the ink spot is out of the water.
- Leave the strip in the beaker for 10 minutes and observe what happens.

Why must the spot of ink be kept above the level of the water?

Black ink is a mixture of different coloured inks dissolved in a solvent. So the different coloured inks are solutes.

These students are investigating what solutes are present in black ink.

The paper absorbs the water. As the water reaches the black ink spot the different coloured inks start to dissolve and are carried upwards with the water molecules. You can get a better understanding of what happens by imagining that the different ink molecules 'hitch' a ride on the back of the water molecules. The inks which dissolve most easily travel furthest with the water. Those that are less soluble travel the shortest distance.

This is a chromatogram of black ink.

Activity

- If your investigation didn't produce a clear chromatogram, look at the one in the photograph.

1 How many different coloured inks are mixed together to make black ink?
2 What are these different colours?
3 Which ink is carried furthest by the water?
4 Which ink is carried the shortest distance by the water?
5 Which ink is most soluble in water?
6 Which ink is least soluble in water?

- Now think about the result of this investigation in terms of solutes and a solvent.

7 What is the solvent used to make black ink?
8 How many different coloured solutes are mixed together to make black ink?
9 What colours are these different solutes?
10 Which solute is carried furthest by the water?
11 Which solute is carried the shortest distance by the water?
12 Which solute is most soluble in water?
13 Which solute is least soluble in water?

Activity

- Repeat the chromatography investigation using red, blue and yellow inks.

Scientists use chromatography to analyse things

Chromatography is a useful technique for telling scientists what substances are present in a mixture. This process is called **analysis**. Scientists use chromatography to analyse a mixture to find out what it contains.

Forensic scientists are people who use scientific techniques to investigate crimes. Criminals sometimes leave traces of blood behind at the scene of a crime. Forensic scientists use chromatography to compare the blood found at the scene of a crime with the blood of different suspects to try and identify which is the criminal.

Forensic scientist is examining clothes for stains that might give clues to the identity of a criminal.

Hospital laboratories analyse medical samples such as blood and urine in order to check a patient's health. If there are any abnormal solutes in the samples, they will show up on the chromatograms. Scientists also use chromatography to analyse new drugs in order to decide whether they are pure and safe to take.

Scientists working in the food industry use chromatography to check the purity of foods and drinks when they are manufactured. Some foods are artificially coloured by using food dyes to make them look more attractive. Chromatography can be used to find out which dyes are present in the food we eat.

Chromatography is used to analyse polluted air and water to find out what pollutants are present.

Activity

Mr Poon was involved in a car accident on a busy weekday in Chaguanas. His problem was that the driver of the other car drove away without stopping. When the police examined Mr Poon's red car, they found some spots of blue paint on its rear bumper which came from the other car. The police arrested three suspects, Mr Mendoza, Mr Roopchan and Mr Hunte, each of whom owned a blue car.
- Explain how a police forensic scientist could use chromatography to prove whether Mr Mendoza, Mr Roopchan or Mr Hunte was the owner of the car which didn't stop.

It is important to remember that chromatography only works if the mixture being analysed is soluble in the solvent being used.

Separating a mixture of solutes

56 Separation techniques in industry

You have learned about various techniques used to separate different substances. These techniques include filtration, evaporation, distillation and chromatography.

Another separation technique used in the laboratory and in industry is **centrifuging**. A centrifuge is a piece of equipment used to separate components in a suspension. Medical laboratories often use a centrifuge to separate substances like blood into its different components. In a centrifuge, a suspension in a container is spun round very fast so that the solid part of the suspension gets flung to the bottom of the container. The liquid part can then be poured off leaving the solid behind in the container.

Filtration, evaporation, distillation, chromatography and centrifuging are also used in industry in order to separate various substances. For example, a variety of separation techniques are used in three of Trinidad's main industries – the sugar industry, the rum industry and the petroleum industry.

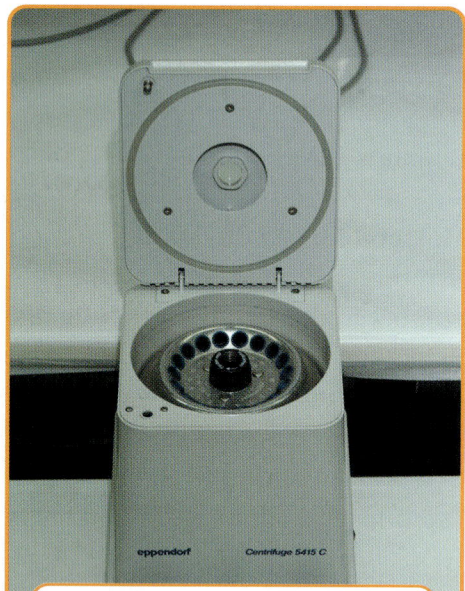

This laboratory centrifuge is used to separate the solid part of a suspension from the liquid in which it is suspended.

Sugar extraction involves lots of chemistry

Sugar is an important crop in many Caribbean islands. It is extracted from the sugar cane plant in a number of different stages. First the cane is cut and then sent to a sugar mill for processing. After this, various chemical processes take place before the final product is obtained.

Did you know?

Sugar cane is crushed between powerful rollers in order to break open the plant cells storing sugar.

This bag of sugar has been produced by of a series of production stages and separation techniques.

Sugar cane is crushed at the sugar mill by being passed through a series of rollers, and cane juice containing dissolved sugar is squeezed out.

↓

Water is sprayed onto the crushed cane before it goes between the last rollers.

↓

The cane juice is sent to large tanks where lime is added.

↓

The mixture of cane juice and lime is heated to its boiling point to extract any impurities which settle to the bottom of the tanks.

↓

The impurities are continually drawn off from the bottom of the tanks and filtered to remove more juice which is sent to evaporators where the water is evaporated off.

↓

The clear juice at the top of the tanks is also continuously drawn off and sent to evaporators where the water is evaporated off.

↓

A special vacuum device then further evaporates the juice leaving behind sugar crystals and a thick syrup known as molasses.

↓

The molasses and sugar crystals are separated from each other in a large centrifuge.

↓   ↓

Molasses is used to make rum.   Sugar crystals are sent to the sugar refinery to be granulated, powdered, or made into cubes for consumers.

A flow chart showing how sugar is extracted from sugar cane.

Activity

- Study the flow chart showing the stages in the manufacture of sugar.
1. How is cane juice extracted from sugar cane?
2. How are any impurities in cane juice removed?
3. What separation technique is used to extract any additional juice from the impurities after liming?
4. What separation technique is used to get rid of the water from the clear juice?
5. What separation technique is used separate the molasses from the sugar crystals?

Separation techniques in industry 145

Rum is made from a by-product of the manufacture of sugar

Most rum is made from the molasses produced during the manufacture of sugar. The molasses is diluted with water and then fermented with yeast to produce alcohol and carbon dioxide. The fermented liquid is then distilled at 78 °C to separate the spirit (alcohol) from the water and any impurities. The distilled spirit is called rum. Rum comes out of the still as a clear, colourless liquid. Sometimes a substance called caramel is added to the distilled rum to give extra flavour. The rum is then stored in wooden barrels which also give it additional flavour. Ageing in barrels and the use of added caramel give the final colour to the rum. Finally, the rum is blended (mixed with other rums) to get exactly the right taste and then bottled ready for drinking.

Activity

- Read the above account of the manufacture of rum.
- Draw a flow chart like the one for sugar manufacture to show the stages in the manufacture of rum.
1. What main separation process is used in the manufacture of rum?
2. Why is distillation carried out at 78 °C?
3. Why does rum change from a colourless liquid to a brown colour at the end of the manufacturing process?

Rum is an important export of Trinidad and Tobago. It is produced by a series of chemical processes and separations.

This equipment is used to separate the products of fermentation by the process of distillation during the manufacture of rum.

Separation techniques in industry

Changing melting points and boiling points

When a solid melts or a liquid boils, the chemical bonds which hold the particles together are broken. The stronger the bonds, the more the energy needed to break them. The stronger the bonds, the higher the temperature needed to break them. The strength of the bonds between particles is different for different substances. This means that the bonds will usually be broken at different temperatures. So different substances melt and boil at different temperatures. The melting point of a pure substance is always the same under the same conditions. The boiling point of a pure substance is also always the same under the same conditions. We know, for example, that pure water always melts at 0 °C and boils at 100 °C at normal atmospheric pressure.

INVESTIGATION

Find out how a solute affects the freezing point of a solvent

- Put 50 ml of distilled water into each of two plastic cups.
- Label the two cups A and B.
- Leave cup A as it is but add one teaspoonful of salt to cup B and stir to dissolve.
- Place both cups in the freezer section of a refrigerator and leave overnight.
- Next morning, remove the cups from the refrigerator and record what you find.

1. Which cup contained a pure substance?
2. Which cup contained a solution?
3. What happened to the contents of cup A?
4. What happened to the contents of cup B?
5. Can you use the terms solvent and solute to describe what this experiment shows?

The presence of a solute in a solvent affects its freezing point. Pure water freezes and pure ice melts at 0 °C. If there is an impurity (such as salt) in the water, it freezes at a lower temperature. The impurity lowers the freezing point of the water. This is true of all substances. So, the presence of a solute in a solvent lowers the freezing point of the solvent. In cold countries people make use of this fact. When ice and snow are expected, the authorities in charge of roads spread a mixture of grit and salt on the roads. When it snows, the salt dissolves in the water forming the snow and forms an impure solvent. This solvent freezes at a lower temperature than 0 °C so no ice is formed on the roads. This makes the roads safer.

> Why do the authorities mix grit with the salt before spreading the mixture on the roads?
> When making ice cream at home, why do you add salt to the ice surrounding the bowl of ice cream mixture?

In cold countries, lorries like this spread a mixture of salt and grit on roads to make the roads safer to drive on.

In cold countries, car engines often need extra protection against freezing conditions. A substance called ethylene glycol is used as an anti-freeze. When this substance is dissolved in water, it lowers the freezing point of the water. The mixture is used in the car engine's cooling system.

The table shows the freezing points of different mixtures of water and ethylene glycol.

% Water	% Ethylene glycol	Freezing point (°C)
100	0	0
90	10	−4
80	20	−9
70	30	−16
60	40	−24
50	50	−34
40	60	−47

148 Changing melting points and boiling points

Activity

- Using the data in the table, plot a line graph to show how the freezing point of water is affected when it is mixed with different concentrations of ethylene glycol. Plot % ethylene glycol along the horizontal axis and freezing point on the vertical axis.

1. When water freezes it expands. How could this damage a car's cooling system?
2. What is the freezing point of pure water?
3. What is the freezing point of a mixture containing 55% water and 45% ethylene glycol?
4. What mixture would you use in your car if the lowest winter temperature was forecast to be −11 °C?
5. Your car's cooling system has a capacity of 6000 cm³. Use your answer to the previous question to calculate how much ethylene glycol you would need to add to the cooling water.

In a mixture of water and ethylene glycol, which is the solvent and which is the solute?

INVESTIGATION — Find out how a solute affects the boiling point of a solvent

- Dissolve one teaspoon of salt in 50 ml of distilled water.
- Half-fill a boiling tube with the salt solution.
- Place a thermometer in the boiling tube. The thermometer must be one that can measure temperatures above 100 °C.
- Carefully heat the boiling tube in a beaker of water over a Bunsen flame.
- Continue heating until the salt solution starts to boil.
- Record the temperature at which the solution starts to boil.

1. At what temperature did the salt solution boil?
2. Did the solution boil at a temperature lower or higher than 100 °C?
3. Using the terms solvent and solute, describe what this experiment shows.

The presence of a solute in a solvent affects its boiling point. Pure water boils at 100 °C. If there is an impurity in the water, it boils at a higher temperature. The impurity increases the boiling point of the water. This is true of all substances. So, the presence of a solute in a solvent increases the boiling point of the solvent.

58 Water – an important solvent in industry

Many important chemicals are made using water as the solvent

You have discovered that water is the most important solvent for all life processes. It is also an important solvent for many industrial processes.

Sulphuric acid is a very dangerous and corrosive chemical

More **sulphuric acid** is produced each year than any other chemical and it is used in most industries. It is used to make a wide variety of other important materials including fertilisers, detergents, dyes, paint, plastics, and soap. It is also the acid usually used in many batteries.

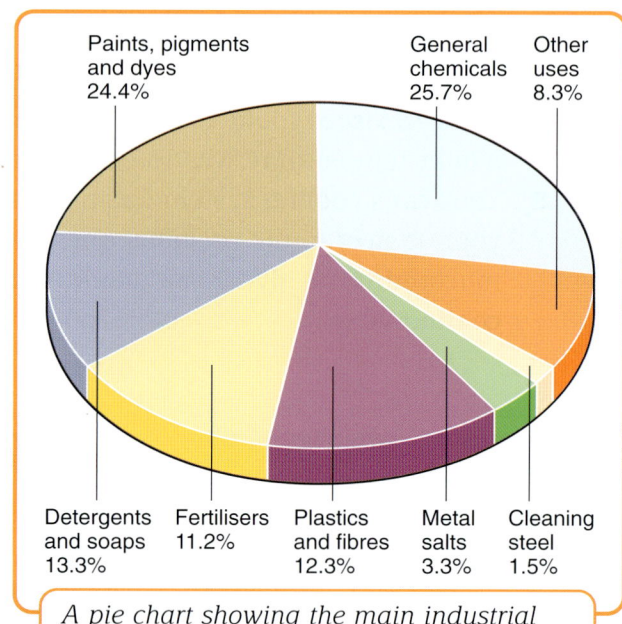

A pie chart showing the main industrial uses of sulphuric acid.
- Paints, pigments and dyes 24.4%
- General chemicals 25.7%
- Other uses 8.3%
- Detergents and soaps 13.3%
- Fertilisers 11.2%
- Plastics and fibres 12.3%
- Metal salts 3.3%
- Cleaning steel 1.5%

Activity
- Look at the warning sign used on all containers and tankers containing sulphuric acid.

What warning do you think this sign gives?

This warning sign is displayed on all containers and tankers containing sulphuric acid.

The manufacture of sulphuric acid requires water as the solvent

The materials used to make sulphuric acid are sulphur, air and water. The process used is called the **contact process** and it is used all over the world.

In the first stage of manufacture, sulphur is burned in air to produce sulphur dioxide gas. This reaction gives out heat and is called an **exothermic reaction**.

Stage 1:   sulphur   +   oxygen   ⇌   sulphur dioxide
            S(s)   + O_2(g) ⇌ SO_2(g)

In the second stage, the sulphur dioxide is cooled and then allowed to react with oxygen to convert it to **sulphur trioxide** gas.

Stage 2:   sulphur dioxide   +   oxygen   ⇌   sulphur trioxide
            $2SO_2$(g)   + O_2(g) ⇌ $2SO_3$(g)

It is difficult making sulphur trioxide because the reaction is slow and reversible. To speed it up, it is carried out under special conditions. It needs to be heated to 450 °C and it also needs a substance called a **catalyst**. The catalyst used is called **vanadium pentoxide**.

The sulphur trioxide gas made in Stage 2 is now mixed with 98% sulphuric acid to give 99.5% sulphuric acid. This is then dissolved in water to give concentrated sulphuric acid. So water is the final solvent used in the manufacture of sulphuric acid.

Stage 3:   sulphur trioxide   +   water   ⇌   sulphuric acid
            SO_3(g)   + H_2O(l)   ⇌ H_2SO_4(aq)

Hydrochloric acid is another important chemical. It is made industrially by burning hydrogen in chlorine to produce hydrogen chloride gas. The hydrogen chloride gas is then dissolved in water to make hydrochloric acid.

Activity
- Find out how **nitric acid** is manufactured industrially, and the part played by water in the process.

Fizzy drinks depend on dissolved carbon dioxide

The fizzy drinks industry makes use of the solubility of carbon dioxide in water. A fizzy drink such as soda water is made by dissolving carbon dioxide in water under pressure. At the end of the manufacturing process, the pressure is kept up by putting a top on the bottle or by sealing the drink in a metal can.

Once a fizzy drink has been bottled and sealed with a top, you can't see anything happening in the bottle. But something is going on, even though you can't see it. Molecules of carbon dioxide are continually coming out of the solution, while other molecules of

The reaction involving carbon dioxide in fizzy drinks is reversible. A lot of carbon dioxide dissolves in water under pressure during the manufacturing process. When the pressure is released by opening the drink, the carbon dioxide comes out of the solution.

carbon dioxide are continually dissolving back into the solution at exactly the same speed. Because of this, the overall change to the amount of dissolved carbon dioxide is zero. However, as soon as the bottle or can is opened, the dissolved carbon dioxide quickly comes out of the solution and appears as a stream of bubbles. The 'fizz' in a fizzy drink is caused by carbon dioxide coming out of the solution.

In the manufacture of fizzy drinks, carbon dioxide is dissolved in water under pressure.

Activity

- Read the paragraphs above about fizzy drinks and look at the photographs and captions.
1. Why is carbon dioxide dissolved in fizzy drinks under pressure during their manufacture?
2. Why should you keep fizzy drinks in a refrigerator?
3. Why do bubbles suddenly come off a fizzy drink when you open the bottle?
4. What would happen if you opened a bottle of fizzy drink and left it for a few hours?

Carbon dioxide also plays a part in the manufacture of beer. It is produced during the making of the beer by a process called fermentation. It dissolves in the water and gives the beer its bubbles. Also, during the manufacture, more carbon dioxide is dissolved under pressure in the beer and this gives the beer its froth when it is poured.

What is in crude oil?

Oil contains energy from prehistoric times

In Year 1, you discovered that oil and natural gas are fossil fuels formed from the bodies of microscopic organisms that lived in the sea millions of years ago. When the organisms died, their bodies sank to the bottom of the sea. Over millions of years, they became buried under thick layers of sand and mud. The dead micro-organisms rotted and formed oil and natural gas deposits. Oil and gas contain stored chemical energy from prehistoric times.

Crude oil is a mixture of different chemicals or compounds. The different compounds in crude oil are called **hydrocarbons** because they are made up of the elements carbon and hydrogen. The different compounds in crude oil contain different numbers of carbon and hydrogen atoms.

FACTFILE

Carbon

Each carbon atom can combine, or link, with four other atoms.

Carbon atoms can join together to form long chains of molecules.

Carbon forms over a million different compounds. There are more compounds of carbon than there are of all the other elements put together.

Your body is built up mainly of carbon compounds.

Life as we know it would not be possible without carbon atoms.

DNA, genes and the genetic code all depend on the properties of carbon.

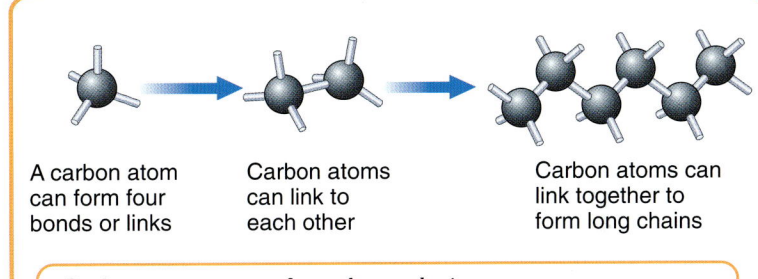

A carbon atom can form four bonds or links

Carbon atoms can link to each other

Carbon atoms can link together to form long chains

Carbon atoms can form long chains.

INVESTIGATION Distil crude oil

This investigation must be done with great care and under close supervision of your teacher. It is important to have a fire extinguisher or a bucket of sand near to hand in case of fire. You must carry out this investigation exactly as your teacher tells you.

You will need to set up your distillation apparatus as the one shown in the diagram on the next page.

- Soak a piece of mineral wool in some crude oil.
- Place the mineral wool in a boiling tube with a side arm.
- Put a rubber bung in the boiling tube with a thermometer (360 °C) inserted in it.
- Clamp the boiling tube over a Bunsen burner.
- Attach a delivery tube to the side arm of the boiling tube.
- Insert the end of the delivery tube in a test tube.

- Place the test tube in a beaker half filled with cold water.
- Light the Bunsen burner and adjust the flame so it is very small.
- Now gently heat the oil-soaked mineral wool.
- Collect any distillate which comes off in the test tube until the temperature reaches 70 °C.
- Now replace the test tube with a new one and continue heating.
- Collect any distillate which comes off until the temperature reaches 120 °C.
- Now replace the test tube with a new one and continue heating.
- Collect any distillate which comes off until the temperature reaches 170 °C.
- Now replace the test tube with a new one and continue heating.
- Collect any distillate which comes off until the temperature reaches 240 °C.

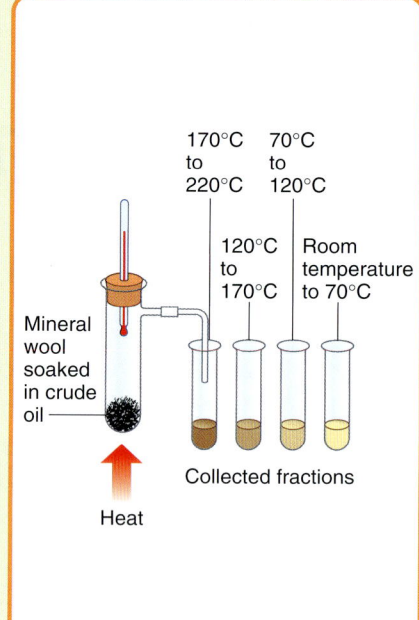

A simple piece of apparatus to separate crude oil into its main fractions.

You should now have four test tubes each containing a different compound from the distillation. You have separated the crude oil into four **fractions**.

INVESTIGATION: Test the properties of each fraction of crude oil

This investigation must be done with great care and under close supervision of your teacher. It is important to have a fire extinguisher or a bucket of sand near to hand in case of fire.

- Look at each fraction you have separated and record its appearance and viscosity (how runny it is).
- Pour each fraction in turn into an upturned tin lid.
- Carefully set fire to each fraction in turn.
- Record how well each fraction burns.
- Record the colour of the flame as each fraction burns.
- Construct a simple table to display the properties of the four fractions of crude oil you have separated. Your table should show properties such as colour of fraction, viscosity, how well it burns and colour and cleanness of flame.

Does your table agree with the table shown here?

Boiling range (°C)	Name of fraction	Colour	Viscosity	How it burns	Colour of flame
20–70	petrol	pale yellow	runny	easily	yellow
70–120	naphtha	yellow	fairly runny	quite easily	yellow, some smoke
120–170	paraffin	dark yellow	fairly viscous	harder to burn	quite smoky flame
170–240	diesel oil	brown	viscous	hard to burn	smoky flame

A table showing the properties of fractions of crude oil obtained by distillation in the school laboratory.

154 What is in crude oil?

Turning crude oil into useful products

In the petroleum industry, oil is split into fractions

In Unit 59 you separated a small sample of crude oil into different fractions or compounds. When you did some simple tests on the fractions, you discovered they had different properties. In order to make crude oil useful on a large scale, it also has to be split into fractions. The different fractions have different properties. This is why the products from the refinement of oil have different uses.

The compounds in crude oil are volatile

Chemists separate the different fractions in oil by a process called **fractional distillation**. Fractional distillation works in a similar way to the method you used in Unit 59 when you distilled a small sample of oil.

Fractional distillation works because the different compounds in crude oil can be made to undergo a change of state. When they are heated they **vaporise** – they undergo a change of state from liquid into gas. But some of the compounds are more **volatile** than others – they vaporise more easily. The very volatile compounds have low boiling points. The less volatile compounds have higher boiling points. So, the more volatile compounds undergo a change of state and vaporise more quickly than the less volatile compounds.

Industrially, crude oil is distilled on a large scale

In the petroleum industry, crude oil is heated in a furnace to over 300 °C. In the furnace, all the different fractions evaporate and become gases. The gases are fed into a metal tower 40 m high called a fractionating column or 'pipe still'. The temperature in the **fractionating column** varies from about 350 °C at the bottom to about 20 °C at the top. The most volatile compounds (those with the lowest boiling points) vaporise first. The less volatile compounds (those with the highest boiling points) vaporise last.

This large tower at the oil refinery in Pointe-à-Pierre in Trinidad is used to separate the different compounds in crude oil by the process of fractional distillation. You can see pipes coming off the tower at different levels. These lead the different fractions away after they have been separated.

As the different vapours pass up the fractionating column, they start to cool down and condense – they turn back into the liquid state. The ones with the higher boiling points cool more quickly and condense nearer the bottom of the column. Those with lower boiling points cool more slowly and condense higher up the column. As the vapour of each compound condenses into a liquid, it is piped out of the tower and collected.

> Where in the column would you expect to find any fractions with boiling points higher than 350 °C?

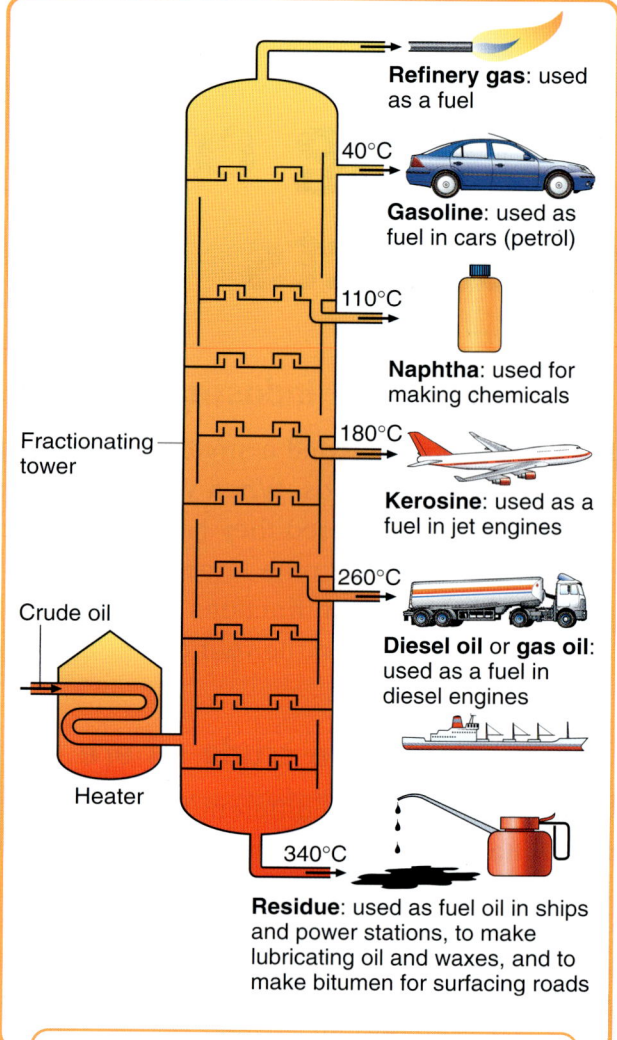

Many different products are obtained from the fractional distillation of crude oil.

Activity

- Look at the photograph of a fractional distillation tower.

1. Which pipe will take off the most volatile fraction?
2. Which pipe will take off the least volatile fraction?

Activity

- Look at the diagram of a fractionating column.

1. Which fraction comes off at the bottom of the column?
2. Which fraction comes off at the top of the column?
3. Does gasoline condense at a lower or a higher temperature than diesel oil?
4. At what temperature does kerosine (paraffin oil) condense?
5. At what temperature does the fuel used in cars condense?
6. Does lubricating oil have a higher boiling point or a lower boiling point than gasoline?
7. Which fraction is used to produce aeroplane fuel?
8. Which fraction is used to make bottled gas?
9. Which fraction is used in building roofs and roads?

Static electricity – electricity at rest

FACTFILE

History

Just over 250 years ago, a man called Benjamin Franklin performed a very dangerous experiment. He attached a large metal key to the string of a kite. Then he flew the kite in a thunderstorm. When he brought his hand near the key, a spark jumped from the key to his knuckle.

Benjamin Franklin was the first person to discover that storm clouds are charged with something called static electricity. He realised that there are two types of unlike charges of static electricity. He called these positive and negative charges. In the experiment the wet string worked like a conductor, carrying electrons (negative charges) from the thunderclouds down towards the key. The electrons then passed through Franklin's body to the ground. Based on this work, Benjamin Franklin invented the lightning conductor in 1752. Benjamin Franklin was very lucky. The next two scientists who tried this experiment were killed!

When you undress before going to bed at night, you can sometimes hear a crackling noise. It often happens when an item of clothing made of nylon rubs against another type of material. If you undress in the dark, you might even see tiny flashes of electricity. All this happens because of the same **static electricity** Benjamin Franklin investigated over 250 years ago.

INVESTIGATION

Make electrons move from one place to another

- Turn on a cold water tap until you get a thin, even trickle of water.
- Rub a plastic fork on your sleeve about 20 times.
- Hold the fork near the trickle of water.
- Observe what happens.

What happened to the trickle of water when you held the fork near it?

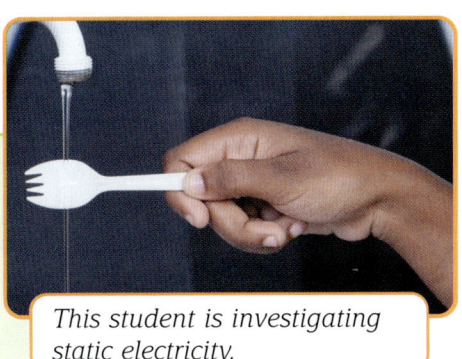

This student is investigating static electricity.

INVESTIGATION — Make an object temporarily attract something else

- Tear a piece of paper into about ten small pieces.
- Place the pieces on the workbench.
- Rub a plastic pen on your sleeve and then hold it near the pieces of paper.
- Observe what happens.

What happened to the pieces of paper when you held the plastic pen near them?

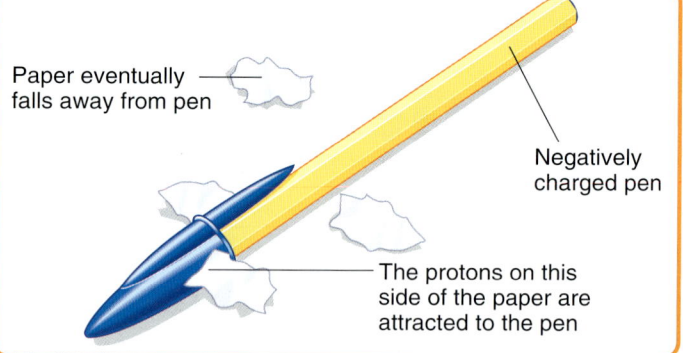

Atoms contain lots of charged particles called protons and electrons

In Year 1, you learned that atoms contain lots of positively (+) charged particles called protons and negatively (−) charged particles called electrons. In an uncharged (neutral) atom, the number of protons equals the number of electrons. Electrons move about in pathways called **shells** or **orbits**. These shells or orbits surround the nucleus. Protons are fixed in the nucleus, in the centre of an atom.

When two things such as a plastic pen and a cotton (or wool) sleeve are rubbed together, electrons move from one to the other. The plastic pen gains electrons from the sleeve. The plastic pen is now negatively (−) charged because it has more electrons than protons. When you hold the pen near a piece of paper, the pen repels (pushes away) the electrons on the part of the paper nearest to it. This leaves the paper with a positive charge at one end so it is attracted to the negatively charged pen and sticks to it. After a while the extra electrons on the pen travel through your body to the ground. The piece of paper is no longer attracted to the pen so it falls off.

> In terms of electrons and charge, can you now explain what happened when you rubbed a plastic spoon on your sleeve and then held it near a trickle of water from the tap?

INVESTIGATION Give objects similar charges

- Rub two empty plastic bottles of the same size against a piece of wool for 10 seconds each.
- Lay one bottle on its side on a flat surface.
- Predict what will happen when you bring the second bottle close to the first.
- Place the second bottle close to the first and observe what happens.
- Record your result.

1. What happened when you placed the two bottles near each other?
2. Was your prediction correct?
3. In no more than 100 words, explain (in terms of electrons and electric charge) what happened in the above investigation.

Activity

Work with a partner.
- Tape two equal lengths of cotton thread to the top of a door frame. Make sure they are spaced about 3 cm apart.
- Blow up two balloons and tie one to each thread so they hang at the same height and are touching.
- Each of you rub one of the balloons simultaneously with a piece of wool.
- Allow the balloons to hang freely and record what happens.

1. How did the balloons behave after being rubbed with a piece of wool?
2. Explain the behaviour of the balloons in terms of electrons and electric charge.

Static electricity – electricity at rest

Static electricity at work

Lightning occurs because of static electricity

In thundery weather, static electricity builds up when falling water droplets and rising ice crystals in a storm cloud rub together. Positive charges build up in the top of the cloud while negative charges gather in its base. The negative charges at the bottom of the cloud also cause positive charges to gather on the ground directly underneath. Eventually, a giant spark flashes out of the cloud and forces its way through the air to the ground below, attracted by the positive charges that have gathered there. This giant spark is what we see as a flash of lightning during a thunderstorm.

When lightning travels from a cloud to the ground, it quickly heats up the air it travels through. As the air heats up, it expands very quickly. It is this expansion of air which we hear as thunder. Light travels much faster than sound, so unless the storm is directly overhead, you always see the lightning before you hear the noise made by the thunder.

A flash of lightning branches out in lots of directions as it makes its way to the ground. Lightning contains a very large amount of electrical energy which is changed into light, heat and sound energy.

Activity

- In Unit 61, you learned about Benjamin Franklin and his kite-flying experiment. Write a letter or send an e-mail back in time to Benjamin Franklin giving him an explanation of the science behind what he observed when he flew his kite in a thunderstorm.

Activity

- Imagine you and a friend have decided to go out and fly your kites. Just as you are getting ready to leave home, the sky clouds over and you hear the rumble of an approaching thunderstorm. What scientific argument would you use to persuade your friend to abandon the idea of flying your kites until the thunderstorm has gone away?

If the electric current in a flash of lightning hits anything on its way to the ground, it burns it. High buildings, such the two towers of the National Bank in Port of Spain, have a metal strip attached to them. The strip runs all the way from the top of the building to the ground and is called a lightning conductor. If a flash of lightning hits the building during a thunderstorm, the lightning conductor takes the current safely down to the ground so the building isn't damaged.

Did you know?

There are cases where people have been hit by lightning and lived through it. One person has even been struck by lightning seven times with no major harm done.

As this model parades on the catwalk, her dress rubs against her body. This causes opposite charges to build up on her skin and the dress material. These charges attract each other and the dress clings to the model's body. Static electricity can make us feel very uncomfortable when clothes stick to us. Clothing manufacturers now produce anti-static materials which help prevent the build-up of static electricity.

A photocopier makes use of static electricity

When you put a document on a photocopier and press the 'copy' button, light is shone onto the document. The light reflects off the white areas of the document but not off the areas covered in print. There is a metal drum inside the photocopier which is charged with static electricity. Light, which is reflected off the white areas of the document, hits the drum and neutralises the charge. No light reflects onto the drum from the parts of the document with print on. The drum remains charged only on those areas where there is print on the document. The surface of the drum is coated with a layer of powdered ink called toner. This toner only sticks to the charged parts of the drum. As the drum spins, the toner is transferred onto the paper, which is also charged, and a copy of the original document is made.

Static electricity at work

Static electricity – a nuisance and a danger

People get all kinds of unexpected shocks

One of the biggest complaints people have about static electricity is that it causes sparks or gives them electric shocks when they touch things or even other people. Most people experience this problem only occasionally, but others get small shocks frequently. The problem occurs when the air is dry and materials rub against each other. Items that commonly rub together to create static electricity are:
- clothes rubbing on skin
- pyjamas or nightdresses rubbing on skin and on sheets in the bed
- clothes rubbing on furniture or car seats
- the soles of shoes rubbing against a rug or the floor.

You can do different things to reduce static electricity

The way to reduce the problem of excess static electricity is to try to get more humidity in the air, and change the materials or modify their surface. Another way is to **earth** yourself (sometimes known as **ground** yourself) before touching things whenever possible. This gets rid of any excess electrons from your body. You need to touch a metal object in contact with the ground (earth) so that electrons can flow from your hand to the ground.

Some people have very dry skin that may cause the build-up of static charges, especially in dry weather. You can use moisturisers or lotions on your skin to reduce these charges. Just putting lotion on your hands may be sufficient, since shocks and sparks usually come from touching objects with your hands.

Some clothing materials create more static electricity than others. When you slide out of a car seat or off furniture in the house, you can create static electricity if the combination of materials is right. You can reduce the static charge by putting a cover on the seat, changing the materials or your clothes, or by spraying things with an anti-static spray.

Nylon night-clothes and bed sheets create static electricity when rubbed together. Wearing cotton pyjamas or nightdresses and using cotton sheets reduces static charge because cotton doesn't develop as much static electricity as artificial fibres like nylon.

When you take clothes out of the tumble dryer, they often cling together. Also, on dry days, some clothes will get an electric charge and cling to your body. There are anti-static solutions you can spray on your clothes to prevent them from holding the electric charge on their surface.

People get shocks from walking on a rug in the house, jumping on a trampoline, or even playing basketball. Some synthetic rubber soles on shoes create a lot of static electricity. You can try experimenting with different shoes to find out which type of sole creates the most (or least) static electricity.

Activity
- Kavita took a maxi-taxi to visit her aunt in Arima. As she was getting out of the taxi outside her aunt's house, she received a mild electric shock. In no more than 100 words, explain why Kavita received a mild electric shock.

A spark can damage the internal electronics of a computer

There are some situations where excess static electricity can damage equipment or even pose a danger. Lightning can damage a building or severely injure or kill a person. A spark can cause an explosion or ruin your computer. In order to limit the danger to computers, computer hard drives are normally packaged in anti-static plastic bags before they are sold.

Normally, when operating a computer, static electricity is not a problem. But if you have been experiencing static electricity causing a spark when you touch things, it is wise to take precautions before touching even the computer keyboard. For example, you should earth yourself by touching a metal object to take away any charges from your body before you touch the computer.

When an oil tanker loads or unloads its cargo of fuel, great care has to be taken in order to avoid causing an explosion because of static electricity.

When a person handles computer boards, it doesn't take much of a spark to damage the circuitry. Technicians who repair computers often have a special pad on the floor and use an earth strap on their wrist to lead away any charges from their bodies. This is to avoid any chance of damaging the computer's electronics with a static electric spark.

Static electricity can be a danger on bulk oil tankers

Static electricity is generated when liquids move in contact with other materials. This occurs when liquids are moved through pipes, mixed, poured, pumped, filtered, or disturbed in some other way. Because of this, static electricity has long been known as a danger during the loading and unloading of oil. There have been a number of accidents involving oil tankers which were caused by a spark setting off an explosion. The spark was caused by the build-up of static electricity.

Static electricity can develop in gasoline filling stations

Filling stations can be dangerous places unless precautions are taken. When large amounts of gasoline are transferred from a tanker into an underground tank at a filling station, there is a lot of friction caused by the gasoline flow. Also, since the fuel is very flammable, a single spark caused by static electricity could cause an explosion. In order to avoid an accident, the tanker uses an earthing device on the hose used to transfer the gasoline. This draws the electric charges away from the gasoline and prevents any static sparks from occurring.

Petrol stations can be very dangerous places

Electrical circuits

Electricity on the move is called current electricity

In Unit 61 you learned that static electricity refers to charges which stay still. **Current electricity** is different. In current electricity, charges are continually on the move. The electricity we use at home, in school, in offices and in factories is current electricity.

Some materials conduct electricity, others do not

Like heat, electricity travels better through some materials than others. A material which allows electricity to travel through it is called a **conductor** of electricity, and a material which doesn't conduct electricity is called an **insulator**. Insulators are also called non-conductors.

Metals are good conductors of electricity

Metals have lots of 'free' electrons and this is why they are good conductors of electricity. Whenever there are more electrons at one end of a conductor than at the other, 'free' electrons in the conductor move as an electric current towards the end with fewer electrons. The difference in electrons between one end of a conductor and the other is called the **potential difference**. This difference is a bit like the pressure difference which causes water to flow through a pipe.

Electricity needs a pathway or **circuit** along which to flow. The circuit has to be **complete**. If a circuit is incomplete, or broken, an electric current will not flow along it.

All these household items use current electricity.

INVESTIGATION

Make a simple electrical circuit

- Put a bulb in a bulb holder.
- Use a connecting lead to connect the bulb to the positive terminal of a cell.
- Use another lead to connect the bulb to the negative terminal of the cell. This completes the circuit.

What happened to the bulb when you completed the circuit?

This simple electrical circuit has two components – a bulb and a cell.

Electrical circuits **165**

Sometimes we need to be able to break a circuit

If we break a circuit, electricity stops flowing. Sometimes it is necessary to do this. We can stop the flow of electricity through a circuit by using a switch. When a switch is closed, the circuit is complete and electricity can flow. When a switch is open, the circuit is broken and electricity cannot flow. When someone asks you to plug in and switch on the television, what they are really asking you to do is to make sure the switch is closed in order to complete the circuit from the power point in the wall to the television set.

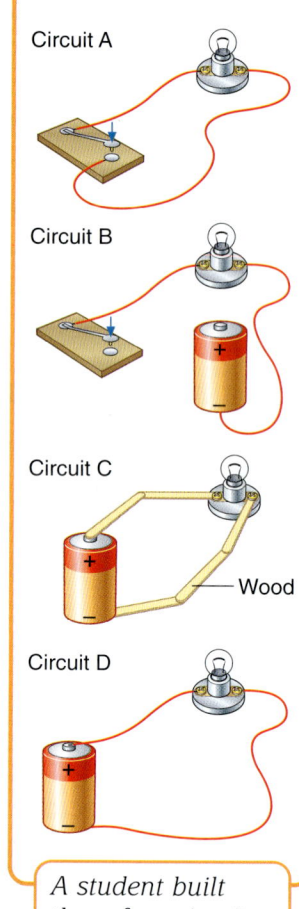

A student built these four circuits to try to make a bulb light up. But some of them won't work!

INVESTIGATION: Use a switch to make and break a circuit

You are going to connect a switch into the circuit you made in the previous investigation.
- Leave the end of the lead connected to the positive terminal of the cell in place, but disconnect the other end from the bulb.
- Connect the end of the lead previously connected to the bulb to one of the terminals of a switch.
- Make sure the switch is open.
- Use another lead to connect the other terminal of the switch to the bulb.
- Press the switch so it is closed.
- Press the switch again so it is open.

1. What happened to the bulb when you closed the switch?
2. What happened to the bulb when you opened the switch?
3. What did you do to the circuit when you closed the switch?
4. What did you do to the circuit when you opened the switch?
5. What happened to the flow of electrons when you closed the switch?
6. What happened to the flow of electrons when you opened the switch?

Activity
- Carefully study the four diagrams and read the caption.
1. In which of the four circuits will the bulb light up?
2. Explain briefly why each circuit worked, or didn't work.

Activity
- Describe how you would make a circuit using a cell, some leads, a bulb and a switch so that the bulb lights up.
- Draw a picture of your circuit.
- Explain what kind of material you would use for the connecting leads in an electrical circuit.

More about cells and circuits

The energy needed to make an electric current flow comes from a cell

An electric current can only flow round a circuit if there is a source of energy to make it flow. This energy is provided by a cell (or cells). The best way to understand how this works is to imagine that the cell provides the energy to 'push' an electric current round the circuit, so a cell works like a kind of 'electron pump'.

A single cell can only provide a limited amount of energy. In some circuits, this is not enough to make a current flow so two or more cells are needed. Two or more cells connected together are called a **battery**. (In everyday language the word 'battery' is often used to mean a single cell. But in scientific language the word 'cell' is always used.)

Activity

- Look at the diagram of a torch.
1. What provides the energy to make this torch light up?
2. How many cells does this torch contain?
3. How many batteries does this torch contain?
4. In the diagram, is the switch open or closed?
5. With the switch in its present position, would the bulb be lit up or not lit up?
6. What would you need to do to the switch to use the torch on a dark night?

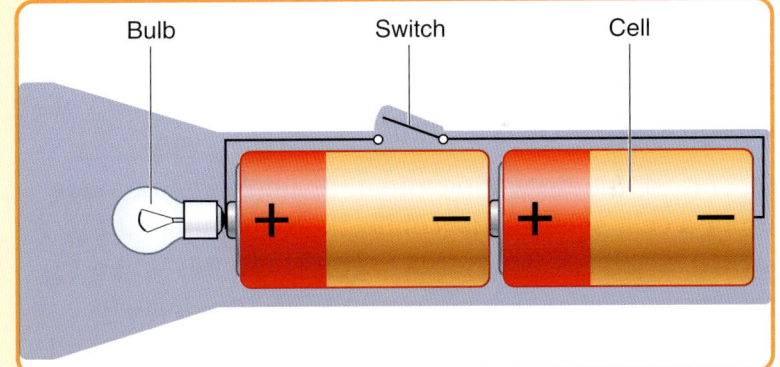

It is often useful to have a battery of cells connected together inside one casing. Shops sell batteries of different shapes and sizes to fit different electrical items.

All cells and batteries carry a printed message

If you look at any cell or battery you can tell how much energy it can supply to a circuit. This information is printed as a figure on the outside of the casing. The figure tells you the **voltage**, measured in units called volts (V). A single cell provides about 1.5 V. A battery of six cells provides 9 V. So voltage is a measure of how much energy can be supplied by the cell or battery to a circuit. Scientists use an instrument called a **voltmeter** to measure voltage.

6 volts   9 volts   1.5 volts

Cells and batteries supply different amounts of energy.

Activity

- Look at the photograph.
1. How much energy can a single cell supply?
2. How much energy can each battery supply?
3. Which would make three bulbs in a circuit glow most brightly?
4. Which would make three bulbs in a circuit glow least brightly?

Did you know?

When you switch on a torch, its light bulb uses about 6 billion, billion electrons every second.

Scientists use symbols to show the components of a circuit

In Unit 64 you drew a picture of a simple circuit made up of a cell, some leads (connections), a bulb and a switch. Scientists don't draw pictures like this when they want to show what a circuit looks like. Instead, they draw **circuit diagrams** using a kind of shorthand. They use small symbols to represent the different components in the circuit and straight lines to represent the connecting leads.

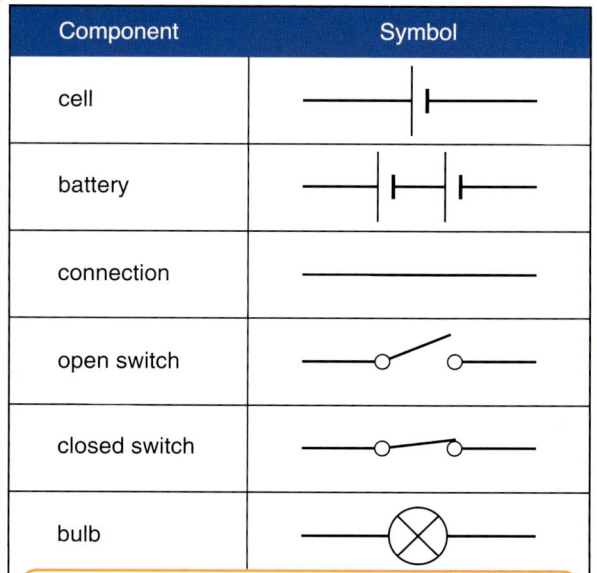

Component	Symbol
cell	—┤├—
battery	—┤├┤├—
connection	———
open switch	—o/ o—
closed switch	—o——o—
bulb	—⊗—

These symbols are used in circuit diagrams.

Activity

- Look at the circuit diagram for a circuit made up of a cell, some leads (connections) and a bulb. (There is a photograph of this circuit in Unit 64.)

- Use symbols to draw a circuit diagram of a circuit made up of a cell, a switch, some leads (connections) and a bulb.

- Use symbols to draw a circuit diagram of the circuit in a torch (like the one opposite).

Activity
- Look at the pictures of the four circuits.
- Use symbols to draw a circuit diagram of each circuit.
1. Which of these circuits have a cell?
2. Which of these circuits have a battery?
3. In which of these circuits will the bulb or bulbs light up?
4. In which of these circuits will the bulb or bulbs not light up?
5. In which circuit do you think the bulb or bulbs will be brightest?

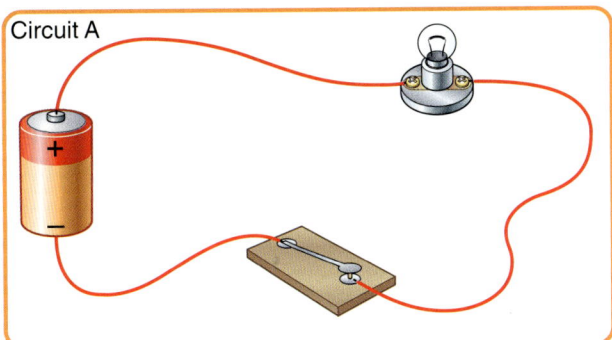

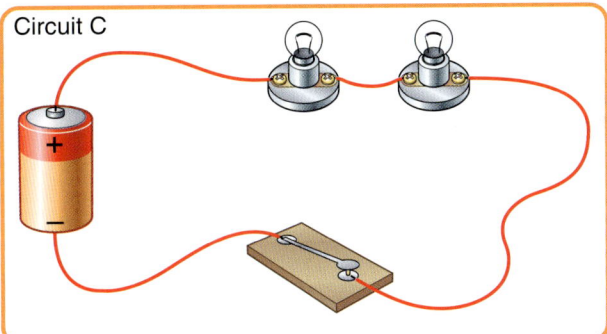

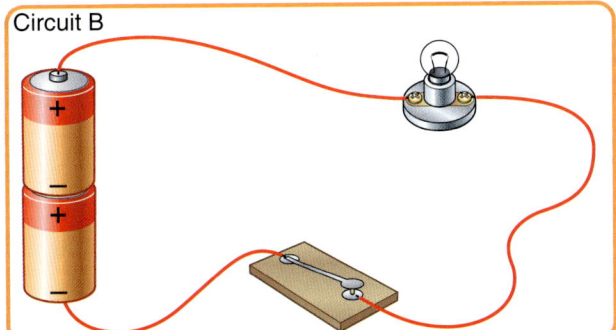

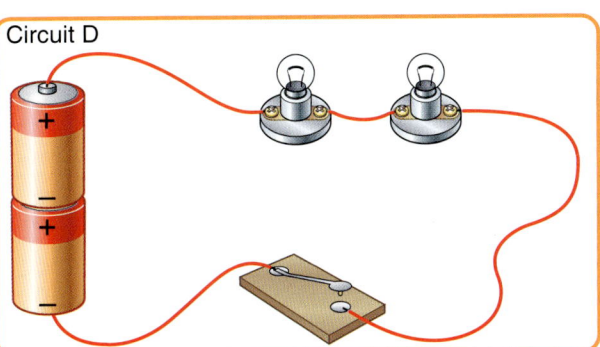

Activity
- Fill in the blanks in the following description.

A torch contains a simple .... with a battery connected to a .... and a bulb. When you want to use the torch you can .... the switch. This .... the circuit and a .... flows from the battery through the circuit and back to the battery. This makes the .... light up. When you don't need the torch any more, you can .... the switch to make the circuit .... Now the bulb is ....

More about cells and circuits **169**

Series circuits

There is only one path around a series circuit

All the circuits in Units 64, 65 and this unit are **series circuits**. In a series circuit, there is only one loop of connecting wire which connects all the components. This means there is only one path around the circuit for the electric current to follow. Because there is only one path, all of the electric current flows through every component in the circuit.

Activity

- Look at the photograph of two bulbs connected in series.
- Draw a circuit diagram of this circuit using the correct symbols.

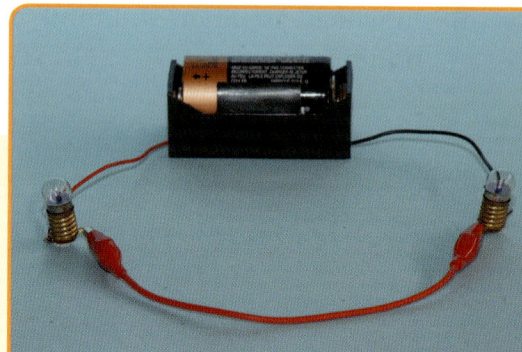

In this circuit, the two bulbs are connected in series.

INVESTIGATION Make a simple series circuit

- Connect one bulb to the positive terminal of a 1.5V cell.
- Connect a second bulb to the first bulb.
- Complete the circuit by connecting the second bulb to the negative terminal of the cell.
1. Do both bulbs light up?
2. Is one bulb brighter than the other or are both bulbs the same brightness?
3. Do you think each bulb is receiving the same amount of electric current?

The strength of an electric current can be measured by an ammeter

You know that an electric current flows around a series circuit from one terminal of the power supply (the cell or battery) back to the other terminal of the power supply. We can use a simple instrument to measure the strength of this electric current. This instrument is called an **ammeter**.

The strength of an electric current is measured in units called **amperes**. Scientists abbreviate this to **amps** or '**A**'. When an ammeter is put into a circuit, it is connected in series with other components such as bulbs. When it is connected like this, all the electric current flows through each component in the circuit including the ammeter.

This is the symbol for an ammeter.

Activity

- Look at the drawing showing an ammeter connected in a circuit.
- Draw a circuit diagram of this circuit.
1. What reading is the ammeter showing?
2. What is the value of the electric current flowing through the circuit?

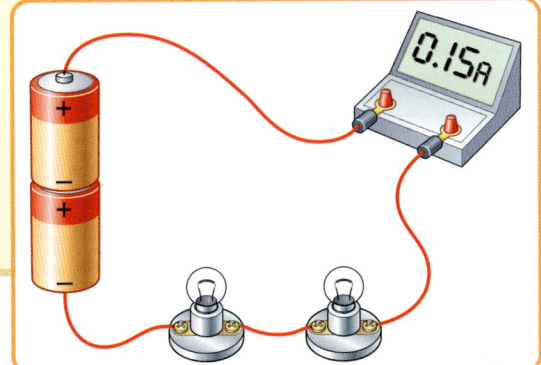

Activity

- Look at the three drawings showing three different positions in which an ammeter can be connected in a series circuit.
1. Apart from the ammeter, how many other components are there in this circuit?
2. What are the other components in this circuit?
3. Are all the components in this circuit connected in series?
4. What is the value of the current flowing round this circuit?
5. Is the value of the current the same throughout this circuit or does it vary from one part of the circuit to another?
6. Does the current get used up as it passes through the ammeter?
7. Does the current get used up as it passes through the other components?

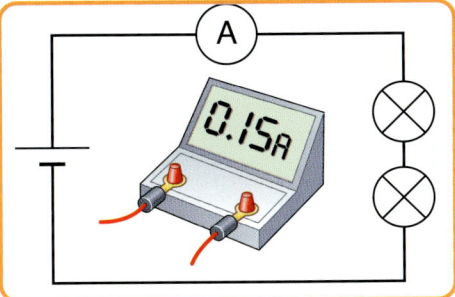 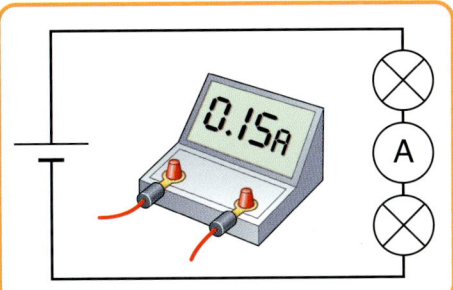 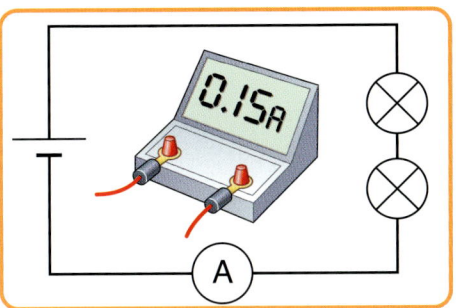

Series circuits

Activity
- Look at these three drawings.
- Count the number of bulbs in each of the three circuits.
- Record the value of the current in circuit A, circuit B and circuit C.

What happens to the value of the current as more bulbs are connected to a circuit?

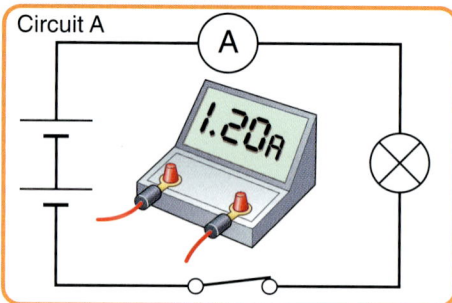
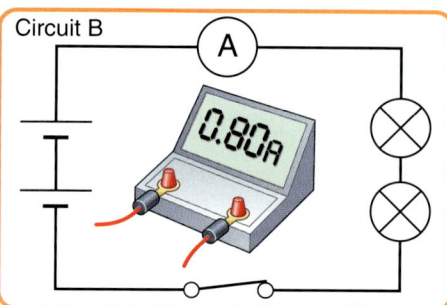
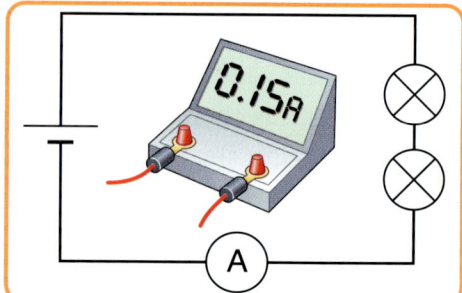

Bulbs resist the flow of an electric current

When you connect a bulb in a circuit, it 'slows down' the flow of the electric current. Scientists say the bulb 'resists' the flow of the current. The bulb acts as a **resistor**. If you add more bulbs to a circuit, you increase the resistance to the flow of an electric current. As you increase the resistance, you decrease the value of a current.

What will happen to the brightness of a bulb if the value of an electric current decreases?
In which of the above three circuits will the bulb or bulbs be most bright?
In which of the above three circuits will the bulb or bulbs be least bright?

Did you know?

1 ampere (or amp) is a flow of about 6 million million million electrons per second past a point in a circuit.

Parallel circuits

A parallel circuit has junctions

In previous units you have studied series circuits. You know that in a series circuit there is only one pathway for an electric current to follow. The other main type of circuit is called a **parallel circuit**. In a parallel circuit there are junctions at various points in the circuit, so an electric current has more than one pathway to follow.

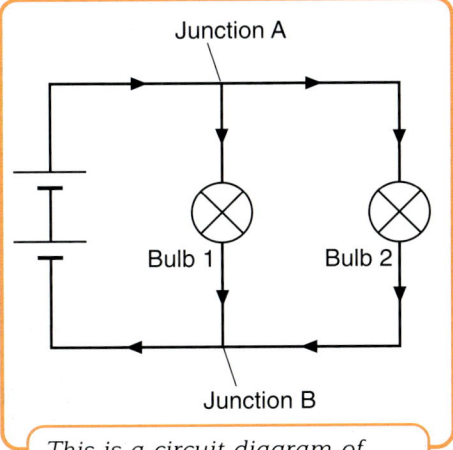

This is a circuit diagram of two bulbs connected in parallel.

Activity
- Look at the diagram of two bulbs connected in parallel.
1. Is the circuit powered by a cell or a battery?
2. How many components are there in this circuit?
3. How many junctions are there in this circuit?

In this circuit, the current leaves the positive terminal of the battery and travels to junction A. When it arrives at junction A, the current divides, so some of it goes through bulb 1 and some goes through bulb 2. At junction B, the current which passed through bulb 1 meets up with the current which passed through bulb 2. Now the joined-up current travels back to the negative terminal of the battery.

Each part of the circuit which takes divided current (one part through bulb 1, one part through bulb 2) is called a **branch** of the circuit.

Activity
- Look at the four circuit diagrams labelled A, B, C and D.
- Record whether each circuit is a series circuit or a parallel circuit.
- Look again at circuit B.
In circuit B, at which point (or points) labelled W, X, Y and Z will the current be at its highest value?

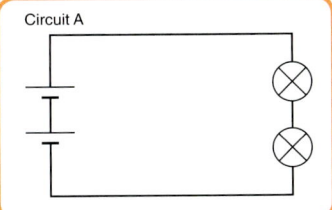
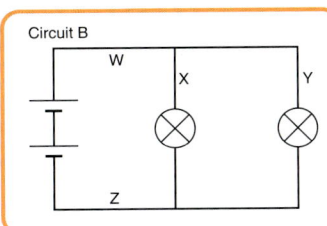
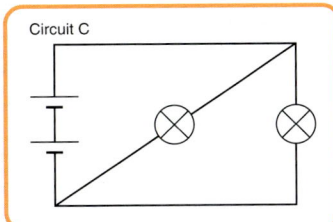
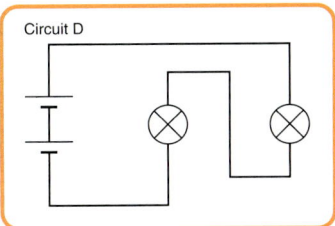

Parallel circuits 173

In a parallel circuit, the current from the battery is equal to the currents flowing through each of the branches added together.

Activity

- Look at this circuit diagram. The two bulbs are identical.
1. Is this a series circuit or a parallel circuit?
2. What is the value of the current leaving the battery?
3. What is the value of the current going down each branch of the circuit?
4. What is the value of the current going through each bulb?
5. What is the value of the current returning to the battery?
6. Is the current from the battery equal to the currents flowing through each of the branches added together?

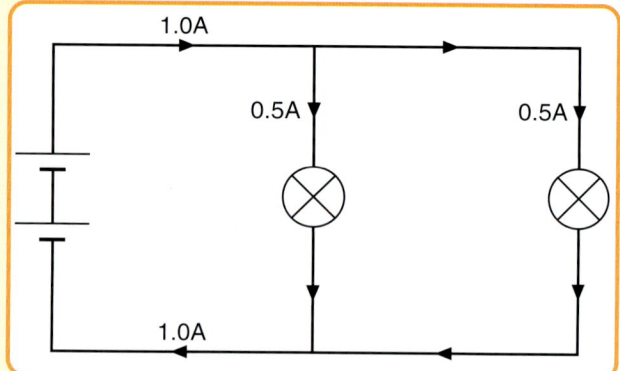

Activity

- Look at this circuit diagram. The three bulbs are identical.
1. What is the value of the current flowing through bulb C?
2. What is the value of the current flowing from the battery?
3. What is the value of the current at position X?
4. What is the value of the current at position Y?
5. Write a simple equation to express the relationship between the current from the battery and the currents flowing through each of the branches in the circuit.

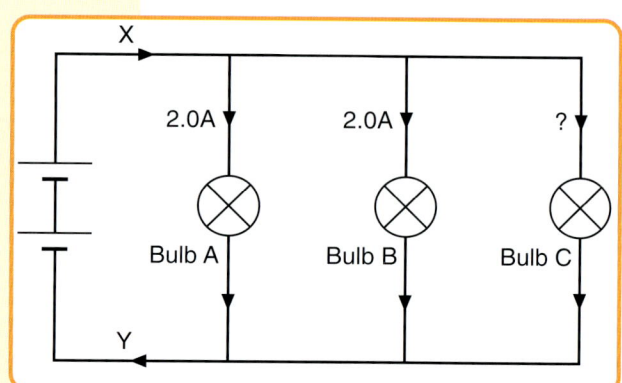

In a parallel circuit, each bulb is connected directly to the power source

If you look again at any of the parallel circuits on this page you will see that each bulb is connected directly to the battery. This means that the voltage across each bulb is the same as the voltage across the battery. This means that all the bulbs are bright. It doesn't matter how many bulbs you connect in a parallel circuit, they will all have the same brightness. When you connect more bulbs in parallel, the current from the battery increases. If you connect a lot of bulbs to a battery in parallel, the energy stored in the battery will be used up very quickly and the battery will become 'flat'.

> If you have three bulbs connected in parallel to a 9V battery, what will be the voltage across each bulb?
> As you add more bulbs in parallel, what happens to: (a) the brightness, (b) the total resistance, (c) the total current through the bulbs, (d) the battery?

Electrical circuits are designed for specific jobs

When electrical engineers design a circuit, they have to decide whether it is better to build a series circuit or a parallel circuit. It all depends on what the circuit is going to be used for. If you want to control each bulb separately, you need to build a parallel circuit. If not, a series circuit will do. A series circuit is also safer because the current passing along it is smaller. It is also the right kind of circuit to use if you want to light several bulbs and the bulbs don't have to be very bright.

> What happens to the other bulbs in a series circuit if one of the bulbs 'blows'?
> What kind of circuit would you want for lights in a house or an office?

Activity

- Imagine that an electrical engineer built two circuits. The first circuit had 20 bulbs connected in series to a power supply. The second circuit had 20 identical bulbs connected in parallel to an identical power supply.
1. Which circuit would have the highest voltage across each bulb?
2. In which circuit would the bulbs be brighter?
3. Which circuit would use most electricity?

Activity

Mr Mendes wants a display of lights for his shop in Port of Spain to celebrate Carnival. He wants his display to have a total of 12 bulbs: three red, three yellow, three green and three blue. He wants to be able to turn all three bulbs of the same colour on and off together. If a bulb of one colour 'blows', Mr Mendes doesn't mind if all the bulbs of the same colour are also off. However, he still wants to be able to switch on the other colours.
- Design a circuit and draw a circuit diagram to give to Mr Mendes so he can build his light display.

Different kinds of switches

A switch is a device for closing or opening a circuit

In Unit 64, you learned that a circuit has to be complete in order for an electric current to flow. If there is a break in the circuit (if the circuit is incomplete), the electric current stops flowing. You also discovered that a switch is a device which allows you to complete or break a circuit. A closed switch completes a circuit. An open switch breaks a circuit.

The diagram shows how a switch is used in the wiring of a lamp in a house. For safety reasons, when changing a bulb in a lamp, it is important that the switch is in the 'live' wire.

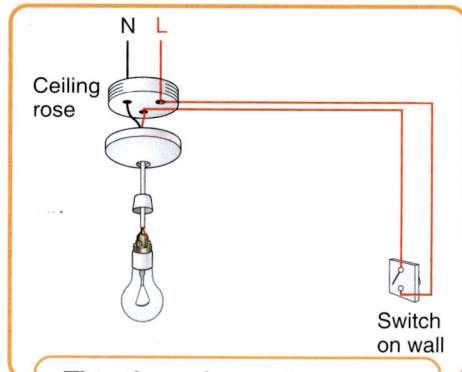

This shows how a lamp is wired to a ceiling rose and a switch. The letters L and N refer to the 'live' and 'neutral' wires from the mains electricity supply.

Two-way switches have a special function

Sometimes it is useful if a lamp can be controlled from two different positions. The lamp over a stairway is usually connected so it can be switched from the bottom of the stairs and from the top. This kind of circuit needs a type of switch called a two-way switch – one positioned on the wall at the bottom of the stairs and one on the wall at the top of the stairs.

Activity
- Look at the circuit for lighting the stairway of a house.
1. Can you control the lamp with either switch?
2. As the diagram is drawn, would the lamp be on or off?

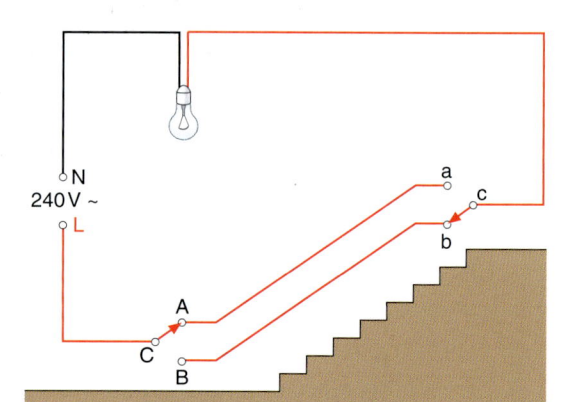

This circuit can be used for lighting a stairway. The two-way switch allows wire C to be connected to either A or B. The letters L and N refer to the 'live' and 'neutral' wires from the mains electricity supply.

A dimmer switch changes the strength of a current

Dimmer switches are often used in household circuits to change the brightness of a bulb or bulbs. A dimmer switch has different settings which control the value of the electric current.

All components resist the flow of electric current

When an electric current flows through a circuit it has to push its way through each component in the circuit. This includes any bulbs

Activity

- Look at the drawing which shows three circuits each with a dimmer switch set to a different setting.
1. What is the value of the electric current flowing through circuit A?
2. What is the value of the electric current flowing through circuit B?
3. What is the value of the electric current flowing through circuit C?
4. Which circuit had the highest value of electric current?
5. Which circuit had the lowest value of electric current?
6. List the circuits in order of the brightness of their bulbs.

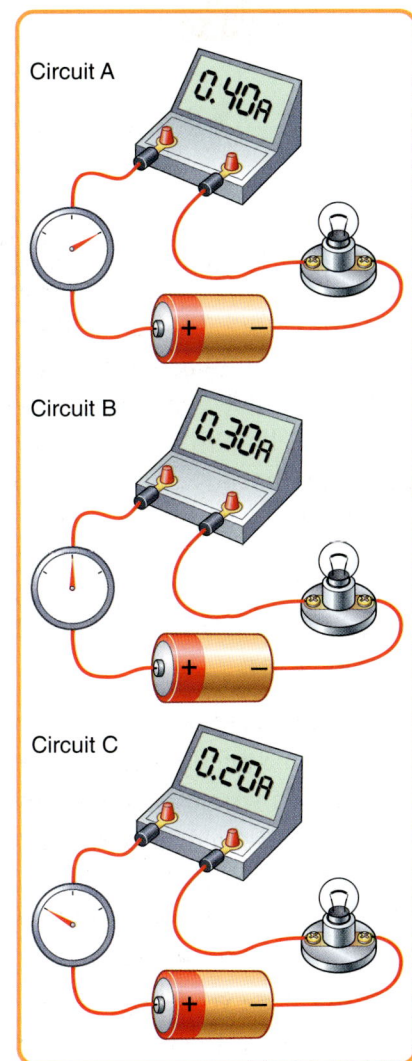

Circuit A

Circuit B

Circuit C

connected in the circuit. Each component acts like a barrier which tries to hold the current back. Each component resists the current. This causes **resistance** in the circuit.

A dimmer switch acts as a resistor but, because its settings can be changed, it is called a **variable resistor**. As you turn the dial of the dimmer switch in a clockwise direction, you decrease the resistance in the circuit. This increases the current and the bulb gets brighter. If you now turn the dial of the dimmer switch in an anti-clockwise direction, you increase the resistance in the circuit. This decreases the current and the bulb gets dimmer.

Anna-May's party

Anna-May was having a birthday party with her friends at home. She wanted to reduce the lighting in the living room to improve the party atmosphere. She decided to use the dimmer switch on the wall.

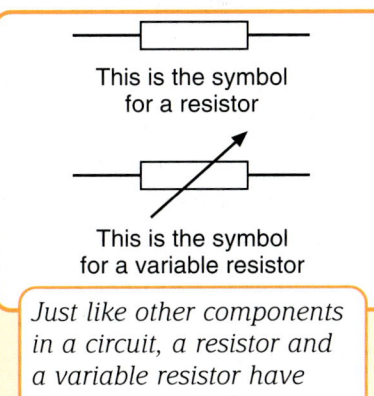

This is the symbol for a resistor

This is the symbol for a variable resistor

Just like other components in a circuit, a resistor and a variable resistor have their own symbols.

Activity

- Read the last two paragraphs carefully.
1. When Anna-May turned the dimmer switch anti-clockwise, did she increase or decrease the resistance in the circuit?
2. When she turned the dimmer switch anti-clockwise, what did she do to the current flowing through the circuit?
3. When she turned the dimmer switch anti-clockwise, what did she do to the lighting in the living room?
4. At the end of the party, Anna-May wanted to put the lighting in the living room back to normal. In no more than 100 words, explain how she did this. Your explanation should mention resistance and current.

69 What is in a cell?

A cell is a store of transportable energy

You know that a cell provides energy to make a current flow around a circuit. This energy comes from chemical reactions which take place inside the cell. So, a cell is a kind of storage tank full of chemical energy. Cells and batteries are useful because they enable you to carry your own energy supply with you and use it to power your portable radio, CD player, torch or anything else you take with you.

A dry cell contains an electrolyte paste and two electrodes

The outside case of a cell is made of zinc. The inside is full of a special kind of paste called an **electrolyte**. Electrolytes are substances which conduct electricity but they are usually liquids. Because a cell contains a paste rather than a liquid, it is called a **dry cell**. In the middle of the cell, surrounded by the electrolyte, is a **carbon rod**.

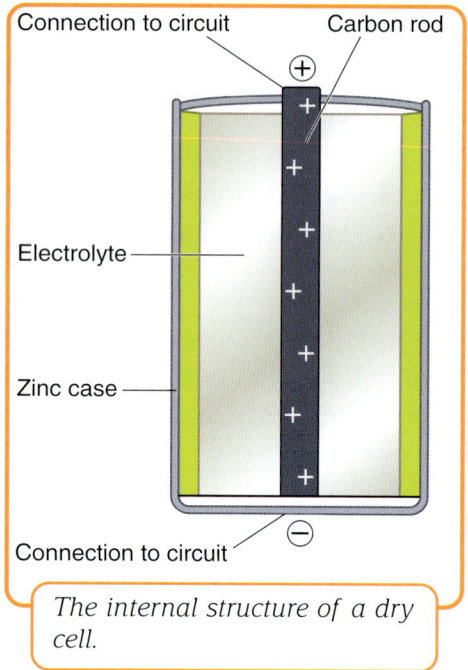

The internal structure of a dry cell.

The zinc case and carbon rod are both structures called **electrodes**. The zinc electrode is called a **cathode**. The carbon electrode is called an **anode**. The electrolyte paste contains billions and billions of positive and negative particles. There is a build-up of negative charges on the zinc cathode and a build-up of positive charges on the carbon anode. The cell stores the charge until it is connected to a bulb or other electrical component to make a circuit. When this happens, the cell pushes electrons round the circuit. In the case of a torch, the electrons give up their energy to the thin wires inside the bulb so the wires get hot and glow.

When the electrolyte is used up, no more current can flow. Now the cell is 'dead'.

A car battery is rechargeable

The battery of cells found in a car contains a liquid electrolyte – it is a wet battery. It is called a **lead–acid battery**. This type of battery doesn't wear out like a dry cell made with zinc and carbon. Instead, it is rechargeable. It provides energy to start the motor. Then it is recharged when the engine is running.

Some types of dry cell are also rechargeable (but those made with zinc and carbon are not).

> **INVESTIGATION** **Make your own cell**
>
> - Stick two pieces of metal that are different into a lemon or an orange – a brass drawing pin and a steel paper clip will do. Make sure they don't touch each other.
> - Connect a length of copper wire to each piece of metal.
> - Connect the other end of each copper wire to a 1.5V bulb in a bulb holder.
>
> Did the bulb light up?

Activity
- In less than 100 words, explain what happened in the investigation above. Use the terms electrolyte, anode, cathode and electrons.

Activity
- Read the new advertisement for Longerbright batteries.
- Design an experiment you could carry out to test Longerbright's claim that their batteries last ten times longer than any other battery on the market.

Longerbright Batteries are best!

Longerbright has now produced the longest lasting battery in the world.

A Longerbright battery in your torch will last ten times longer than any other battery on the market.

Always buy Longerbright batteries.

Activity

- Show your experimental design for the above activity to your teacher.
- When your teacher is satisfied with your experimental design, write a letter to the Managing Director of Longerbright describing your experiment and telling him or her what you think of the long-lasting claim in Longerbright's advertisement.

The electric eel can give a powerful shock

The electric eel is a large fish which lives in rivers in South America. Most of its body is made up of an organ that produces electricity. Its electric organ consists of a series of modified tail muscles similar to a battery of cells connected in series. Like a battery, the electric eel has two opposite poles (the head and the tail). When its electric organ discharges, the voltage flows from either the head or the tail. After delivering a strong shock, the electric eel has to recharge its batteries from the energy it gets from its food. An electric eel can generate as much as 600 V. This more than two times the voltage that comes out of a wall socket at home. The electric shock it can give is strong enough to kill a human!

Did you know?

An electric eel has been known to knock down a horse crossing a stream from 6 m away with its electric shock.

The electric eel uses its electricity for navigation and for stunning and killing its prey. It finds its way by producing electric signals. It detects the echoes made as the signals bounce back and these help it find its way in muddy water.

Good and bad conductors of electricity

Metals have lots of free electrons

When you built circuits, you used connecting leads made of metal (copper wire) to join up the different components in a circuit. The copper wire carried the current around the circuit. In Unit 64 you learned that metals have lots of free electrons and this is why they make good conductors of electricity. Now you are going to investigate whether materials other than metals also conduct electricity.

INVESTIGATION: Find out if other materials conduct electricity

- Construct a simple circuit to include a 1.5 V cell, a bulb and a switch.
- Test the circuit by closing the switch to see if the bulb lights up.
- Now connect other materials into your circuit, one at a time. You can try a plastic ruler, a piece of string, an eraser (rubber) and a wooden splint.
- Construct a table like the one below.
- Record in the table whether the material connected into the circuit is a good or bad conductor of electricity.

Test object	Material	Does the bulb light up?	Good or bad conductor?
ruler string eraser splint			

This circuit has been set up to find out if a liquid conducts an electric current.

INVESTIGATION: Find out if liquids conduct electricity

The photograph shows an experimental set-up to investigate whether a liquid conducts electricity.

- Construct a simple circuit using a 1.5 V cell, a bulb and a switch. Use a lead 30 cm long to connect the cell to the bulb.
- Test the circuit by closing the switch to see if the bulb lights up.
- Now put the switch in the open position.
- Cut the lead connecting the cell to the bulb half-way along its length.
- Remove 5 cm of the plastic insulation from the two cut ends of the lead to expose the copper wire inside.
- Half-fill a small beaker with tap water.
- Dip the two exposed ends of the copper wire into the tap water in the beaker. Do not let them touch.
- Close the switch and record what happens.
1. Did the bulb light up when you closed the switch?
2. What does this investigation tell you about tap water?
- Now repeat the investigation using different liquids. You can try distilled water, salt water, methylated spirit, oil, lemon juice and copper(II) sulphate solution. Make sure the beaker is thoroughly washed out before you try each new liquid.
3. Make a table to show which liquids conduct electricity and which don't conduct electricity.

182 Good and bad conductors of electricity

INVESTIGATION | Find out if voltage affects a liquid's ability to conduct electricity

- Repeat the above investigation, but this time try connecting a 4.5 V battery into the circuit and then a 6 V battery in place of the 1.5 V cell.

Does a liquid conduct an electric current better if the amount of energy supplied to a circuit is increased?

Any liquid which conducts electricity is called an **electrolyte**. When electricity is passed through an electrolyte it changes it. This is called **electrolysis**.

Tap water can be made to conduct electricity

Water and solutions in water appear to be poor conductors of electricity when tested with a low voltage cell or battery. But at higher voltage they become good conductors of electricity. Tap water contains small amounts of dissolved substances. At higher voltage the dissolved substances in tap water make it a good conductor of electricity. In fact, at the voltage supplied to a wall switch or a wall socket at home, tap water becomes such a good conductor of electricity that it becomes dangerous!

Why shouldn't wall switches be fitted in bathrooms?
Why are string-pull switches safer to fit in bathrooms?
Why shouldn't power points (wall sockets) be fitted in bathrooms?
Why should the string of a string-pull switch in a bathroom always be kept dry?
Why should you never touch a wall switch with wet hands?
Why should you always make sure your hands are completely dry before you plug an electrical device into a power point (wall socket) at home?

Activity

Mercury is a metal which is a liquid at room temperature.
- Predict whether mercury would be a good or bad conductor of electricity.
- Design a simple investigation to find out if your prediction is correct.
- Discuss your design with your teacher as part of a class discussion.
- When the class has agreed a design, ask your teacher to carry out the investigation as a class demonstration.
1. Is mercury a good or bad conductor of electricity?
2. Was your prediction correct?

71 Magnetism

Magnets and magnetism

FACTFILE

History
About 2500 years ago, people discovered a very strange type of rock with an amazing property. If positioned in a certain way, it could pull another piece of the same type of rock towards it. If it was turned round, it could also push the piece of rock away from it. In other words, it could attract and repel rock of the same kind. The Ancient Greeks called this strange rock lodestone. It was also discovered that a piece of lodestone could attract some other substances.

Lodestone displays the property of magnetism

Nowadays, scientists know much more about the amazing property of lodestone. They call this property **magnetism**. Magnetism is a type of force called a **magnetic force** which occurs in only a few substances. It occurs in the metals iron, nickel and cobalt. It occurs in lodestone because this is made of an iron compound called **magnetite**.

Activity
Here are two facts about Greek shepherds who lived over 2500 years ago:
1. They sometimes found their sandals seemed to 'stick' to the ground when they walked over bare, rocky hills tending their sheep.
2. The leather soles of their sandals were held in place with small, iron nails.
- Use the two facts to explain, in no more than 100 words, why the sandals of Greek shepherds sometimes seemed to 'stick' to the ground as they walked.

Scientists classify materials according to their magnetism

Scientists now classify materials into three different groups depending on the force of magnetism. The three groups are **magnets**, **magnetic materials** and **non-magnetic materials**.

Magnets – these contain the element iron or a compound of iron. Lodestone is a type of magnet. Magnets can attract and repel each other. Magnets attract magnetic materials.
Magnetic materials – these include certain metals such as cobalt, iron, nickel and steel. They are attracted to magnets but not to each other.
Non-magnetic materials – these are not attracted by magnets. They include all non-metals. But some metals are also non-magnetic, for example aluminium and copper.

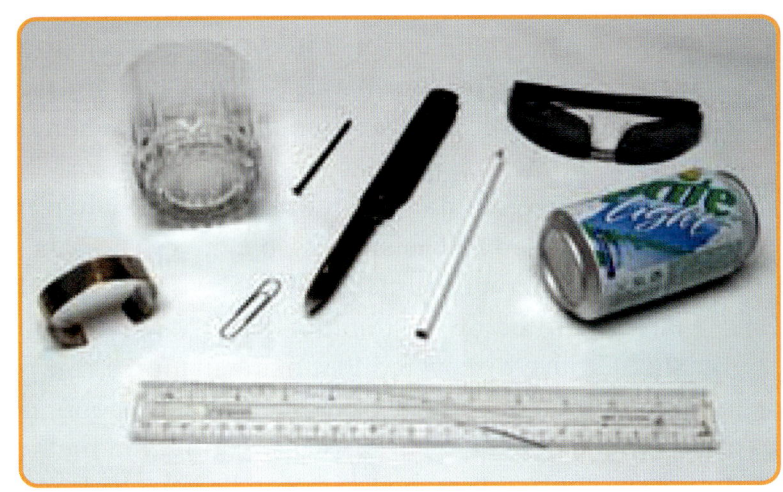

You can see that iron is in two of the three groups. Iron behaves as a magnetic material when it is 'unmagnetised'. But it can also be 'magnetised' to make it into a magnet. The molecules inside the iron are arranged differently in the two cases (there is more about this in Units 72 and 75).

Activity

- Look at the photograph.
- Divide the items displayed into magnetic and non-magnetic materials.

INVESTIGATION
Find out what magnetic force passes through

- Tie a paper clip to the end of a piece of cotton thread.
- Position a magnet so one end overhangs the top of your work bench.
- Dangle the paper clip near the end of the magnet.
- Record what happens.
- Place your hand between the magnet and the dangling paper clip and record what happens.
- Place a plastic ruler between the magnet and the dangling paper clip and record what happens.
- Place a sheet of paper between the magnet and the dangling paper clip and record what happens.
- Place a thin sheet of iron between the magnet and the dangling paper clip and record what happens.

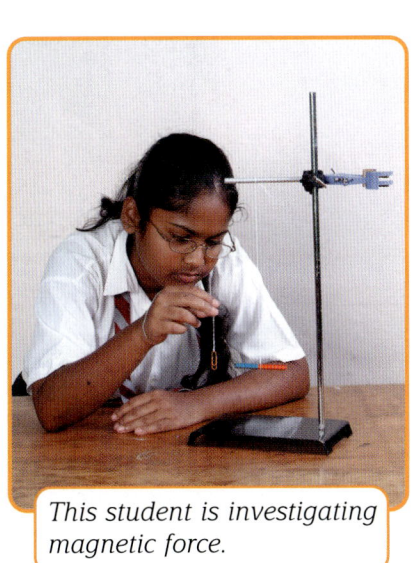

This student is investigating magnetic force.

Magnets and magnetism 185

1. Was the paper clip attracted to the magnet when the two were separated by your hand?
2. Was the paper clip attracted to the magnet when the two were separated by the plastic ruler?
3. Was the paper clip attracted to the magnet when the two were separated by the sheet of paper?
4. Was the paper clip attracted to the magnet when the two were separated by the thin iron sheet?

You should have discovered that magnetic force can pass through non-magnetic materials such as skin, bone, plastic and paper. You should also have discovered that magnetic force cannot pass through magnetic materials such as iron.

5. Would magnetic force pass through a thin sheet of aluminium?
6. Would magnetic force pass through a thin sheet of steel?
7. How would each of the following behave if it were placed near a magnet:

a microscope slide, a brass paper fastener, a plastic spoon, a steel knife, a piece of copper pipe, a photographic negative, a steel needle, a plastic mug?

A refrigerator is made of thin steel and is usually painted white. 'Fridge' magnets are often used to decorate the front of a refrigerator door and make it look more attractive, especially for young children. They consist of colourful wooden or plastic shapes with a small magnet attached on the back. They vary in appearance but popular shapes include animals, numbers and letters of the alphabet.

What does the fact that a 'fridge' magnet attaches to a painted refrigerator door tell you about paint and magnetic force?

Activity
- Design a simple experiment to find out if magnetic force is affected by distance.
- Show your plan to your teacher.
- When your teacher is happy with your plan, carry out your experiment.
- Write a complete account of what you did and the results you obtained.

What conclusion did you come to about the effect of distance on magnetic force?

'Fridge' magnets attach to the outside of a refrigerator door because of the force of magnetism.

More about magnetic force

In Unit 71, you discovered that magnetism is a force. You also discovered that only certain substances are magnetic or can act like magnets. Magnets only attract other magnets and magnetic materials. They can't attract anything else.

INVESTIGATION Find the poles of a magnet

- Suspend a bar magnet by means of a piece of cotton thread so the magnet hangs horizontally.
- Spread about 30 small steel pins evenly over a piece of card.
- Place the card and pins directly under the suspended magnet.
- Slowly bring the card up towards the bar magnet making sure that the magnet always hangs above the middle of the card.
- Record what happens.
1. What happened when the pins were brought close to the suspended magnet?
2. Did the magnet attract pins equally along its length?
3. Which parts of the magnet attracted most pins?
4. Where do you think the magnet's magnetic force is strongest?

This student is investigating where the poles of a magnet are.

A magnet always has two poles

The parts of a magnet where its magnetic force is strongest are called the **poles**. The poles of a bar magnet are found at either end. The two poles are always different. Early explorers observed that when a magnet was allowed to hang freely, it always came to rest with one end pointing towards the Earth's north. They called this the 'north-seeking pole' or **north pole** for short. The other end of the magnet always points to the Earth's south. They called this the 'south-seeking pole' or south pole for short. Early explorers used this discovery to make a compass.

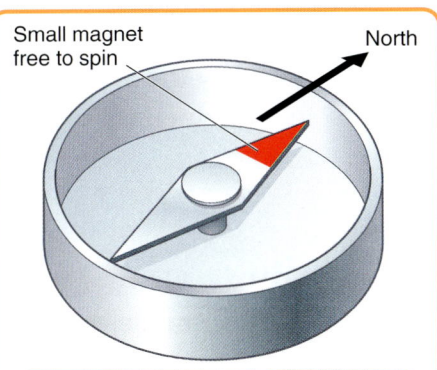

A compass is a device which contains a magnet which can spin round. It has a north pole and a south pole.

> **INVESTIGATION** **Play with magnetic poles**
>
> - Bring the north poles of two bar magnets together and record what happens.
> - Now bring the north pole of one bar magnet towards the south pole of the other bar magnet and record what happens.
> 1. Do similar poles of a magnet attract or repel each other?
> 2. Do different poles of a magnet attract or repel each other?
>
> Two similar poles (north–north or south-south) are called **like** poles. Different poles (one north, one south) are called **opposite** poles.

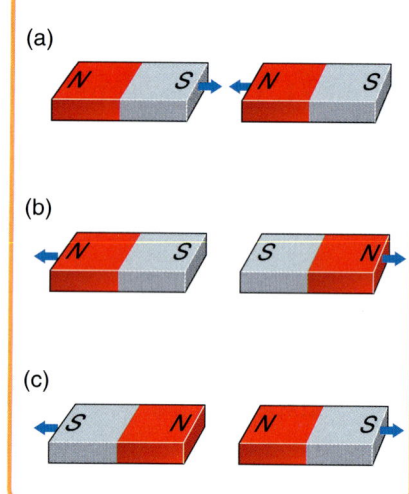

 **Activity**

- Look at the diagram of the magnets.
Are the magnets in diagrams (a), (b) and (c) attracting or repelling each other?

Molecules inside a magnet behave in a special way

In the diagrams below, the molecules in a magnet are represented by matchsticks. Each 'matchstick molecule' works like a tiny magnet in its own right. It has a north pole at its head and a south pole at the other end. A piece of unmagnetised iron can be represented as a jumble of 'molecular magnets' which are so mixed up that their magnetic forces cancel each other out. This is shown in diagram (a).

In diagram (b), the 'molecular magnets' line up with their north poles pointing in exactly the same direction. This is how the 'molecular magnets' in a magnetised piece of iron are arranged.

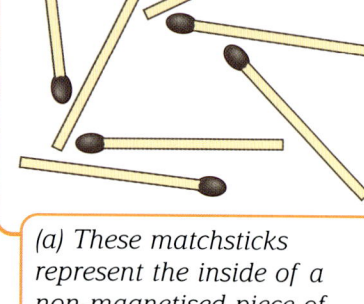

(a) These matchsticks represent the inside of a non-magnetised piece of iron.

 **Activity**

- Design a simple experiment to compare the strengths of two different magnets.
- Show your plan to your teacher.
- When your teacher is happy with your plan, carry out the experiment.
- Write a complete account of what you did and the results you obtained.

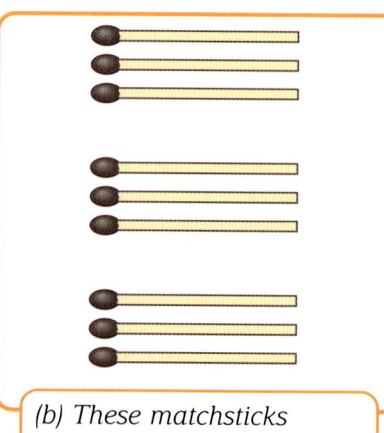

(b) These matchsticks represent a magnetised piece of iron (a magnet).

Magnetic fields

All magnets have a magnetic field

There is a region around every magnet which has an effect on magnetic material. This region is called the magnet's **magnetic field**. Although we normally can't see this magnetic field, there is a way to make it become visible.

INVESTIGATION: Make a magnetic field become visible

- Place a bar magnet on the workbench.
- Lay a piece of thin white card over the magnet. Make sure the magnet is underneath the centre of the card.
- Sprinkle some iron filings as evenly as you can over the white card.
- Gently tap the white card with your finger.
What happens to the iron filings after you tap the card?
- Draw a diagram of the pattern you can see around the magnet after you tap the card.

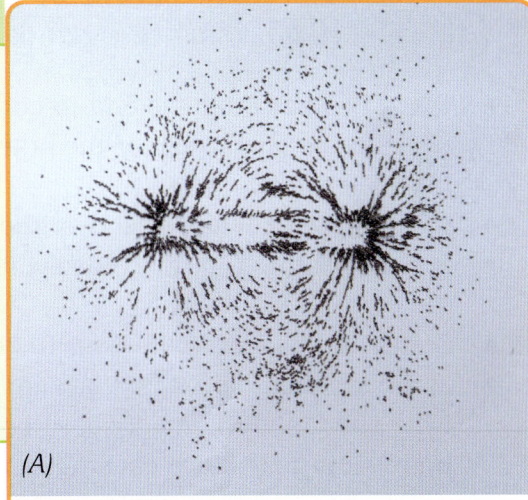
(A)

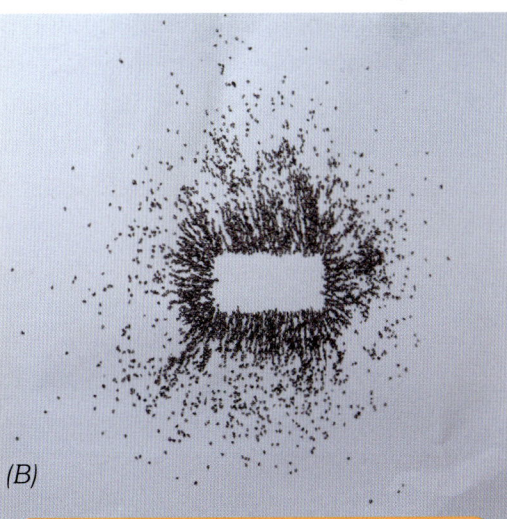
(B)

The photographs show patterns of iron filings around a weak bar magnet (A) and a strong bar magnet (B). Iron filings help to make a magnetic field visible.

Magnetic fields vary in strength

The pattern made by the iron filings after you tapped the card shows the magnet's magnetic field. The lines making up the pattern are the **lines of magnetic force** around the magnet. Not all magnetic field patterns are the same. They differ depending on the strength of the magnet. We can use the pattern made by iron filings to compare the strengths of two different magnets.

Activity

- Look at the two photographs of different magnetic fields.
- Make a drawing of each in your notebook.
1. Are the patterns showing the two magnets' magnetic fields the same shape?
2. Does a weak magnet have the same-shaped magnetic field as a strong magnet?
3. Are the lines of magnetic force the same for a weak magnet and for a strong magnet?

The number of lines of force indicates the strength of a magnet. Where the magnetic force is stronger, the magnetic field shows more lines and the lines are closer together. Where the magnetic force is weaker, the magnetic field shows fewer lines and the lines are further apart.

Activity

- Look at the two photographs on page 189 again. Where is the magnetic field of a magnet strongest?

 **Look at magnetic fields at the poles**

- Place two bar magnets end-to-end so the north pole of one is close to the south pole of the other. Leave a gap of about 2 cm between the two poles.
- Lay a piece of white card over the two magnets.
- Sprinkle some iron filings as evenly as you can on the card.
- Gently tap the card with your finger.
- Make a drawing of what you see.
- Now rearrange the magnets so both north poles or both south poles face each other and repeat the investigation.

1. What happens to the magnetic field between two opposite poles when they face each other?
2. What happens to the magnetic field between two like poles when they face each other?

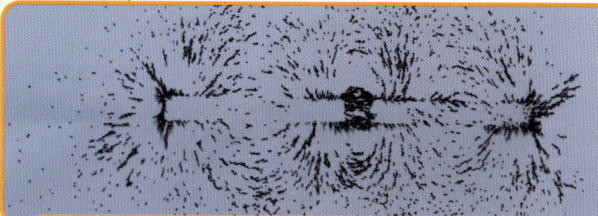

This shows the magnetic field pattern formed by iron filings when opposite poles of two bar magnets face each other. Opposite poles attract and the magnetic field between them is strengthened.

Activity

- Using the results you obtained from the investigation and the information shown in the two photographs, complete the following sentences using these words:

  attract   repel   magnetic   strengthened

  The opposite poles of two magnets .... each other, and the magnetic field between them is ....

  Like poles of two magnets .... each other.

  There is a zero .... field point between them.

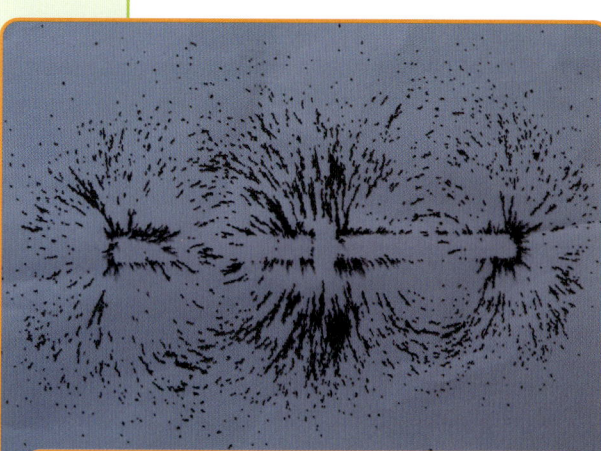

This shows the magnetic field pattern formed by iron filings when like poles of two bar magnets face each other. Like poles repel each other and this creates a zero magnetic field point between them.

Making an electromagnet

Electricity can be used to make a magnet

When an electric current flows through a wire, the wire behaves like a magnet. The metal in the wire doesn't have to be magnetic. Any piece of metal wire behaves like a magnet when an electric current passes through it. A magnet made by using electricity is called an **electromagnet**.

This girl is experimenting with electricity and magnetism.

INVESTIGATION: Pass an electric current through a coil of wire

Handle batteries with great care and always follow instructions.
- Wind a piece of insulated copper wire 20 times round a pencil to make a coil.
- Leave about 10 cm of straight wire at each end of the coil and remove about 1 cm of the insulation from each end.
- Connect one end of the coil to the positive terminal of a 6 V battery and the other end to the negative terminal to make electricity flow through the wire.
- Place a small compass close to the coil and record what happens.
1. Did the compass needle move when you placed it next to the coil?
2. Was the coil magnetic?
- Now try to pick up some paper clips with your coil.
3. Did the coil behave like a magnet?

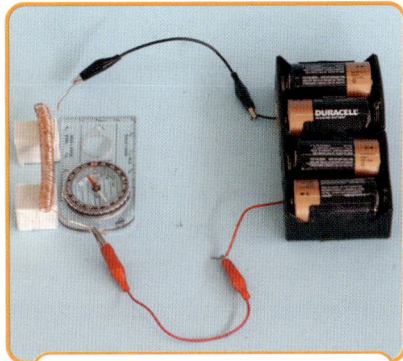

A compass needle is affected by an electric current flowing through a wire coil. This shows the coil is magnetised.

The coil you have just made became magnetic when you attached it to the battery terminals and an electric current flowed through it. Using a compass demonstrated this. The only sure way to detect if an object is magnetised is to see if it repels a compass. However, the coil's magnetic field was very weak. It was such a weak electromagnet that it probably wasn't able to pick up even a single paper clip.

Activity
- Design a simple experiment to investigate what happens to the magnetic field of a coiled electromagnet if you increase the number of coils.
- Check you plan with your teacher and then carry out the investigation.

> **INVESTIGATION** **Make a stronger electromagnet**
>
> - Repeat the previous investigation but replace the pencil in the coil with an iron nail.
> - Try using this electromagnet to pick up some paper clips.
> 1. Was this electromagnet able to pick up some paper clips?
> 2. Does enclosing an iron nail inside the coil make a stronger electromagnet than in the previous investigation?
> - Now disconnect one of the terminals.
> 3. What happened to the electric current when you disconnected one of the terminals?
> 4. Does the electromagnet work when one of the terminals has been disconnected?

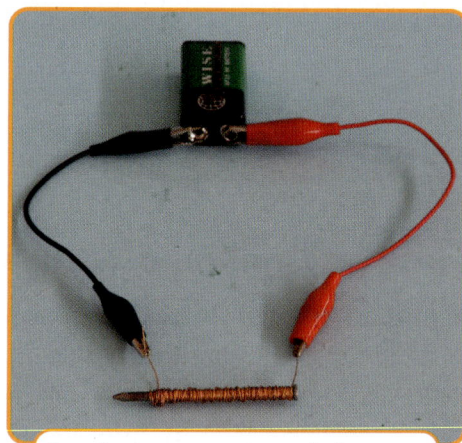

An electromagnet made by using an iron nail inside the coil.

Electromagnets vary in strength

Some electromagnets are so weak that they have a problem even picking up a small paper clip. The first electromagnet you made was probably like this. But others are much stronger. Some industrial electromagnets are strong enough to pick up large pieces of metal and even a whole car!

You can change the strength of an electromagnet by changing the size of the electric current. The larger the current, the stronger the electromagnet. You have already discovered that a wire carrying an electric current produces a weak magnetic field around it. A wire coil produces a magnetic field pattern similar to that of a bar magnet. When you place a piece of iron inside a wire coil and pass an electric current through it, the iron also becomes magnetised. The magnetic field of the iron core adds itself to the magnetic field of the coil. This is why a wire coil enclosing a piece of iron makes a stronger electromagnet than a coil by itself. This is why the second electromagnet you made was much stronger than the first.

It is important to choose the right material when making an electromagnet. Magnetic materials such as iron lose their magnetism when the current is switched off. These are called **soft magnetic materials**. Steel stays magnetised when the electric current is switched off. Steel is called a **hard magnetic** material.

> **Activity**
> - In no more than 100 words, explain why electromagnets made with iron are temporary magnets.

192 Making an electromagnet

Things which affect magnets and magnetism

INVESTIGATION Make a magnet

- Place an iron nail on a piece of white paper.
- Stroke the nail from its head end towards its pointed end 20 times with the north pole of a bar magnet.
- Now try to pick up some pins with the nail.

1. Was the nail able to pick up some pins after it had been stroked with a magnet?
2. What did you do to the 'molecular magnets' in the nail when you stroked the nail with a magnet?

When you stroked the nail in one direction with the north pole of a magnet, the 'molecular magnets' in the nail started to reposition themselves. Their south poles were attracted to the magnet's north pole. The more you stroked the 'molecular magnets' in the nail, the more they lined up with their south poles facing in the same direction.

3. After you finished stroking the nail, in which direction did the south poles of its 'molecular magnets' point?
4. After you turned the nail into a magnet, which end was its north pole?
5. After you turned the nail into a magnet, which end was its south pole?

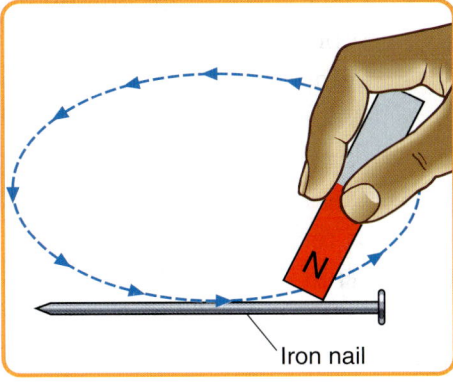
Iron nail

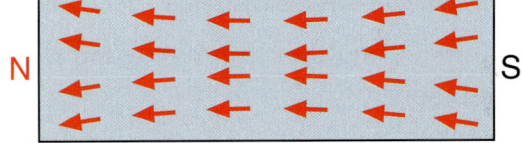
Magnetised iron

This is what your iron nail looks like inside after you have finished stroking it with a magnet. Most of the 'molecular magnets' in the nail point in the same direction and the nail is magnetised.

Activity
- Design and carry out a simple experiment to test whether your answers to questions 4 and 5 above are correct.

INVESTIGATION: Find out what happens when you heat a magnet

You must carry out this investigation under the strict supervision of your teacher. Alternatively, your teacher may prefer to do this experiment as a class demonstration.

- Take the iron nail which you magnetised in the previous investigation and hold it tightly in a pair of tongs.
- Heat the nail in the flame of a Bunsen burner until it starts to glow red hot.
- Place the red-hot nail on a fireproof mat and allow it to cool down. You must allow the nail to cool completely before carrying on with this investigation.
- When the nail has completely cooled, try to pick up some paper clips with it.

1. Does the nail work like a magnet after it has been heated to red heat?
2. What does heating a nail to red heat do to its magnetism?

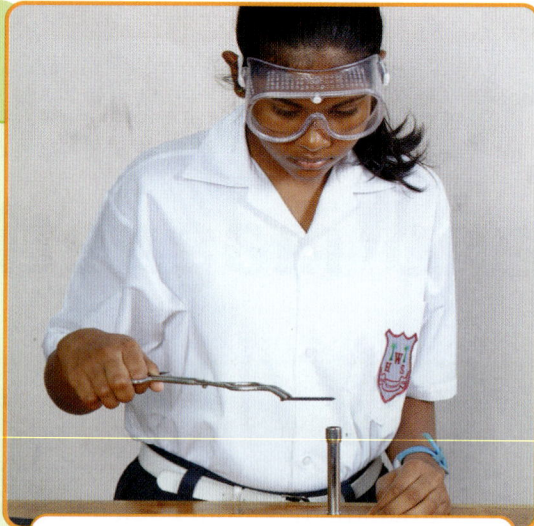

This student is investigating the effect of heat on the magnetism of an iron nail.

INVESTIGATION: Find out what happens when you hit a magnet

- Magnetise another iron nail using the same technique as you did before.
- Test your nail to make sure it has become a magnet.
- Now hit the magnetised nail with a hammer several times.
- Test the nail again to see if it still behaves like a magnet.

What happened to the nail's magnetism after you hit it several times with a hammer?

In Unit 72, you discovered that when something is magnetised, many of its molecules behave like tiny 'molecular magnets' with their north poles pointing in one direction and their south poles pointing in the opposite direction. In an unmagnetised object, the 'molecular magnets' are jumbled up. Their north and south poles point in all directions, and their magnetic forces cancel each other out. In order to destroy magnetism, you need to jumble up all the 'molecular magnets' again. You can do this by heating a magnet until it is red hot and letting it cool down. You can also demagnetise a magnet by hitting it with a hammer.

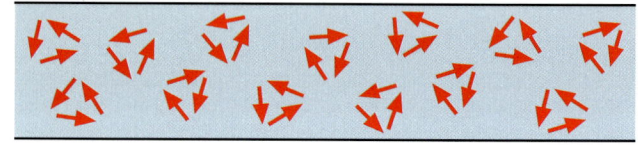

This is what your nail looks like inside after you have finished heating it or hitting it with a hammer. Heating or hammering the nail makes some of its 'molecular magnets' change position and point in different directions. When this happens, the nail becomes demagnetised.

Magnetism in the workplace

Magnetism is used in many different ways

Large, powerful electromagnets are used in industry to move heavy objects made of steel and iron. In hospitals, doctors sometimes use a strong electromagnet to remove splinters of iron or steel from a patient's eye. Magnetic inks are made by mixing tiny magnetic particles with a liquid. The mixture is used as a magnetic coating (a kind of paint) to make magnetic tapes for tape-recorders and video players and floppy discs for computers. Credit cards and debit cards have a magnetic strip which stores important information about the cardholder.

Magnetism is used to separate steel from other materials during the recycling process. Steel is a magnetic material because it contains iron. Aluminium is not magnetic, so aluminium is left behind.

Engineers use magnetic liquids

Magnetic ink can be mixed with oil to make a magnetic liquid which doesn't dry out. This is then used to detect tiny cracks which sometimes develop in steel pipes. Even the smallest cracks can be dangerous, especially if a pipe is carrying harmful liquids which might leak out if the crack gets bigger. Engineers first magnetise the pipe by putting a wire coil round it, which they then pass an electric current through. Once the pipe is magnetised, engineers then paint the outer surface with the magnetic liquid. If there is a tiny crack, some of the magnetic lines of force leak out of the pipe at the
point where the crack is. The magnetic liquid shows up the position and shape of the crack so it can then be repaired.

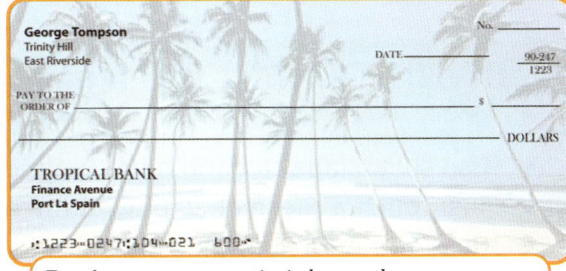

Banks use magnetic ink on cheques so that they can be passed through a machine and sorted automatically. The machine detects the magnetic field around each number printed on the cheque. It detects information about the cheque number, the bank sort-code number and the customer's bank account number.

EPaint has to be applied evenly

Steel is used in the manufacture of many items including cars, ships and bridges. Unless it is protected properly, steel rusts and corrodes, especially if it is exposed to wet weather. Items made of steel are usually protected by a layer of paint. In order to give proper protection, the paint must be sprayed on evenly over the whole of the surface. No part of the surface must be missed during the spraying. The layer of paint covering the surface of a car is usually about 0.2 mm thick. During the car's manufacture, this has to be checked with a paint gauge. The gauge uses a spring balance and a magnet.

Electromagnets have many uses

Most electric machines in use today rely on electromagnets whose power can be switched on and off by means of an electric current. Electromagnets have many uses, ranging from lifting heavy metal objects, to providing propulsion for levitating trains and making telephones work. Electric motors and generators also work because of electromagnetism.

'Magnetic' trains use electromagnetism

A **magnetic levitation** (MAGLEV) train uses electromagnetism to 'float' above the rail. As magnets on the underside of the train pass conducting coils on the track, the coils become temporary magnets. Their magnetic force repels the magnets on the underside of the train so the train is pushed away from the track. This makes it 'float' above the track. This reduces friction between the train and the track. The train moves forwards because there are permanent electromagnets on the track. The train is attracted by the electromagnets ahead and repelled by those behind it. In this way, it is pulled forward.

This magnetic levitation (MAGLEV) train works by means of electromagnetism.

INVESTIGATION Use a paint gauge

- Use sticky tape to hang a bar magnet from a spring balance.
- Just touch a piece of steel with the magnet.
- Record the force (in newtons) needed to pull the magnet away from the steel.
- Now place a sheet of paper between the steel and the magnet. This represents a layer of paint.
- Again measure the force needed to pull the magnet away from the steel.

Did you need a bigger or a smaller force to pull the magnet away when it was separated from the steel by the sheet of paper (the pretend paint)?

Magnets in the home

Magnets have many uses around the home

Most homes contain examples of magnets and magnetism at work. Magnets are used as magnetic catches to keep cupboard doors shut. Refrigerators and freezers have a magnetic strip all round the door. The strip keeps the door closed tight so the cold air is kept inside. Electromagnets are found in many objects in the home including switches, bells, buzzers, telephones and hi-fi equipment. Even in the immediate home surroundings magnets are at work. For example, a magnet is fitted in the oil sump tank of a car engine in order to attract any tiny bits of steel that wear off the moving parts of the engine. This prevents the bits from going back into the engine and causing damage.

Activity
- Make a list of all the devices in your home which use magnets and magnetism.

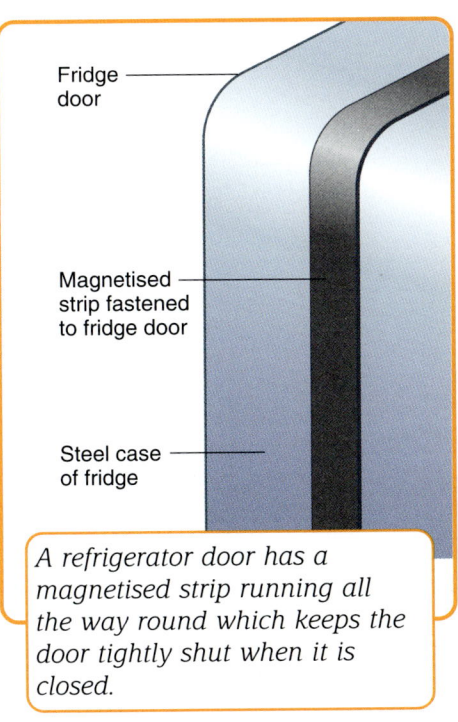

A refrigerator door has a magnetised strip running all the way round which keeps the door tightly shut when it is closed.

An electric doorbell works because of magnetism

Whenever you ring a doorbell or somebody rings your doorbell at home, a small electromagnet is activated.

Activity

- Look at the diagram of an electric doorbell and its circuit.
- Try to work out what happens when the bell-push is pressed down. (You may need to look back at the work you did on circuits in Unit 64.)

1. What is the state of the circuit when the bell-push is not pressed down?
2. What is the state of the electromagnet when the bell-push not pressed down?
3. What happens to the circuit when the bell-push is pressed down?
4. What happens to the electromagnet when the bell-push is pressed down?
5. What happens to the springy metal strip, iron bar and hammer when the bell-push is pressed down?
6. When the springy metal strip, iron bar and hammer react to the bell-push being pressed down, how does the state of the circuit change?
7. When the state of the circuit changes, what happens to the state of the electromagnet?
8. When the state of the electromagnet changes, what happens to the springy metal strip, the iron bar and the hammer?
9. When the springy metal strip, the iron bar and the hammer react to the change of state of the electromagnet, what happens to the circuit?
10. What happens to the circuit and the electromagnet when the bell-push is no longer pressed down?

How an electric doorbell works.

When an electric doorbell is activated, lots of things happen

When the bell-push is in the normal position, the circuit is broken and no current flows through the electromagnet.
When the bell-push is pressed, the circuit is complete and a current flows through the electromagnet.

198 Magnets in the home

When the current flows, the electromagnet attracts the springy metal strip holding the hammer.

When the hammer moves and hits the bell, it breaks the circuit at point X.

When the circuit is broken, the current stops flowing and the electromagnet turns off.

When the electromagnet turns off, the springy metal strip with the hammer moves back and completes the circuit again at point X. Now the cycle starts all over again.

When the bell-push is no longer pressed, the circuit is broken again and it remains broken until the bell-push is pressed again.

Tape recorders contain an electromagnet

In a cassette tape recorder, sounds are recorded as a pattern of magnetised particles on a plastic tape. The recording is done by a part of the cassette player called the recording head. The recording head is a small electromagnet. When a recording is being made, the magnetised particles on the tape are arranged into different patterns as the tape passes over the recording head. The millions of magnetic particles on the tape make it possible to store large amounts of information. The patterns of rearranged particles on the tape can then be read by another part of the cassette recorder called the playback head. This converts the information stored in the magnetised particles back into sound.

The plastic tape in the cassette is covered with magnetic particles of iron oxide or chromium oxide.

INVESTIGATION: Distort the sound on a cassette tape

- Record a short piece of music on a cassette tape.
- Wind the tape back to the start and remove it from the cassette recorder.
- Carefully unravel the first part of the tape and run a magnet over it a few times.
- Carefully wind the tape back into the cassette and then play it back.

1. Is the sound on the tape the same as the piece of music you recorded?
2. What did you do to the magnetic particles on the tape when you ran a magnet over it?

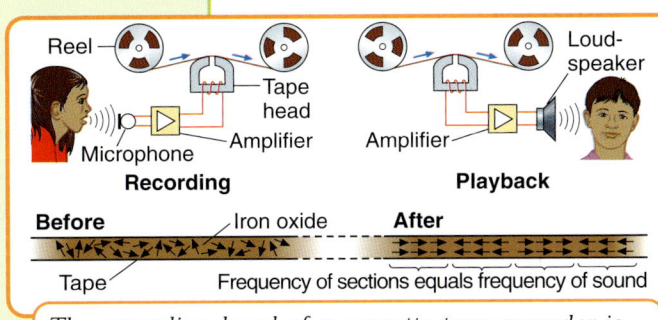

The recording head of a cassette tape recorder is an electromagnet which rearranges the magnetised particles on the tape into patterns.

Magnets in the home

Magnetic Earth

The Earth behaves as if there were a gigantic bar magnet inside it. Its magnetic field has exactly the same pattern as the magnetic field of a bar magnet. However, such a magnet cannot really exist because the centre of the Earth is too hot. Scientists think the Earth behaves like a giant magnet because of its structure and the way the different layers from which it is made move round.

The Earth's core is made of metal, mainly iron. The outer layers, the mantle and the crust, also contain some metallic rocks. The mantle and crust move around at different speeds from the metallic core. As these layers move over each other, they behave like a gigantic generator which produces electric currents in the core and a magnetic field around the Earth itself.

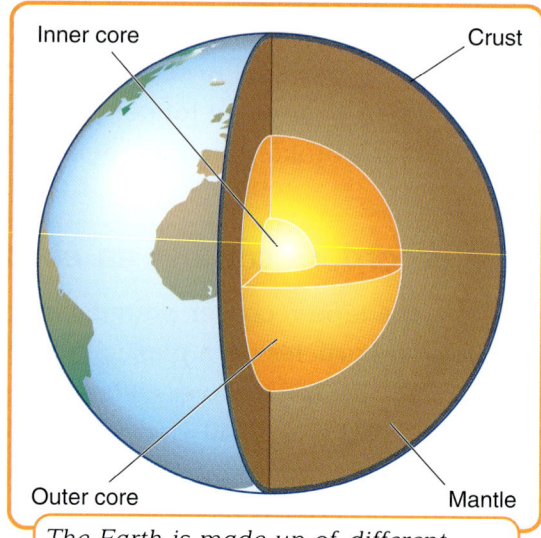

The Earth is made up of different layers with an inner core.

This is a diagram of the Earth with an imaginary magnet inside it and a magnetic field surrounding it. Note that the imaginary magnet is arranged at an angle to the Earth's north–south axis. Also note that the south pole of the Earth's imaginary magnet is in the northern hemisphere and its north pole is in the southern hemisphere.

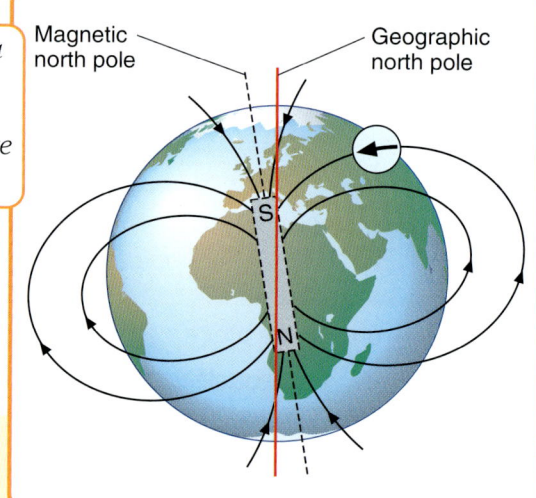

Activity
- Look at the diagram showing the Earth's magnetic field.
- Work with a partner and take turns to point out to each other where the Earth's geographic south pole is and where its magnetic south pole is on the diagram.
1. Is the Earth's geographic north pole in the same place as its magnetic north pole?
2. Is the Earth's geographic south pole in the same place as its magnetic south pole?

200 Magnets in the home

INVESTIGATION — Observe the behaviour of a freely suspended bar magnet

- Tie a piece of strong cotton thread round the middle of a bar magnet.
- Carefully adjust the thread so the magnet is balanced and hangs horizontally.
- Hang the magnet from the arm of a retort stand and allow it to come to rest.

When a suspended bar magnet is at rest, does it always point in the same direction?

In Unit 72, you learned that early explorers discovered that when a magnet was allowed to hang freely, it always came to rest with one end pointing towards the Earth's north. You also learned that early explorers used this discovery to make the first compass. A compass consists of a needle enclosed in a container with a transparent top cover. The compass needle is a small bar magnet which is suspended so it can spin round. The needle has a north pole and a south pole.

In which direction does the north pole of a compass needle point? How does a compass needle behave in relation to the Earth's imaginary internal bar magnet?

Activity
- Find a detailed map of Trinidad in your school atlas.
- Find Princes Town on the map and place a small compass on it.
- Rotate the map and the compass so that the compass needle points to 'N' on the compass and 'north' on the map.
1. In which direction is Tunapuna from Princes Town?
2. If you wanted to travel from Princes Town to Rio Claro, in which direction would you go?
3. If you wished to travel from Princes Town to San Fernando, in which direction would you go?

Some animals are magnetic travellers

Scientists believe they may have solved the mystery of how birds migrate long distances without losing their way. They now think that birds can actually see the Earth's magnetic field. New research

Magnetic Earth 201

suggests that a bird's eye can detect magnetism as well as light. It is thought that birds see the Earth's magnetic field in much the same way as they see coastlines, rivers, trees and other familiar objects. One idea is that a bird's brain superimposes a picture of the Earth's magnetic field on the landscape below – rather like the 'head-up' displays found in modern fighter jets. Humpback whales migrate from one side of the world to the other. They also probably sense the Earth's magnetic field to help them swim in the right direction.

The leatherback is the biggest of all turtles. It sometimes gets washed up on Caribbean beaches.

Atlantic leatherback turtles probably migrate from the Caribbean Sea along the warm Gulf Stream to the east coast of Canada. After this, scientists are not sure where the turtles go, but they think they may cross the North Atlantic and swim down the west coasts of Europe and Africa. Then, they cut back across the Atlantic to their Caribbean breeding grounds. If this is their route, it means they cover a journey of about 15 000 kilometres in a single migration. Some scientists think that leatherbacks sense the Earth's magnetic field to help them find their way.

Australian compass termites make tall mounds which they always build on a north–south axis. Each mound has two narrow sides and two wide sides. The narrow sides always face north and south. This arrangement means only a small amount of the mound's surface is exposed to the hot, midday Sun. The big surfaces of the wide sides, which face east and west, catch the cooler early morning and late evening Sun. This arrangement is designed to keep the mound cool during the hottest time of the day. Scientists think that compass termites may use the Earth's magnetic field to line up their mounds on a north–south axis.

Science dictionary for Book 2

acid rain
rain water with sulphur dioxide and oxide of nitrogen dissolved in it

adolescence
the time when boys and girls start to become adult aerobic with air

aerobic
respiration with air

air sac (alveolus)
a tiny bag at the end of the tubes from the nose and mouth

alveolus (air sac)
a tiny bag at the end of the tubes from the nose and mouth

amino acid
protein after the first stage of digestion

ammeter
instrument for the measure of amperes

amp (A)
abbreviation of ampere

ampere
unit of measurement of electrical current

anaerobic respiration
respiration without air

analysis
he breakdown and description of the component parts of a solution or mixture

anode
the electrode that electrons flow out of to rejoin the circuit – in a dry cell this is a carbon rod

aquatic animals
animals that live in water

artery
blood vessel carrying blood from the heart to the rest of the body

atrium
the top chamber of the heart

auditory nerve
nerve which carries information about sound

balance reflex
automatic muscle action used to correct balance

ball and socket joint
joint such as shoulder or hip

battery
a group of charged cells

blind spot
the area of the eye which with no light receptors because it is where the optic nerve leaves the eye to go to the brain

blood pressure
a measure of how hard the heart has to work to move blood around the body

blood vessel
tube in the body carrying blood to and from the heart and lungs

branch
section of parallel circuit

calcium
mineral found in milk and other foods

203

calcium carbonate
limestone

calcium hydrogen carbonate
compound formed by reaction between dilute carbonic acid and calcium carbonate

canine
strong pointed tooth for gripping food

capillary
tiny blood vessel used to deliver food and oxygen to cells and remove waste from them

carbohydrate
energy-producing compound of carbon with hydrogen and oxygen found in food such as bread, potatoes and sugar

carbon dioxide
gas compound of carbon and oxygen emitted in respiration and combustion

carbon monoxide
gas compound of carbon and oxygen emitted in combustion

carbon rod
the core of dry cell, forming anode

carbonic acid
rain water after dissolving carbon dioxide and other gases on its way to the earth

cardiac muscle
muscle of the heart

cartilage
firm elastic tissue, a main component of bone

catalyst
substance which speeds up chemical reaction

catalytic converter
device fitted to cars to reduce emission of carbon monoxide

cathode
electrode at which electrons go into a cell – in a dry cell this is the zinc case

cell
container holding electric charge

centrifuge
machine rotating at high speed to separate components in a suspension

cerebellum
the base of the brain, dealing with balance

cerebral hemisphere
half of the cerebrum

cerebrum
the largest part of the brain

cervix
the lower, narrow portion of the uterus where it joins with the top end of the vagina

chemical weathering
the action of carbonic acid on stone

chromatogram
a coloured picture showing the breakdown of solutes

chromatography
a technique to separate different solutes from a solution

circuit
pathway along which electric charge can flow

circuit diagram
set of symbols to describe an electrical circuit

circulatory system
the heart and three types of blood vessel

cochlea
spiral cavity in the ear connected by auditory nerves to the brain

combustion
burning

complete
unbroken

concentrated
having a high proportion of solute

condensate
the substance produced by the process of condensation

condensation
the process of gas becoming liquid

condenser
apparatus used to collect condensed water after evaporation

conductor
material which allows electric charge to flow through it

contact process
process used in the industrial manufacture of sulphuric acid

contract
shrink, become tense

coronary artery
the blood vessel supplying blood to the heart

current electricity
flow of electric charge

deamination
the process which takes place in the liver of breaking down excess amino acids into urea

decibel
unit of measurement of the loudness of sound

deficiency
shortage

detergent
cleaning agent

diaphragm
a big flat muscle at the base of the chest

digestion
the system which breaks food down for use by the body

dilute
having a low proportion of solute

dimmer switch
switch containing a variable resistor

disease
illness

distillation
the process of separating and collecting a solvent

DNA
nucleic acid that contains the genetic instructions specifying the biological development of all cellular forms of life

dominant eye
the eye you use more strongly

double circulatory system
the way the blood is pumped around the human body

dry cell
container holding electric charge without using water

ear bones (hammer, anvil and stirrup)
bones which vibrate in response to sound

ear canal
the gap between ear bones leading to the eardrum

Eustachian tube
a protective tube behind the eardrum

earflap
the part of the ear outside the head

earth (ground)
send excess electrons out of the body

electrolyte
substance which conducts electricity

electromagnet
magnet created by use of an electric current

electron
subatomic particle carrying negative electric charge

embryo
unborn child during the first two months of growth

enzyme
a catalyst producing chemical reaction

ethylene glycol
substance used in anti freeze to lower the boiling point of water

Eustachian tube
tube connecting each eardrum to your nose and throat

eutrophication
build up of nutrients in water which speeds up algae growth, using all available oxygen so that water becomes stagnant and unable to support life

evaporation
the process of liquid becoming vapour

excrete
to remove waste from the body

excretion
removal of waste from the body

exothermic reaction
giving out heat

faeces
undigested food got rid of as waste from the body

fallopian tube
tube from the ovary used to carry eggs to the uterus

fat
important element of food for warmth and energy, found in food such as meat, dairy products and oil

fatty acid
fat in food after the first stage of digestion

fibre (roughage)
indigestible material in food which helps digestion of other foodstuff

foetus
unborn child during the final seven months of growth

forensic scientist
scientist using analysis to investigate crime

fraction
part

fractional distillation
separation of fractions of a substance by boiling

fractionating column
equipment for separating the fractions of crude oil

frequency
a measure of the number of sound waves produced every second

gaseous exchange
swapping one gas for another by osmosis and diffusion

gene
unit of heredity in chromosome

genetic code
the code which controls DNA

genetically linked
caused by some change in the genetic code

glucose
a sugar

glycerol
fat in food after the first stage of digestion

ground (earth)
send excess electrons out of the body

ground water
the water lying in the soil which feeds lakes rivers and springs

haemoglobin
chemical found in red blood cells

hard magnetic material
magnetic materials which do not lose magnetic force when electric current is switched off

hard water
water containing high proportion of calcium hydrogencarbonate

heart
the group of muscle which pumps blood around the body

hereditary
passed from one generation to another in the genes

hertz (Hz)
unit of measurement of frequency of sound

hinge joint
joint such as knee and elbow

hormones
chemical messengers from one cell (or group of cells) to another

hydrocarbons
compound of hydrogen and carbon

hydrochloric acid
hydrogen chloride mixed with water

hydrophilic
loves water

hydrophobic
hates water

hypertension
medical condition of dangerously high blood pressure

impulse
electrical currents passing from nerve cells to the brain

incisor
biting tooth

infectious
passing easily from one person to another

insulator
material which does not allow electric charge to flow through it

iodine
a mineral important in the regulation of the body's function

iris
a muscle which controls the amount of light entering the eye

kidney
the main waste remover of the body

lacteal tube
tube leading from the intestine, to carry digested fat through a villus, to the lymphatic system

lead-acid battery
battery using liquid electrolyte

lens
the layer at the front of the eye which focuses light onto the retina

lifestyle
the way we live

ligament
the material which joins bones together and joins bones to muscle

like poles
similar poles on separate magnets

lime scale
build up of calcium carbonate deposited by heated hard water

line of magnetic force
the pattern of a magnetic field

lodestone
rock made of magnetite

lung
organ used in respiration to take in oxygen and get rid of carbon dioxide

lymphatic system
body system for absorbing fat and fighting infection

magnet
an object with magnetic force

magnetic field
the area around a magnet where it has effect on magnetic material

magnetic force
strength of magnetism

magnetic levitation
system using electromagnetism to drive trains

magnetic material
material which responds to magnetic force but is not a magnet

magnetism
force causing certain substances to attract or repel each other

magnetite
magnetic iron oxide

medulla oblongata
part of the brain, joined onto the spinal cord which controls heartbeat and breathing

metabolic waste
waste produced by cell activity in the body, e.g. carbon dioxide, urea and bile pigment

milk teeth
the first teeth a baby grows

mineral
elements in food essential for healthy growth and living such as iron, calcium, iodine and magnesium

molar
large back tooth for chewing

mucus
protective, sticky liquid produced in the respiratory system

nerve
this carries information from receptors to the brain

neurone
nerve cell in the brain

nitric acid
oxide of nitrogen dissolved in water

non-aqueous solvent
solvent that does not use water

non-magnetic material
material which does not respond to magnetic force

north pole
end of free hanging magnet which points north

nutritional table
table printed on food packaging to give information on the proportion of different foods present

obese
dangerously overweight

obesity
excess weight as an illness

oesophagus
the tube leading from the mouth to the stomach

oestrogen
a female hormone

olfactory bulb
the group of smell receptors in the roof of the nose cavity

opposite poles
different poles on separate magnets

optic nerve
the nerve leading from the back of the eye to the brain

orbit (shell)
the pathway used by movement of electrons

organ
a group of tissues that work together

organic solvent
carbon based solvent

oscilloscope
a machine which turns sound waves into electrical patterns

osmoregulation
control of gas exchange in animals

ovary
organ where eggs (ova) are stored in a woman's body

ovulate
produce eggs

ovum (pl. ova)
single cell egg produced by a woman

oxidation reaction
chemical reaction involving oxygen

oxide
binary compound of oxygen

oxygen debt
a lack of oxygen caused by anaerobic respiration in strenuous exercise

oxyhaemoglobin
haemoglobin loaded with oxygen

parallel circuit
electrical circuit where the current divides and flows through separate components

penis
the male sexual organ

peristalsis
the squeezing action of the oesophagus which pushes food towards the stomach

permanent hardness
hardness of water caused by calcium sulphate and magnesium sulphate

permanent teeth
the second set of teeth, usually grown between the age of six and ten

plasma
the water content of blood used to carry digested food for repair of the body's cells and for energy

platelets
a component of blood used to stop the loss of blood from wounds

pole
part of magnet where its force is strongest

potential difference
difference in electrons between one end of a conductor and the other

premolar
grinding teeth next to the canines

protein
important element of food for growth and repair, found in food such as meat, cheese and pulses

proton
subatomic particle carrying positive charge

puberty
the point when sexual maturity is reached

receptor
sensitive cells in a sense organ which receive information

red blood cells
oxygen carriers in the blood

reflex action
a physical response to stimulus, occurring before the brain has time to process information

relax
stretch, lose tension

renal artery
the main blood vessel supplying blood to the kidney

renal vein
the main blood vessel taking blood away from the kidney

resistance
slowing down of electrical current by components of a circuit

resistor
component of circuit which slows down electric current

respiration
breathing, the chemical reaction using oxygen to create energy in the body

respiratory system
the body system consisting of two lungs and the tubes that lead from them to the nose and mouth

retina
the area at the back of the eye which picks up light stimuli and passes them along the optic nerve to the brain

ribs
protective bones around lungs and other organs

roughage (fibre)
indigestible material in food which helps digestion of other foodstuff

salinity
saltiness

saliva
spit

salivary amylase
the enzyme in saliva which breaks down food ready for swallowing

scent
smell

scrotum
the sacs holding the testes outside the body
secondary sexual characteristicsother changes occurring in adolescence which show maturity is developing

semen
a mixture of sperm and fluid from the prostate gland

sense organ
an organ in the body which receives information about changes in the environment (stimuli)

series circuit
electrical circuit where the current flows through all components in sequence

shell (orbit)
the pathway used by movement of electrons

skeleton
the framework of bones which keeps the body in shape and protects delicate organs

skin
protective organ covering the whole body

soap
substance which encourages dirt to dissolve in water

socially transmitted
passed on by people by the way they behave

soft magnetic material
magnetic materials which lose magnetic force when electric current is switched off

soft water
water containing low proportion of calcium hydrogencarbonate

solute
substance which has been dissolved

solution
mixture of solute and solvent

solvent
material in which other substances can dissolve

solvent glue
glue which uses volatile solvent as a base

sound wave
the pattern made in the air by vibration from sound

south pole
end of free hanging magnet which points south

specialised
adapted for a particular purpose

sperm
a single cell seed of a new human produced by a man

sperm ducts
tubes carrying sperm to the penis

spinal column
backbone

static electricity
the imbalance of positive and negative charges in a material

stereoscopic
taking in information through two separate points

stimulus (pl. stimuli)
change in the environment

sucrose
a sugar

sulphuric acid
sulphur dioxide dissolved in water

sulphur dioxide
chemical resulting from sulphur mixing with oxygen in the air

sulphur trioxide
gas produced when sulphur dioxide is mixed with oxygen

sweat gland
glands which produce sweat to cool the body

system
a group of organs that work together

taste bud
a small bump on the surface of the tongue containing tiny taste receptors

temporary hardness
reversible hardness of water caused by calcium hydrogencarbonate

testis (pl. testes)
the organ which makes sperm cells in a man

testosterone
a male hormone

tissue
a group of cells which specialise in the same activity

trachea
tube from the nose and mouth to the lung for taking in air

urea
liquid waste from the body

urethra
a tube running down the centre of the penis, carrying sperm

urine
waste material drained from the body through the kidney

uterus (womb)
organ where a baby grows inside the mother

vagina
tube from the uterus, through which sperm enter the uterus and through which the baby is born

valve
structure in the heart controlling the flow of blood from one chamber to another

vanadium pentoxide
catalyst used in production of sulphur trioxide

vaporise
change from liquid to gas

variable resistor
part of electrical circuit which can be adjusted to increase resistance to current

vein
blood vessel carrying blood back to the heart

ventricle
the bottom chamber of the heart

vertebra (pl.vertebrae)
a single bone in the spinal column

vibrate
make small movements caused by sound

vibration
small movement caused by sound

villus (pl. villi)
tiny structure on the inside of the intestine, used to absorb digested food

visible spectrum
the band of colours that humans can see

vitamin
elements of food essential for normal growth and nutrition

Vitamin A
found in carrots, paw-paw and mango

Vitamin B
found in liver, brown bread, brown rice and green vegetables

Vitamin C
found in most fresh food, especially fruit

Vitamin D
found in oil, liver, eggs and fish and sunlight

volatile
evaporating rapidly

volt
unit of measurement electrical charge

voltage
measurement of electrical charge

voltmeter
instrument to measure voltage

white blood cells
used to fight infection

windpipe (trachea)
tube from the nose and mouth to the lung for taking in air

womb
organ where a baby grows inside the mother

Index

A
acid rain 128–9, 132
aerobic respiration 47–8
age, disease and 106
AIDS 106
air sacs 44, 45, 46
aluminium 132
amino acids 72, 78
ammeter 170, 171
anaemia 75, 105
anaerobic respiration 48
arteries 56
arthritis 106
atoms 158
atrium 50

B
balance 29–31
batteries 167–9, 178–80
beer manufacture 152
blind spot 15–16
blood cells 58–9
blood circulation 56–7
blood pressure 54
Body Mass Index (BMI) 108–9
boiling points 147–9
bones 90–2, 93–4
Braille 39
brain 32–3
bulbs in circuit 172, 174–5

C
calcium 60
calcium carbonate 123, 124
calcium hydrogencarbonate 125, 126, 127
capillaries 56, 57, 77, 81
carbohydrate 60, 64, 73–4
carbon atoms 153
carbon dioxide 42, 45, 151–2
carbonic acid 123–4, 125
cartilage 93, 97
catalytic converters 129
cells, living 6–7
centrifugation 144
chemical weathering 124
chest 42–3
chewing 68–9
chromatography 141–3
circuit, electrical 165–6, 167–9, 176–7
    diagram 173
    parallel 173–5
    series 170–2
    symbols 168–9

circulatory system 50, 54
cochlea 27
colour vision 14
compass 187
concentrated solution 117
condensation 138
condenser 139
Contact process 150
cost of illness 110–12
crude oil 153–6

D
Dead Sea 117
deamination 81
deficiency diseases 105
detergents 136–7
diabetes 112
diaphragm 42, 43
diet 60–1, 62–3
digestion 68–70, 76–8
digestive system 71–2
dilute solution 117
diseases 104–6
distillation 139–40
dominance, brain and 36
dominant eye 16–17
dry cell 178
dry cleaning 137

E
ear bones 27
ear canal 27
ear flaps 26
eardrum 27, 28
ears 26–8
electric current 170–1
electric doorbell 199–200
electric eel 180
electricity 157–9, 165, 181–3
electrodes 178
electrolyte 178
electromagnet 191–2, 197
electrons 158
embryo 85
enzyme 68
epidemic 104
ethanol 134
ethylene glycol 148
Eustachian tube 28
eutrophication 131
evaporation 138
excretion 79
eyes 10

F
faeces 72
Fallopian tubes 84
fats 54, 74
fatty acid 72
fermentation 146
fertilisation 85–6
fibre (roughage) 60, 72, 73
fingerprints 37
fizzy drinks 151–2
fluoride 131
foetus 85
food tests 64–5
fractional distillation 155–6
frequency 25

G
gases, solubility 118, 120
genes 88
genetic modification 89
genetically linked diseases 106
gills 118, 119, 120
glucose 48, 64, 72, 77
glues 134
glycerol 72
glycogen 77
goitre 75

H
haemoglobin 59
haemophilia 88, 106
hairs, on skin 37–8
Harrison's Cave 123–4
hearing 25
heart 49–50, 54–5, 111
heart-lung machine 55
heat 9, 40, 48
HIV virus 106
hormones 83
hospitals, cost of 110–11
hydrocarbons 153
hydrochloric acid 151
hypertension 54, 107

I
impulses 33
In Vitro Fertilisation (IVF) 87, 88
industrial diseases 106
infectious diseases 104, 105
insulator 165
iodine deficiency 75
iris 15
iron 75

J
joints 95–7

K
kidneys 80, 81–2

L
large intestine 72
lens 10
lifestyle, health and 54–5, 106, 107–9
ligaments 95, 99
lightning 160–1
lime scale 127
limestone 123
liver 77–8
loadstone 184
loudness 25
lungs 42–3, 44–6
lymphatic system 77

M
magnetic Earth 201–3
magnetic fields 189–90
magnetic force 184, 187–8, 189–90
magnetic levitation (MAGLEV) train 197
magnetism 184–6, 193–4
    uses 195–7, 198–200
magnets 185, 188, 193–4
malaria 104
medulla oblongata 33
melting points 147–9
metabolic waste 79–80
minerals 60, 75
movement 101–3
mucus 44
muscles 49, 98–100

N
neurones 32
nitrates 131–2
nitric acid 128
non-aqueous solvents 137
non-magnetic materials 185
nose 18
nutritional information 60–1

O
obesity 107, 109, 112
oesophagus 70, 71
oestrogen 83
olfactory bulb 18
optic nerve 10
organ 7
organic solvents 137
oscilloscope 25
osmoregulation 122
osmosis 121, 122
ovaries 84
ovulation 84
ovum (ova) 83, 84, 85
oxidation reactions 47
oxygen 42, 45, 47–8, 59
oxyhaemoglobin 59

P
penis 84
peristalsis 70
plasma 58, 59
platelets 58
poles, magnetic 187–8
pollution 119, 130
protein 60, 64–5, 73, 78
protons 158
puberty 83
pulse rate 51–3
pulsometer 51

R
rain water 123
rainbow 14
receptors 8
reflex action 34–5
relaxation, muscle 98–9
reproduction 83–4
reproduction technology 87–9
resistance, electrical 176–7
respiration 42–3, 44, 47–8
retina 10
rib cage 92
ribs 42, 43
rum manufacture 146

S
salinity 117, 121
saliva 68
saturated solution 113
scents 18
scrotum 83
semen 84
sense organs 8–9
sensors 38
sewage 131
sex–linked disease 88
sexual maturity 83
sickle cell anaemia 106
skeleton 90–2
skin 37–9, 40–1, 90
skull 92
small intestine 72, 76–7
smell, sense of 9, 18–20, 23
soaps 136
socially transmitted diseases 106
solubility 113, 118, 120
solutes 133–5, 138–40, 141–3
solution 113
solvent 113, 133–5, 138–40
sonar system 8, 9
sound 24–5
sperm 83–4, 85
spinal column 92
stalactites 124
stalagmites 124
starch, test for 64
static electricity 157–9, 160–1, 162–4, 181–3
stereoscopic vision 13
stethoscope 52
stimulus 8
stomach 7, 71
sugar extraction 144–5
sulphur dioxide 128
sulphuric acid 128, 150–1
surface area 114, 115
swallowing 69–70
sweat 41
switches 166, 176–7
system, organ 7

T
taste, sense of 21–3
teeth 66–7
temperature, body 40–1
testis (testes) 83
testosterone 83
3–D vision 12–13
tissue 7
tongue 21, 22
touch 38–9
toxins 104
trachea 42

U
urea 78, 81
urethra 84
urine 78, 81, 82
uterus 84

V
valves, heart 50
vaporisation 155
veins 56, 57
ventricle 50
vertebrae 92
vibration 24
villus (villi) 76–7
vision 9, 10–11, 12–13, 14
vitamins 60, 74–5
volatile compounds 155
voltmeter 168

W
water 116–17
    fresh 117, 122
    ground 130–2
    hardness of 125–7
    life in 118–20, 121–2
    sea 116, 117, 121
    as solvent 118, 150–2
    tap 125–7, 183
weight, balance and 29
wheels 102–3

Acknowledgements

We would like to thank the following for permission to reproduce photographs:
Alexis Rosenfeld/Science Photo Library, Alfred Pasieka/Science Photo Library, Andrew Aiken/Rex Features, Andrew Syred/Science Photo Library, Anthony Mercieca/Science Photo Library, Art Wolfe/Science Photo Library, AWC Images/SIME/Photo Access, CCI Archives/Science Photo Library, BP, Chan Myung Gu/maxppp, Chris Martin Bahr/Rex features, Chuck Brown/Science Photo Library, Daniel Gomez@naturpl.com/Photo Access, David Scharf/Science Photo Library, DASPHOTOGB@aol.com (DavidSimson/B-6940Septon), Dr Morley Read/Science Photo Library, Duif du Toit/Touchline Photo, Empics Eric Grave/Science Photo Library, Getty Images/ Touchline Photo, Giovanni Simeone/SIME/Photo Access, Hitachi Ltd, Inpra, Jacques Jangoux/Science Photo Library, James King-Holmes/Science Photo Library, Jeremy Bishop/Science Photo Library, Jinnah Ali and Nazim Mohammed (Trinidad and Tobago), Karen Ahlschläger, Kent Wood/Science Photo Library, Landbou Weekblad, Martin Bond/Science Photo Library, Martin Dohrn/Science Photo Library, Michael Abbey/Science Photo Library, Microscopix, NASA/Science Photo Library, Noboru Komine/Science Photo Library, PA/Empics, Paul Rapson/Science Photo Library, Pauline Rowles, Peter Menzel/Science Photo Library, Philippe Psaila/Science Photo Library, Photo Access, Photolibrary, Profimedia/Touchline Photo, Rex 7t, 140b, 147t, Rothamsted Experimental Station, Science Photo Library, Sheila Terry/Science Photo Library, Sidney Moulds/Science Photo Library, Simon Fraser/Science Photo Library, Sleeping Cat/Touchlife Images, Spehner-Joubert/Phanie, St Mary's Hospital Medical School/Science Photo Library, Touchline, TRL Ltd./Science Photo Library, Vanessa Vick/Science Photo Library, Vincet Munier/naturpl.com/Photo Access, Voisin/Phanie, Wendy Lee.